4-17-69

MOVEMENT
IN
PSYCHOTHERAPY

MOVEMENT
IN
PSYCHOTHERAPY

Psychomotor Techniques and Training

by Albert Pesso

New York · New York University Press
London · University of London Press Limited
1969

1499055

To My Family

CONTENTS

INTRODUCTION

This book is intended as an aid in the effort being directed toward the uses of the body and body movement for educational and therapeutic ends. Systematic "Psychomotor Techniques and Training" is the name used to identify the specific techniques outlined in this book. The core of the motor and spatial sensitization techniques grew out of my long experience performing and teaching dance with my wife, Diane Pesso. Our subsequent conscious application of these techniques toward therapeutic ends attracted the interest of Dr. Charles A. Pinderhughes, Chief of Psychiatry Research at Boston Veterans Administration Hospital. His interest led to the formation of a research team under his supervision at that hospital in 1964. The team consisted of Dr. Pinderhughes, a psychoanalyst; Dr. Leo J. Reyna, an experimental psychologist and behavior therapist; Mr. James Pederson, Chief of Recreation, and myself. Four years of systematic inquiry into the processes involved at the Veterans Administration in psychomotor and training led to further sophistication of techniques and the development of a rational design and conceptual framework. Five years of clinical practice with normal people, and four years at McLean Hospital produced practical experience in the use of the method with a wide range of people. This book will deal mainly with actual practices and concrete examples of their use. Articles now being completed at the Veterans Administration Hospital will deal with the conceptual framework and rational design.

These techniques are widely applicable and are not the least intended solely for use with psychiatric patients. Other such nonverbal techniques and methods are very successfully being used in sensitivity training and encounter groups. Most noteworthy among these are the methods being used and developed at Esalen Institute by William Schutz and Bernard Gunther. Charlotte Selver, Mary Whitehouse, Ann Halprin, Marian Chace, and others have contributed their own approaches to the widening application of dance-based experience to the ends previously mentioned. In psychiatric application of movement, mention must be made of Dr. Alexander Lowen and his bio-energetic techniques, and the neo-Reichian understanding and use of movement and body armour must not be ignored. Pioneer efforts by many others now going on are too numerous to mention here.

Many of the exercises of psychomotor training will no doubt appear familiar to those who have worked with dance and movement. No claims are being made for total originality in this book. I owe much to my teachers and those of my wife, Gertrude Schurr, May O'Donnell, Martha Graham, William Bales, Merce Cunningham, Martha Hill, Barbara Mettler, and Jose Limon. Readings of Delsarte, Duncan, Shawn, Stanislavsky, Noverre and Fokine contributed to the development of certain viewpoints. Reading of Freud, Jung, Adler, Sullivan, Horney, James, Watson, and Skinner long before I had any thought of becoming a therapist certainly influenced my psychological thinking. Perhaps what is most original is the use and relationship of the materials within the approach.

The goal of this book is to present the logical and sequential series of steps that may be followed using this technique, not with the idea that a psychomotor therapist will be produced from a reading, but with the idea that someone knowledgeable in his own field might select what is usable and meaningful to himself while seeing the place of that portion within the whole. This brings us to the form in which the book was written. The book proceeds from the very first meeting of a group, and follows the group through all the steps that would lead it toward becoming a working therapeutic entity. Each step is described in detail, as if to a trainee, to underline the meaning behind each step and each decision the group leader makes. The book is not limited to those interested in nonverbal therapies; it should be valuable to all who are involved in groups and group behavior. This material has proven valuable to psychiatrists, psychologists, social workers, nurses, occupational therapists, sensitivity group leaders, teachers, ministers, recreation therapists and activity therapists, as well as students of these subjects.

Systematic psychomotor training has three stages. The first stage deals with the sensitization to motoric impulses, the second with sensitization to the spatial placement of others visually with the inclusion of tactile exploration. The final stage deals with the handling of emotional feelings and events, using the skills in the first two stages in what are called "structures."

The first stage is basically intrapsychic. The goal is to give the group member skills and tools to apprehend how he feels and behaves under the stimulus of different motor impulses. In psychomotor training, motor impulses are polarized in three different categories: reflexive, voluntary and emotional. Attempts are made to move purely in each one of these modalities, not only to develop skill, but to teach the use of these modalities as self-diagnostic techniques to determine the state of the emotions.

The second stage is basically interpersonal. It teaches an individual to be more aware of the emotional impact of gestures and the placements of one or more individuals. It includes training in what is called accommodation. Accommodation assists in the elicitation of emotions by arranging the appropriate expected reaction to each emotion by other members of the group. The basic assumption here is that for an emotion to be successfully processed motorically, three things must take place. First, a specific emotion and circumstance must be recalled or experienced. Second, the body should be permitted to be moved as spontaneously as possible in response to the stimulus of that experience. Third, the environment should react as if the action produced by the emotions was effective. This appropriate environmental reaction is contributed to by the act of accommodation.

The third stage is both intrapsychic and interpersonal and handles emotional motoric expression in a controlled manner called a structure. In a structure the target figures of all emotional expression are polarized into good and bad figures. Negative accommodators stand in for the negative aspects of real life figures such as parents, contemporaries, siblings, and so on, and respond appropriately to rage reactions of the person emoting. Positive accommodators stand in for idealized figures who represent the wished-for ideal parents, contemporaries, siblings, and so on. Negative accommodators provide greater cathartic release of emotions and positive accommodators provide corrective experiences to replace old frustrating and harmful experiences.

This method provides a means of experiencing more of one's "organic" self as a living, moving organism and not only as a thinking, conceptualizing, verbalizing being. Although man's concepts and way of seeing things evolves and is evolving rapidly, man's organismic self has remained constant for as long as man has been man. Yet each culture has made different assessments as to what man's organismic or given self is and forces or allows himself to act accordingly. Psychomotor training attempts to come into contact experientially with this organismic given, without recourse to cultural concepts and preconceptions. Thus one hopes by this method to verify what one is organismically and then upon this foundation build the intellectual, rational and verbal superstructure which is the gift given only to man and which allows only man to adapt, vary, and evolve according to changing external conditions.

MOVEMENT
IN
PSYCHOTHERAPY

CHAPTER

1

Psychomotor training is most effectively practiced with a group but is also useful practiced on a one-to-one basis. For the moment let us consider the group and that this is the time of the very first meeting of the group. Each individual on first arrival to the room does not know the other participants or the leader of the group.

Experience has shown that the first meeting is tension-producing before the fact as no one knows for certain what the psychomotor activity will entail, and usually some are fearful. This is apparent by the type of commentary made, the nervous laughter, the stiffness of movement and the generally unrelaxed look of a person entering any new activity.

Psychomotor training adds to this as the participant is aware that he will be dealing with his emotions in some way and that he will be dealing with his body too, both of which are potentially anxiety-producing to many people. The group leader has the opportunity, therefore, of applying himself at once to this tension as he can begin, even before the beginning, to communicate nonverbally to the new-comer.

What can the leader say nonverbally at this time? He can and should set the stage for all that is to come in later sessions by his choice of room, his choice of clothes, his choice of posture and position in the room, and his relationship with those of the group who have arrived before the latest newcomer previous to the formal beginning of the activity.

I do not intend here to make a list of the type of clothing one should wear, the exact type of room one should select, etc., but I wish to make clear the underlying intent and philosophy behind the specific choices each group leader will make. A psychomotor group leader, ultimately, will be allowing and encouraging the expression of all that there is to express in an individual, good, bad, or whatever. The theme of all that the newcomer sees and responds to is that here he will be allowed to be himself, that the answer is yes, that he will be liked regardless of what he does, that he is safe, and that satisfaction is possible. These attitudes are not lies as they will be acted upon in future "structures."

These attitudes can be used in all forms of teaching and in the present context they can be called Psychomotor Attitudes. The argument can be called forth that the above is unrealistic and that not everything one does is acceptable, that one cannot hurt and kill or destroy, and so on. With this I most heartily agree. We are faced with a contradiction. First I state that one thing should be the case and that these are not lies, then I flatly agree with the opposite statement. We have arrived at the heart of psychomotor training. It attempts to make all impulses realized muscularly, all, including the desire and ability to kill and destroy, but it structures these impulses just short of their final consequences and supplies the doer of the impulse with sufficient facsimile, called accommodation, to satisfy his need for efficacy.

Now we seem to be talking about pretending or play-acting. The group member, obviously, is only pretending to kill and murder, etc., for surely he realizes that his accommodators are not really hurt or dead. Surprisingly, we have found that this accommodation is emotionally quite satisfying and more importantly relieves the doer of guilt as he realizes that he has not actually "done" those things but has simply given vent to the impulses to do those things. Now we have solved the contradiction. It is to the newcomer's impulses that we say be yourself, the answer is yes, and so on. We are not lying to the impulses, we are simply "structuring" them in a new way. And, paradoxically, this new way is not, to the doer, false and unsatisfying for not being totally "real." This kind of doing may not be real to the rational part of a person but is quite real to the emotional. It is because of this difference, between the rational and irrational, that psychomotor training works at all.

Yet, there is another kind of doing which even though emotional in appearance is not "real" to the doer and this is "real pretending" or pantomime which is not impelled from within and is without affect. We will discuss this later when we examine the voluntary mode of moving. However, let it be understood that it is emotional movement that was inferred above when satisfaction occurred and "reality" of response was felt.

It should be apparent from the above discourse that as in all organic things the whole is implied in all of the parts, no matter how small. All of psychomotor training is implied in the being and bearing of the leader, the relationship of the leader to all participants, the room and objects in it, and so on. All these elements should imply and lead toward the basic core of psychomotor techniques touched on above.

More specifically, the room can be quite varied, from a living room to an empty space; but the objects, if any, left in the room, the amount of space available, the manner in which the leader moves or does not move about the room, suggests to the newcomer his own potential future behavior in that room. Does the room imply restraint or does it imply freedom? The same question is pertinent regarding the personality of the leader.

The floor should be easy to sit on, being carpeted or cleanly swept. The leader could be sitting or standing when the newcomer arrives but his greeting and introduction should be relaxed and unofficial, for his future (the leader's) behavior will be important as a catalyst and not so much as an authority figure, although the leader must have sufficient authority to implement the limitations to total acting out that were mentioned earlier. Arrivals can be encouraged to sit or lie on the floor, not by direct invitation but by imitation. All that I have suggested should be implied because it is natural for the leader to behave so, not because he spells it out in so many words and forces himself and others to act in this manner.

Some people entering a new situation seek guidance in how to behave in that situation, some people prefer to step back and watch, some people adopt safe patterns of behavior that they have used before in similar circumstances, some people become disoriented and anxious to a degree that they can hardly behave at all. The group leader must judiciously adapt his own behavior and greeting permitting each to settle comfortably in whatever mode they seem to be aiming for, yet be fully prepared to guide the confused newcomer into a relaxed entrance into the room and into the soon-to-be group. The watchword here for the leader is flexibility and his communication nonverbally and, indirectly, verbally should be tolerance.

When it is time to formally begin the session and all the participants have arrived, the group leader can indicate this by standing and moving to the section of the room he has decided to work from. The criterion is to select a place where one can easily be seen and heard by all and the group is not forced to form in some hierarchical way, for example, in rows. My preference is that the group should not be too much above eight in number and usually that number of people tend to naturally form into a single circle or arc about the leader. My tendency is to let the circle form loosely providing each member with the opportunity of selecting his own distance from other members of the group and the leader.

At this point I find it valuable to use words to prepare the group for what is to come. This moment sketches out the boundaries within which we will work and creates a sense of the limitations within which they, the group, will move. This provides them with freedom within the boundaries and limitations which safeguard them from their possible fear of uncontrollable impulses. Without such a clarification and limitation, members of the group might feel anxiety, the anxiety of facing the unlimited unknown coupled with anxiety of loss of control. What I wish to emphasize is that a group leader should take it upon himself to explain and delineate such boundaries as shall exist. Just what boundaries and limitations and how this is expressed should be up to the discretion of the individual group leader. However, I shall spell out in detail what I have found to be a satisfying way for me to begin. I shall direct my remarks to the reader and the reader can imagine for himself how they would sound in the conversational framework of the actual session in the teaching process.

After the circle has formed or been formed, I elect to sit or stand, depending on my mood and the appearance and mood of the group and explain that I shall take a moment to describe the dimensions of the activity. The gist of what is said, if not the style, is as follows: Today and through the course of this activity we will be attempting to develop in all of you sensitivity and awareness in two broad areas: sensitivity to how a movement impulse feels from within, and the sensitivity to how movement and placement of those about and around you make you experience subjective changes of emotion and expectation. The sensitization of movement impulses from within will be followed by developing skill and control in moving, in response to those impulses. The general categories of impulses that we will explore are: reflex, voluntary and emotional. We will work very slowly in the movement impulse area, beginning first with reflex movement stripped as much as possible from voluntary and emotional impulses; then voluntary movement, stripped as much as possible of reflex and emotional movement; and finally, emotional movement stripped as much as possible of reflex and voluntary movement. The aim of this phase of the program is the acquisition of the ability and skill of moving at will from one movement modality to another.

Concurrent with this training we will be developing sensitization to spatial placement utilizing other members of the group in a controlled fashion, on a one-to-one basis and on a group basis. Using controlled circumstances, each member will be able to manipulate spatially other members individually and collectively, to determine which placements and which groupings have what effect on his emotions and expectations.

Most of the early sessions of the activity will be devoted to developing the skill of moving from one modality to another, giving you the capacity of expressing spontaneously in movement whatever emotion you choose, and also the capacity to turn off the emotion and move in either the voluntary or reflex modalities, at that time ignoring the quality of the emotion being experienced. Freedom and spontaneity are certainly among our aims, but that does not mean we will not also practice control, for it is necessary in psychomotor training that each member be ultimately free to choose the time and place and nature of the emotion he intends to deal with. Our aim is articulation, flexibility, spontaneity, and control of the motor expressions of the body with no aspect being over-accentuated.

I also wish to say that you need not justify to the leader or other members of the group the emotions that you may express during these sessions. The circumstances surrounding the emotion, the associations the emotions arouse in you, are yours and yours alone unless you wish otherwise. Your emotions and your expression will not be discussed and focused upon unless you choose. However, if at any time you feel a compulsion or desire to reveal what it is you have or are experiencing, you can do so informally during or after the session, but this is entirely individual. Emotions and feelings being expressed make one feel vulnerable and it is our intention to reduce this fear of vulnerability by making it clear that "exposure" is not one of the elements of this activity.

I do not wish to restrain anyone's freedom but for the above reasons I must request that members of the group refrain from comment following any and all expressions of feeling and emotion and allow each member to experience his emotion without the incorporation and intrusion of someone else's emotions or insight. In this activity, the experience is primary. If there is to be insight our experience shows that it follows the expression naturally and inevitably without assistance from the leader or other members. If a member wishes to discuss his insight, that is his prerogative to do so, openly, casually, and at his own discretion.

To turn my attention and remarks to the reader once again, let me say that I have never, to my knowledge, expressed exactly what I have written above to any group and I probably never shall, but the essentials of what I have stated are always incorporated in opening remarks on the first sessions.

The group is now ready to begin, and the very first element to be learned is the species stance. (I shall continue to direct my remarks to the reader.) The species stance is a cornerstone of psychomotor training. It is the point from which all else arises. It is both a skill and a barometer of emotional impulse and levels of control. It is a dropping of defenses and inhibitions and a giving up to gravity and the body-righting reflexes. It can indicate levels of trust of one's impulses and reactions to others' (spatial) presence.

Specifically it is a stance resulting from relaxation, or attempt at relaxation, of all the skeletal muscles short of falling to the ground. It is not a controlled stance but a stance that is achieved naturally by the maximum relaxation of voluntary controls. It is not an expression of a state of mind, but an expression of the lack of a state of mind.

The group member is instructed to remove, as much as possible, all thoughts and feelings from his mind and allow his mind to go blank. In this respect the body in the species stance is not a vessel for the expression of the emotions; it is an empty vessel, not inert and unmoving, but oscillating in a continual duet between gravity and the body-righting reflexes. In some respects it is akin to the stance one would observe in a fatigued individual who is attempting to sleep while yet standing, or an inebriated individual simply attempting to stand. In both these cases one can infer that certain cortical processes are dulled and the stance is one of the resultants.

In the species stance these cortical processes could be considered to be consciously inhibited. This stance is the first instance in psychomotor therapy and training of the use of a conscious process of awareness in the service of freedom and the reduction of inhibition. Ordinarily awareness connotes inhibition and restraint, but here these two elements, usually found entwined, are separated and made independent of one another. Awareness is separated from inhibition and is used as a selective process and not as a muscular process. Awareness used in this manner will be discussed in the other modalities at a further time.

The reader familiar with hypnosis will by now be considering whether the species stance is similar to the preparatory stance used in that process. This may be but with the important distinction made above. The group member doing a species stance is not directed to give up his awareness and directed to relinquish his control to someone else. Never in psychomotor therapy or training is one trained in the skill of removal of his own responsibility for his own actions. No one ever makes a move that is not internally initiated by the group member doing it. In fact, all of the practice in the movement modalities is done to reinforce this point. The group member himself and he alone gives "orders" that result in his body movement. This develops self-mastery and not the relinquishment of self-control that is required by hypnosis. It is clear, therefore, that though the external look of the stance is similar to that of hypnosis, its internal state and final purpose is directly opposite.

Specific instructions for the attainment of the stance include directions to let the arms fall to the side, let the head drop allowing the chin to fall to the chest, let the stomach muscles loose and allow the stomach to protrude. Notice the use of the words "fall," "let," and "allow." These are specifically used as they point toward giving in to gravity, rather than "putting" the body parts in those positions. "Putting" would suggest voluntary movement. "Letting," etc. would suggest release of voluntary control.

For some people the stance itself is an important new learning. Never before, perhaps, have they let their body go except when falling asleep. It is surprising to these people that they do not find it easy to let go. Their controls are insistent and persistent, their minds a whir of activity. They have seen themselves as highly self-controlled and had not wondered if they were not masters of the controlling mechanisms. If these people shortly learn to let go, they gain a new delight in finding that even when their conscious control is off, all is not gone, for they discover that there is something else besides their control—their body-righting reflexes. As I sometimes add, they find that when they let go that their arms and head do not fall off, but stay securely attached.

Strangely, it would seem that some people are busily holding all their parts together as if they would fall off if they didn't consciously do something about holding themselves together. To these people the species stance is both a threat and a revelation. I should not belabor this point however, for the average individual has little difficulty doing the stance even though he has never attempted it consciously before. Yet there are elements in all of us that are committed to control and we can all learn the lesson that our consciousness does not have to "do" everything.

The species stance is a step toward movement efficiency valuable not only to the average person but also, and particularly, to the dancer. Does the arm have to be brought down or can one trust gravity to bring it down? This can mean a real saving of energy both mental and physical. Dancers who have been trained in strict styles find it very difficult to let go, for it is absolutely contrary to all they have struggled to attain; conscious control of their bodies. However, if they learn to let go, they become more articulate and more graceful, for grace is efficiency and how is one to be efficient if one does not use all the energy at one's disposal, including gravity?

They become more articulate, for they can change the range of their effort from control to flow, to control again.

It would be oversimplification for me to suggest that by merely having people attempt the species stance all those marvelous results would ensue. Not so. Those who cannot relax are not changed by being told to relax. This is my argument with relaxation therapy. Certainly there is an interaction between body and mind, but the rewards of mental relaxation are not so directly related to bodily relaxation. If one is relaxed mentally, certainly the body tends to be more relaxed, and if one is relaxed bodily, certainly the mind tends to be more relaxed. Yet this relationship is not rigid. There is more to it than this. One must ultimately get to the cause of the tension and deal with that; then perhaps the body will respond to the command, "relax." This getting to the cause of the tension is one of the aims of psychomotor training. Yet, the getting is half the battle; the rest is the expression and resolution of the tension and that shall have to wait till later.

I have given the instructions for the attainment of the species stance and now I would like to describe what the stance looks like to the observer. The person doing the stance correctly is not static. His body is oscillating irregularly as his reflexes erratically move his torso back over the center of gravity and over his feet. As one relaxes in the stance there is a tendency to go too far in one direction falling forward or back. There seems to be relatively little oscillation from side to side. If there were no oscillation in the stance, the group leader could assume that there were more conscious controls being applied to maintain this stability or that the group member was concentrating on something. Both of these factors tend to limit the movement of the oscillation.

You remember that one of the instructions for the achievement of the stance was that one was to empty the mind as much as possible of thoughts or feelings. Experience shows that feeling states or concentration on specific thoughts tend to produce tension which limits relaxation and produces stasis in the interaction between gravity and reflexes. You can see then that the stance provides a unique test of whether one can "turn off" thoughts or feelings. For in one respect or another the body responds to one's state of mind.

Each thought or feeling produces, or in my terms, "programs" a potential response to it, in action. This programming must get the body into readiness and this readiness is discernible in the attenuation of the oscillation.

It is interesting to me in this context to find that mental patients who are considered "depersonalized" have the ability to do a successful species stance, whereas many other mental patients do it poorly. The depersonalization must do in an uncontrollable fashion what the healthy person is attempting to do in a controllable fashion. Depersonalization must include the concept of separation between what is felt and what one does bodily. The normal person doing the species stance successfully is not feeling strong emotional urges but has the capacity to turn his attention away from strong emotional feelings for the time being. The depersonalized person is, wishing to or not, turned off from strong emotions or awareness of strong emotions. He does not, as does the normal person, have the option of turning back *on* those feelings. His psyche and his body are to that extent out of his control and his illness has forced him to relinquish this much of his sovereignty.

The normal person is normal to the extent that he does not have overly powerful emotions which he cannot control. If he cannot control them consciously, then unconscious controls are utilized, and those unconscious controls can be looked upon as symptoms of his illness.

Let us not, however, leap to the conclusion that whoever does not do the species stance well is therefore potentially or actually mentally ill. This is by no means the case. Experience shows that a good percentage of normal people do it relatively poorly. It would seem to be a truer measure of efficiency.

It does seem to indicate that those who do it poorly are forced by the nature of their constitutions or circumstances to use more energy than is necessary to carry themselves through their lives. It could be possible that this energy could be successfully and satisfyingly used in other endeavors. I must say that this last is in the nature of conjecture as I have no absolute proof of this. But many tests over a period of time have indicated to me that there is some basis in fact for this hypothesis. As group members express and resolve their conflicts in movement, their species stance improves and they report that their feeling state is more relaxed in their everyday lives.

The spine in the species stance is more curvilinear than usual. The trunk is upright but the distance between the neck and hips is closer than usual, with the chest collapsed and hips slightly thrown forward. On first try some members of the group tend to fall forward from the hip placing the head and chest forward of the feet and the center of gravity. The most efficient species stance, in terms of maintaining an unstrained balance, is achieved by allowing each segment to slump downward, not forward or backward, toward the next segment. This giving in to gravity causes the least strain, the least expenditure of effort, as any posture with body parts away from the center of gravity is tension-producing and energy-consuming.

Some new group members find it difficult to slump or allow themselves to slump to this extent, not from physical disability but from not being able to see themselves, or have others see them in that not terribly attractive posture. Here is where the name, species stance, becomes relevant. It is not a particular person's stance, a particular individual person with a definite personality and manner of presenting himself to the world. In the species stance a person is not expressing his individual self, but more, he is expressing his species self. Only his human nervous system and structure are relevant in the species stance. This is a test, then, of whether he can, for the moment, give up his individual self, not to another as was discussed earlier, but to his own reflexes, the reflexes possessed by every other member of the species.

As the group member is instructed to let go of all of the muscles as possible in attempting the species stance, the appearance of the head and arms should be completely limp. Gravity should be given in to and the head should slump to the chest with the chin against the chest and the facial muscles relaxed. The arms should hang perpendicularly from the shoulders with the fingers relaxed and not tense.

The average person doing the species stance appears relatively symmetrical laterally. Evidently when all muscles are relaxed the tonus of the antagonistic muscles in the trunk and around the spine neutralizes the pull of each side, resulting in this symmetry. Interestingly, tests of chronic, long-term, male mental patients show the greatest deviance from the normal symmetry. Another interesting difference in this class of patient is in the amount of tension shown in the hands—they are clenched or partly closed. The tonus of these patients' antagonistic muscles is evidently uneven, possibly due to their long-term preoccupation with powerful feelings and emotions which they cannot control and which they cannot express bodily, directly. It might be said that their poor species stance is an indirect expression of their emotions.

Another clue to indirect expression of the emotions in the species stance can be found in eyelid flutter. Ordinarily the eyes are closed during the stance. Experience shows that open eyes tend to make one aware and interested in one's surroundings and this interest results in the changed "programming" of potential behavior during the stance. As explained earlier, this factor tends to dampen the oscillation in the stance.

Some people doing the stance exhibit quite rapid eyelid flutter with the eyes closed. I take this as a sign of emotions indirectly expressed or perhaps an expression of the struggle between the wish to open the eyes and see what is happening and the wish to give in totally and be relaxed. Closed eyes during the species stance are evidence to me of trust. One is relaxed and vulnerable in the stance and closed eyes demonstrate that one is trusting others present not to do harm. Some group members, who demonstrated marked eyelid flutter in the stance in the first few meetings, showed distinct lessening of flutter after several months. This could have been caused by increased trust of the group members or by a lessening of the force of repressed emotions.

Among chronic mental patients there is a greater tendency to keep the eyes open and the head raised during the species stance than among "normals." However, some chronic mental patients do drop their heads and close their eyes during the stance but show other deviations from the normal, such as poor symmetry, clenched fists, and so on.

Other clues to underlying unexpressed, or indirectly expressed emotion can be found in movements of the mouth and jaw during the stance. The group leader can note for himself, for future use,

whether there is pursing of the lips, biting or sucking, teeth clenching, licking or other mouth movements. Invariably, those movements become more overtly expressed and more relevant at some future time in a structure.

For instance, someone who shows teeth clenching in a species stance might very well find that in a structure he wishes to bite some figure in that structure. At that time he will be able to directly express this biting and have his negative accommodator react appropriately. I have yet to describe what is meant by an accommodator and a negative one at that, but I shall leave that term for later explanation, leaving the reader with a small indication and a larger wonder for what is to come.

The fingers are another source of action to watch. Some people will have, quite unconsciously, a good deal of movement of the fingers during the species stance. I see this as another "spillover" of the emotions. It should be said that one of the aims of psychomotor training is the reduction of "the reservoir of the undone." Figuratively speaking, some people have such a large "reservoir" of unexpressed emotions, that, given a moment of stillness and relaxation, the emotions "spill" out. Those people probably rarely stay completely still, perhaps due to the constant pressure of their emotions toward expression. Then, during the relaxed stillness of parts of the body in the species stance, this imbalance between expression and control is highlighted by the unconscious action of the fingers, mouth, eyes, or whatever.

Often I have seen group members break from a species stance and then, seemingly irrelevantly, rub their eyes or their mouths, or do some other like movement. I have learned to pay attention to those gestures as they regularly relate to whatever emotions the group member has just then been experiencing. Sometimes the movement suggests wiping or rubbing the eyes as in crying, or bringing the hand to the mouth as in finger sucking.

What is the group leader to do with his observation of all this unconscious movement? Directly and immediately, very little. The group leader can use this knowledge in developing the speed and direction of the group. He can at some time in the future suggest areas of expression that will be pertinent to those members of the group

who have exhibited this indirect expression. He can at best get the
sense of the feeling tone of the group and then proceed with a greater
awareness of where the group is.

The use of this material should be individual and indirect and
rarely used to point out to the group member what is inherent in it.
There are times when it is valuable for the group member to have
this knowledge brought to his attention if the leader feels that the
group member can more directly express this emotion in an appropriate structure. This is a sensitive region and the group leader should
proceed knowing the difference between manifesting a hidden stance
indirectly and being able to accept and then directly express can be
emotion. Here the group leader is on his own and only member is in
can help him make a decision as to whether or not s elbow to bend
is ready for such feedback.   perpendicular to
There is no doubt that there is much to learn from
member do the species stance, yet, the raising which
the above into thinking that participates with
very first meeting. The is
one slowly and laboriously learns to identify certain
ways that specific group members do the stance over
a   time. However, an experienced group leader can scan
group seeing the stance and, having years of watching and
and behind him, pick up the most pertinent uses listed
the group.

Just as true is the fact that one is always fact that his
members what is relevant and what is not over group member
time. One should not make final, absolute assessment
as people change so their species stance changes. The group leader
should not be frozen in his own judgments and be unable to perceive
the changes however subtle they may be. For the stance is
group leader's means of measuring some kinds of change and he
be aware of all the small variations that could be relevant.

The reader should now recall that it is still the very first meeting
of the group, although much has been said applying the stance to
further meetings. The group members have been in the stance for
perhaps two minutes in silence, possibly punctuated by low register
instructions from the group leader. When it is apparent that the

group has reached a point where most of the members have done the stance as well as can be expected at the first meeting and some of the members may even be showing evidence of rising emotions and interest in the rest of the group, the group leader can ask the group to resume a normal attentive posture.

The point to be noted here is that if the group is left too long in the stance they may continue to hold it superficially while harboring an annoyance and an intense desire to rise up to a normal position. If the leader allows the stance to go on much beyond this point he may ʰᵃᵗively difficult to get the attention and cooperation of ʰᵉ the remainder of the session, for their unexpressᵉᵈ anger ᶜctive hindrance to their perception of what will be ndition is allowed to arise by the leader's inadvertᵉᵗion to one member of the group (due perhaᵖˢ ʰᵉʳ's unusual difficulty in attaining the stance) beyoⁿᵈ ʰᵉ stance for the total group, that uilibrium-producing action. e." Fiᵉˡᵈ ᵃᶜtion at the group make some body violent movement or total body tension at thᵉ ᵉⁿᵈ rience shows that this violent movement or total tensᵉ reduces unspoken and even unconscious annoyance and ᵗᵒ ᵍ the group to proceed. However, the most effectiᵛᵉ ᵃᶜtiᵒⁿ all times is to balance his attention between oup to such an extent that this condition s not arise.

ᵃⁿ exaggeration on my part to describe the above ly but it is clear to me that such sensitivity to minute changes iⁿ the group are necessary to final development of a successfully funcᵗioning group in this medium. Another point worth oᵗe relative timidity of group members on the first ng. One might wonder why a member would continue doing ᵗstance beyond the "normal" limit. Possibly because he is not yet are of his own "normal" limit and is waiting to be told what to do next.

Although I am going through a very definite series of steps that I myself employ in handling the first meeting, clearly there are many other ways that can be used than the ones I have delineated. I write of my own sequences, since I can then elaborate on the dynamics of each move for the reader's knowledge of the principles behind each move. Anyone who is a successful teacher will have his own series of steps which are in sensitive balance to one another. A good teacher should be aware of the subtle meanings in each step he makes.

The group, still in the arc or circle formed at the outset, is now facing the leader. I take this moment to describe how I will raise the arms and hands of each member of the group while he is in the species stance, which will shortly be resumed. This moment can be used effectively to correct general mistakes in the doing of th____ and to point out how they can be overcome, so that t? _ some investment in doing the stance again. While each me_ the stance I raise his arm from the wrist, allowing hi_ at approximately ninety degrees with the upper arm per_ the floor and close to his body.

Before raising the arm I describe the purpose of th_ is to determine whether the group member either p_ or resists the leader's effort in this raising. When anyone is in a position such as the species stance, one is quite vulnerable as described earlier. Therefore, when someone touches a person in that stance, it is natural that there would be a reaction, either startled or interested. The person in the stance, not informed of the fact that he was going to be touched, would probably make either of the two response_ _ above.

Here then is the point: after being informed of the _ arm is going to be raised in the species stance, can the gro_ still turn his attention from the fact of his being touched and his arm raised yet effectively continue the stance? Can he "turn off" his emotional, and one could almost say, "instinctual" response in this position and still trust the toucher? Here are some questions the leader can keep in mind while testing. Does this stance become less relaxed and his arm tense? Does he raise the arm just slightly ahead of the leader keeping only minimal contact with the leader's hand? Does his elbow lock forcing the leader to raise the entire arm from the shoulder? Does he remain passive, allowing the leader the total use of the arm, giving the leader the feel of the total weight of the arm? Do his eyes open and watch the leader raising his hand? Do his eyelids flicker at an increased speed? Does his arm tremble? Does his mouth begin to move?

The responses listed above occur with relative frequency in groups. The "healthier" the group, the more likely will the group display relaxation and trust. Less healthy groups will display some of the above and experience shows that almost all chronic mental patients display many of the above responses.

The species stance is a "zero" point; a point at which the group member theoretically feels and expresses the least and where he controls the least. The arm raise represents a new factor and one can then measure against this theoretical "zero" anything beyond it that occurs. A group member instructing his body to remain limp and when touched, becomes tense somewhere, signifies that some emotions are not under control. The leader can tell that there is tension, and so can the group member. There is no secret about it and there is no covering the fact. It is plain and observable without being subject to counterfeit with any success. I have yet to see anyone "fake" a species stance, and no amount of practice will develop the capacity until the internal conditions are changed, that is, the person being tested is no longer harboring strong emotions.

Sometimes a group member will report that he felt tense as he heard the group leader walking close to him. He may also say that he tried to relax his arm during the raise but that he could not succeed. We have now an effective barometer for measuring changed affect and tension. Some group members who raise their arms in participation with the leader raising their arms, report that they are attempting to "help" the leader place their arm where he wishes. It is this type of report that developed the concept of compliance without trust. The subject wants to help and is not willing to "let" the leader do the raising.

This is seen in extreme degree with chronic mental patients. Merely describing what will be done with the arm sets the patient's arm in motion, almost as if the patient were hypnotized. This is total compliance and this type of patient, long accustomed to custodial care, is totally compliant but in a non-trusting way. The lack of trust shows when the actual arm raise is attempted. The most minute pressure on the skin and even the hairs of the arm is enough to set the arm in motion prior to actual lifting. The tester has almost to follow the patient's arm up if he is to maintain contact with it. This can be understood as an effort to avoid contact on the part of the patient, as well as compliancy. This may be the case too with "normals" who dislike contact and respond by raising the arm with a minimum of effort, or even no effort, by the leader.

One should not jump to conclusions however, for the first meeting with a group is tension producing and many group members show marked change even within the first hour as they relax during the activity. Also there may be other factors producing these responses having little to do with the conjectures listed above. The group member might not understand the instructions and respond poorly, there may be some muscular or nervous condition which does not permit the "normal" response, and so on. It is only when the response remains consistent over a period of many meetings that one can draw some conclusions. Even then one should be cautious and refrain from closing one's eyes to other possibilities.

All that was elaborated above regarding the raising of the arm can be equally applied to the raising of the hand. When the arm is raised so that the forearm is parallel to the floor, the hand should hang loose and relaxed from the wrist. A gentle shaking of the forearm by the leader should produce a flopping action of the hand with no resistance or control from the group member. Neither should the group member show any resistance in the arm being shaken. A point worth noting is the correct manner of raising and moving the arm. Care should be taken that the raising should be done as described earlier with the upper arm remaining able to be perpendicular to the floor, otherwise the group member may find it impossible to maintain the stance as he is being pulled too far forward over and beyond his feet. The shaking too should be up and down rather than forward and back for the same reason. A group member doing the species stance properly would be thrown completely off balance producing a reflex catching of balance, interfering with the proper execution of the stance.

If the group leader uses the right hand to raise the group member's arm, he then uses the left hand to raise the group member's hand, while the right hand remains where it is, supporting the weight of the group member's arm. The hand raising shows different properties than the arm raising and is subject to greater variation from person to person. Some of this variation is a function of the muscular strength and flexibility of the group member. Group members who do gymnastics or work which develops a strong grip tend to show relatively inelastic responses in the fingers as the hand is raised. The group leader must make mental note of the differing responses of all the members of the group so that any changes will be measured against that individual member's past performances rather than with a universal norm.

After the hand is raised, by the fingers, to the highest point without straining by the group leader, he lets it drop and notes whether the group member assists in lowering the hand or whether it drops naturally due to gravity and the elasticity of the muscles and ligaments of the hand and fingers. Some group members will make a very conscious motion of lowering the hand and others will allow the hand to drop completely limp and the subsequent motion and reaction of the dropping is noticeable by the group leader.

A relaxed hand will fall at one speed and with a bouncing motion at the end, but a tensed hand will either go down slowly if it is controlled or too forcefully if the group member is trying to imitate the force of gravity or is responding with emotion. Occasionally, a group member will leave the hand in the same position even after the group leader has taken away his own hand from supporting it. This condition, however, is most frequently found in some depressed chronic mental patients. Their hands have a tendency to remain rigidly in the position placed and often they must be instructed to lower the hand to the original position even after several seconds have elapsed. They seem completely unaware of the force of gravity acting on their hands.

Amongst normals, if a group member does leave the hand stationary for a moment after release, he usually finds himself laughing as if "caught," so obviously is he aware of what should happen. This is not so with the above mentioned patients, who even after several tries and consistent instructions as to what should happen, do not vary their performance.

Roughly speaking the dropping of the hand represents the existence or lack of existence of trust in gravity and willingness to give in to it, just as, once again roughly speaking, passive relaxation of the arm and hand during the arm and hand raise signifies trust in the lifter. To elaborate one step further in this trust element, the oscillation factor in the species stance demonstrates trust in one's reflexes. Therefore, the species stance and the arm raise gives one a three way measurement of trust: trust of gravity, trust of another, and trust of one's reflexes. Trust does not appear to be a single factor, for there are those who show very well in one area of trust and yet not in others.

The trust in gravity shows up more simply and clearly in the subsequent dropping of the arm. Some hands drop due to the elasticity factor spoken of earlier, but no arms drop due to any significant elasticity factor. The muscles surrounding the elbow joint are not significantly stretched and taut at the ninety degree angle, so when the arm is released by the group leader it is primarily gravity which determines the dropping of the arm. Frequently, on the first meeting there will be a minute hesitation following the release of the arm before the arm drops, also the natural pendulum action of the arm will be inhibited. Once this is pointed out the average group member will allow the appropriate relaxation to take place permitting the normal swing of the arm from the shoulder joint. Those group members who have difficulty in relaxation will attempt to imitate the pendulum swing but this is apparent to the group member himself and to the group leader, for the rhythm is obviously wrong and motion obviously forced.

Once again, chronic depressed mental patients frequently exhibit the same rigid maintenance of position following the release of the arm by the tester as was found in the hand release. The arm remains stationary although the tester no longer supports it and the patient often must be instructed to lower the arm. These same patients sometimes recognize that the arm should fall down and attempt to put it down at "fall" speed, but the motion is obviously a counterfeit. To repeat, these patients seem relatively unable to respond and give in to gravity, perhaps due to the constant tension in their muscles, for sensitivity to gravity seems to be coupled with relaxation.

Each group member is tested in turn by the group leader for the amount of tension in the arm and hand during the raising. Not infrequently a group member will demonstrate varying degrees of tension between the right and left arm. Although I have found no unexceptionable rule to this, it seems that if a group member is right-handed and he shows a disparity between the right and left in terms of tension, the right hand and arm tends to participate in the lifting and be unable to go completely limp. The group leader can give individual members specific suggestions that would tend to assist them in relaxing the tense arm such as consciously contracting those muscles with an image or feeling that would be suggested by that tension. If the group member does the stance correctly he is told to wait until the rest of the group has finished before indulging in an activity that might be distracting to the rest of the group. The point here is to release the member from continuing needlessly in the stance or to give some new reason for continuing the stance for further learning or benefit.

If the testing of individuals appears to be taking undue amounts of time, the remaining untested members can be told to remain in the stance or come to a normal stance depending on their own desires. This concern for each member of the group and the appropriate response by the group regarding this concern will be elaborated on in greater detail at a later time, as this is an important element in the proper functioning of the group.

Following the testing of the arm relaxation the group leader can demonstrate the testing of the shoulder and torso relaxation via the torso twist. You recall earlier that the symmetry of the body in the stance is a function of the equalizing action of the antagonistic muscles surrounding the spine and torso. This torso twist test is a measure of the group member's willingness and ability to "give in" to those muscles' action following the group leader's turning of his shoulders during the stance. It is also a test of the group member's willingness and ability to "let" the group leader turn his shoulders without his own participation or resistance just as in the arm raise.

The group leader can have one of the group members turn his (the group leader's) shoulders to demonstrate this. The group leader should instruct this group member to pull one shoulder forward while pushing the other shoulder back turning the shoulders about the center of gravity. If the turning is done incorrectly the subject turned will be thrown off balance and his balance-righting reflexes will come into play, distorting the return of the shoulders to center. When the group member does this correctly, he and the rest of the group can see the group leader's shoulders swing back to center and beyond and oscillate from side to side with diminishing force and finally come to rest in the symmetrical species stance.

Having a group member test the group leader in this demonstration has negative as well as positive aspects. Negatively it gives the group members a model to imitate, and imitation implies control rather than "letting." However, this negative result is easily overcome by the group leader's subsequent testing of each individual, for he can point out the difference to the group member who will shortly be able to ascertain the difference between "letting" and "imitating." Positively it demonstrates that the leader can do what he asks the members to do and that a member can do the testing as well as the leader, for shortly each member will be asked to test another member. This test, then, is a means of introduction to the next phase.

Before the group tests itself, the group leader instructs them to return to the species stance in order for him to test their shoulders as described above. The relaxation of the shoulders and the torso is a much more difficult task than the relaxation of the arm and hand. Very few new members are able to achieve this. Most tend to assist the leader in the turning of the shoulders and find that even when the leader has taken his hands off that they have not relaxed sufficiently to return to center. They may also attempt to purposefully swing their shoulders in the manner observed, but the leader can point out this difference. This imitation effect does not feel as "right" ordinarily and the group member is quick to note the difference himself.

For the extreme contrast, chronic mental patients in this particular test show certain features similar to the manner in which they do the arm and hand raise test. Many, after being turned to one side, remain in that position until instructed to return. Some return slowly by short degrees to an approximation of the center but not the center itself, either too far to the right or left, indicating that this was a "chosen" and not a "felt" return where there would be little chance of error.

An odd response has been demonstrated by a small number of patients that is worth noting. When their shoulders are turned to the side they do not allow the torso to be twisted but move their feet in the direction of the turn and turn in effect their entire body in the direction indicated. When the hands are removed from their shoulders they take little steps and turn themselves back to the original direction. This is their version of the "imitation" which somehow ignores or excludes the twisting effect. I do not know what to attribute this to beyond their general rigidity and lack of tonus, as well as lack of understanding.

Some of the errors noted in "normal" group members' responses include a turning of the head as the shoulders are turned; a raising of the shoulders when they are touched; a stiffening of the arms during the turn; and a general tensing of the body during the turn. Frequently, group members will comment on specific feelings that are provoked during this test such as: I remembered someone pushing me around when I was little, and so on. Such comments point out the relationship between certain body postures and certain memories.

If tensions do occur during the test, the leader can give some of the same suggestions given earlier during the arm lift test, such as to consciously tighten as much as possible the tense area, and so on. This conscious tightening returns an element of volition to the unconscious tension and is one step toward bringing it back under control, much as turning in the direction of a skid brings a veering car under control. This simple act, however, is not sufficient to solve the entire problem of tension or we would not have to go any further than we are in the first session, but it points the way toward the conscious desire to release the tension exhibited in the body as a conscious "*in*tension." The structuring and acting out of those unconsciously exhibited tensions is the ultimate aim of the activity; thus, the small and somewhat random manner of dealing with these tensions is not the end but simply the first step toward the end.

Once the leader has tested the shoulders and torso of each member of the group, he can explain to the group how to go about testing one another. Each member is instructed to pair off with the person beside him having one do the species stance while the other tests the arms and then the shoulders of the other. When one has completed testing he is then to do the species stance while the other tests him.

The instructions for testing can be given as spelled out earlier in this chapter emphasizing care to be taken not to pull or push the one tested off balance, and so on.

The moment that the group breaks into couples is an interesting one. Until this time the focus has been on the leader with each member attempting to apply the instructions to do the stance. Each member during the stance is alone with his subjective feelings, fears, curiosities, wonders, and so on. The leader has been important because he is the central figure relating to all of them. Now, for the moment, he drops away while each one relates directly with another member of the group. The entire atmosphere of the room changes abruptly.

This previously quiet and concentrated group is now busy talking, laughing, and relating. It is an important time for learning. Each member can now see and feel another member of the group; see how he does the species stance and compare it to how his felt, for he cannot see himself do the stance. He can check another person as he was checked, see how it feels to be touched in the stance by another person than the leader. He can ask himself if there was a difference and wonder at the difference. He can see the difficulty in letting shoulders relax or arm hang limp on another person as on himself. He may talk to the other person and inquire how it feels to be touched in the stance, tell the other person how he feels, discover new ways of lifting the arm or turning the shoulder for other effects or results. In other words he has the chance to relate and to give and receive feedback on his responses and performance during the stance.

A subtle point to note is that he has also been given the license to touch another human being in a neutral and nonthreatening way. This is the group's first formal exposure to touch and experience shows that this moment is usually greeted with levity and a kind of heightened awareness. Perhaps this is only so in our culture which is not a particularly tactile one. Potential behavior relating to the vulnerable posture of the person doing the species stance is aroused and this may be the force behind the heightened emotionality in evidence at this time. In the case of testing a member of the opposite sex, fewer hostile emotions may be aroused adding to the excitement. Whatever the exact reasons the moment of pairing off and testing causes a relaxation of the group in terms of concentration on subjective states and a heightened interest and excitement related to touch and vulnerability. The one tested finds that his vulnerability has not produced pain or injury and the tester finds that he is trusted.

The group also finds that they can learn from one another and not only from the leader. An important teaching point apropos of the group learning from one another is for the leader to refrain from correcting or criticising the species stance or any other skill too much and to allow the group member to learn from the other members of the group. This is not to say that the group leader should indiscriminately withhold information from the member, but that he should realize that his criticism has great force and that too much of it can have a negative reaction on a group member, whereas a group member's criticism has less force and is more easily taken and assimilated.

After each couple has played the part of tester and tested, the leader can instruct the group to form couples again but with different partners. This changing of partners spreads the interest of each member of the group toward other members of the group. If the group is small enough the retesting and recoupling can go on until each member of the group has tested and been tested by every other member of the group. This can exhaust the fund of knowledge to be gained from the testing at this time and care should be taken that it is not continued too long to the point of exhaustion of interest in the activity. Now that the entire group has touched one another a new group sensation and awareness can be discerned. The group is a little more relaxed, there seems to be less fear of the unknown or unexpected, there is the beginning of a kind of camaraderie resulting from all having gone through the same kind of experience together. A small step in the process of developing a group trust has been made.

CHAPTER

2

When the group is ready to return its attention to the leader, the leader can note for himself whether each member is back in the original position in the circle or whether he has chosen to change it. Most group members will reassume the original position, but some will alter theirs. The leader can note that some group members are now closer to one another than they were before and some further away. Some will be closer to the leader and some further from him. This gives some small indication as to whether the group member is more or less involved in other members of the group or the leader. The placement is an unconscious indicator in the approach-avoid continuum. Some group members will have already found that this activity is too threatening and will be partially withdrawing and some will have made an internal commitment to the activity and be drawing closer together.

The next step involves the teaching of the torso twist initiated by the person doing the species stance. In the previous chapter, the manner of testing the species stance by turning or twisting the torso of the person doing the stance was demonstrated. Now the twisting is initiated by the group member himself by a forceful and sudden twist of the hips to one side and then immediately relaxing again. If the species stance can be called the "zero" state, then the torso twist can be considered "zero plus one." The "plus one" in this case is the capacity to use voluntary movement for a short segment of time and then to quickly relax, allowing the body to respond to the centrifugal force, gravity, action of the antagonistic muscles in the trunk, and to the reflexes which are activated, all of which move the body in a particular way following the sudden twist and relaxation of the torso.

The "plus one" should be only plus one and not a plus of more than one by which I mean a greater expenditure of energy than that required to do the movement. The question to be asked here is, can one control one's energy impulses on a volitional basis sufficiently to avoid the "radiation" of that impulse to other parts of the body other than the one intended and for a greater length of time than one intended? Also, can one turn the body without the use of emotional imagery and emotional energy? Some people who are carrying about a large amount of unexpressed emotion do the torso twist in an explosive fashion with far more energy and feeling than they had anticipated and called for. It is almost as if the feeling took the opportunity to "jump out" at the first opportunity.

After an explanation of the torso twist to the group the leader can demonstrate it. To do it properly, one waits until one is maximally relaxed in the species stance with the head slumped to the chest, the arms hanging loosely at the sides and the stomach muscles relaxed and the hips slightly thrust forward. (Frequently, beginners in their haste do not initially do a good species stance thus making it unlikely that they will do the torso twist properly.) Once the leader has relaxed to this maximal point in the species stance, he executes a sudden twist to the left or the right with his torso, causing his arms to fly out to the side by the centrifugal force of the twist. His head will be flung to one side too by the same action. The turning action must be done suddenly and turned off equally suddenly to force the arms away from the body and then to allow them to swing in a pendulous manner from the shoulder socket. The torso itself springs back to the center and beyond due to the elasticity of the muscles surrounding the spine and the trunk. There is a diminishing swing left and right of the shoulders and torso, and finally the forward and back oscillation natural to the species stance manifests itself and the "zero" point is resumed.

What is the point of this exercise? We have reached or attempted to reach the "zero" point of the species stance, allowing the reflexes to manifest themselves in movement. Theoretically the group member doing the stance is "doing" nothing and expressing nothing. He is "letting" movement of a certain kind occur. Where do we go from the point of no volitional movement? We go to a point with a minimum amount of volitional movement that would cause other forces, that is, centrifugal force and gravity, to come into play, which could occur if the arms, head, and shoulders were relaxed enough to allow or let them come into play. Therefore, an attempt to do a quick "on-off" kind of action would allow us to go one small step away from the zero point without including other factors which we may not be aware of or over which we have no control.

The following are what the leader examines when the group members attempt the torso twist: Can the member turn his torso without initiating the movement elsewhere? Can he move forcefully enough to cause the arms to be flung out from his body? Are his arms relaxed enough so they can be flung from his body? Do his arms merely "imitate" the motion he saw the leader "allow" to occur? Can he terminate the force of the movement or does he remain tense due to the first contraction of the muscles? In that event how long does it take him to resume the maximal point of the species stance? Does he toss his head to one side instead of turning his torso? Do his arms swing pendulously from his shoulders? Do his hands stay relaxed throughout or do they tense up as a result of the first expenditure of energy? Does the trunk swing back easily from side to side or does the group member do an obvious imitation of the turning back of the torso? Does the group member remain stationary, twisted to the right or left following the initial twist without returning to the center point unless he makes a conscious volitional action to do so? Altogether, these elements add up to whether the group member can use his energy effectively and his capacity to relax instantaneously. This exercise gives him a skill which teaches him to be able to relax and let certain kinds of movements occur which before he perhaps could only *make* occur. (All this is possible of course once he removes the tension from his body through direct expression of the emotion tacitly expressing itself there.) The torso twist is very much like the species stance except one other factor is added, therefore, "zero plus one."

As the group practices this movement the leader can notice quickly those who can do this well and those who cannot. Generally, those who do the species stance well in the first place can be expected to do the torso twist more successfully than those who do the species

stance poorly. Those whose arms tend to raise without the effort of
the tester when being tested in the species stance can be expected to
have arm action independent of centrifugal force and the force of
gravity in the torso twist.

The leader should have the members of the group separate somewhat at the mass attempt at the torso twist, for the arms, if the
twist is done properly, can swing out with a good deal of force and
those standing too close to one another can get hit. When this is
mentioned ther can be a certain number of good-natured or humorous attempts at purposely hitting neighbors. The leader, by his own
humorous response to this, paves the way toward greater tolerance
of other hostile or aggressive expression that can be done without
guilt or embarrassment. This humorous response to the potential
hitting of one's neighbors is a germ of the experience of function
pleasure—that pleasure or relief concomitant with the bodily expression of strong emotion.

Frequently, there will be a member in a group who will do the
torso twist with an emotional component added. This emotional
component varies with each individual. He may turn suddenly and
forcefully as if striking at someone behind him with his arms. In
this the head may participate and the expression of the face might
change in relation to the emotion felt. When questioned as to whether
emotion was felt this member might mention that indeed he did
feel angry but that when he started he had not intended to express
or feel any anger. It should be clear however that this person's anger
is always ready to act as a "rider" to neutral or innocuous movement
that it can attach to. This would be another example of "spillover."
The emotional reservoir is too full; it needs to be emptied by whatever movement modality is available.

Another member might throw his head back and his face to the
ceiling as if startled or about to shout. Others may turn the body
slowly with the face lifting in a kind of ecstatic expression. Of
course the slow movement would not cause the head to lift at all
and therefore the head lift must be caused by emotional feeling.
Others might move hardly at all in the torso indicating a certain
timidity or tentativeness in their movement. This small movement
is not necessarily an expression of emotion, but more a lack of energy

and force. Frequently this type of person is slow in being able to do emotional movement, letting it be known that they are experiencing inhibition. Often if there is emotional expression in the torso twist it will be relevant to that person's meaningful constellation of experience and feeling, hence it is wise for the leader to watch and note for and to himself what is occurring so that he might be of assistance at some future time in developing a "structure."

When there is emotional expression of some kind it is only necessary for the leader to indicate that fact to the group member manifesting it without elaborating on what he thinks the emotion might be. At this point in the activity it is important that the torso twist be worked on for its control and lack of emotionality. The clarification of emotion and its direct expression is for a later date. In the early meetings of the activity the torso twist is valuable as a barometer of "spillover," as a means of pointing out to people areas to work on, such as learning to relax the arms, learning to turn the body around rather than just to the side, learning to "pull out" or remove emotion and learning to turn off the amount of energy expended. The individual group member soon learns when he is doing it correctly, giving him another means of determining for himself his emotional tension level.

After the group members have worked on accomplishing this action for a sufficient period of time and when it is clear that little more would be gained from continuing on with it during the first session the group leader can call for the attention of the group so that he might teach them the next skill.

Before going into that I would like to point out to the reader that as often as possible the group members are taught each skill in such a manner that they might be able to assess for themselves when they are doing it properly or not. His criticism should always be aimed toward giving each member of the group mastery of all the techniques with himself as judge so that his dependence on the leader would diminish over time and he would be able to rely on his own judgment. The leader should naturally avoid harsh criticisms and damaging statements that would turn the group member away from his own self-reliance.

The next skill to be taught is the fall catch. When the center of gravity of a person doing the species stance falls either too far forward or too far back of the feet a reflex action occurs that would tend to place the weight back over the feet. When the distance that the center of gravity falls beyond the feet is small the resultant reflex action on the legs is small, usually merely the rising up slightly onto the toes if the falling is forward or the rocking back onto the heels with toes lifting up and knees stiffening if the falling is backward. If the distance beyond the feet is even greater than just described the reflex action results in a small step forward or back. If it is even greater than that the reflexive action is even more forceful with a resultant sudden step forward followed by a series of shorter steps if the weight is falling forward or a sudden staccato series of abrupt steps backward on the heels if the falling is backward.

Most individuals can easily inhibit this series of reflex catches, and most individuals can avoid them altogether if they wish, and fall forward until they catch themselves on their hands or flat back if there was someone behind to catch them or they were on a trampoline. What is to be worked on in psychomotor training is the development of sensitivity to each level of catch with the concomitant ability to "give in" to this reflex action without inhibiting it or participating with it on a volitional imitative base. Here, the attempt is made to polarize the reflexive action as much as possible, removing conscious control and emotional expression to the same extent attempted in the species stance itself. The difference now, however, is that greater force and action is called for by the fall reflexes than by the body righting reflexes which mediated the center of gravity by moving the torso forward or back over the feet.

It is difficult to continue relaxing even while the body is falling forward and to allow the subtle, easily dampable reflexes to motivate the legs to move. What compounds the difficulty is that in order to do the most violent fall catch response one must first dampen or not respond to the earliest order of reflex catches, so that the fall catch exercise is seen to have a dual purpose: one, to sensitize one to the low register reflex impulses allowing one's self to respond to them; and, the second, to have the capacity to dampen and be selective to different orders of reflexive responses.

The group is facing the leader waiting to hear instructions on how to do the fall catch, which the group leader can describe in the terms outlined above. The group is instructed to resume the species stance and to allow the center of gravity to fall a small amount beyond the feet and to note the tendency to rise up on the toes or to rock back on the heels and stiffen the knees depending on the direction of the fall. This they can be permitted to do for several minutes until they become accustomed to it. Then the group leader can demonstrate the next step of allowing the center of gravity to go so far beyond the feet that a step is necessitated. Following the demonstration the group is asked to attempt it.

Most group members will have no difficulty in doing these first two steps of the fall catch, although a small percentage will report that their toes are "gripping" the floor and they find they cannot allow their center of gravity to move enough beyond the feet to force a reflexive rise on the toes. This particular minority might include those who tend to collapse at the waist and drop their torso forward rather than rise up. Others might find that the normal oscillations that would provide the momentum for a further falling forward is reduced when they know that they are going to allow their weight to fall more forward. That is, they find that they become too self-conscious and that their controls then turn on, reducing the oscillations and reducing reflexive responses.

Often, the average person who does succeed in allowing for the rise on the toes or the rocking back on the heels will also find a tendency to move his arms in a protective manner, preparing to catch his weight on his hands in the direction he is tending to fall. Occasionally, a group member who knows that the "proper" way to respond is by rising onto the toes, will do that rising in a voluntary and nonreflexive manner. This should be pointed out to that member so that he can become cognizant of the fact that this is not the way to do it in order that he can direct his attention to the subtle reflex impulses which he is apparently ignoring.

Finally, the group leader can demonstrate the furthest and most active point of the fall catch. The leader makes certain that there is sufficient room in the direction of his fall so that he will not fall onto someone or some object, for the entire action usually covers a good deal of space. The leader, in demonstrating, permits his normal oscillation in the species stance to continue until he finds himself falling slightly forward. He permits this forward falling to continue, damping or repressing the early righting reflexes until he reaches a point where he permits or allows his reflexive response to occur. In the process of falling forward, the group leader maintains a columnar posture, in that he does not allow himself to bend at the waist, but keeps the relationship between his shoulders and hips constant. At the lowest point of this columnar fall or tilt, a sudden lurching step forward takes place followed by a series of shorter, less violent, steps which end in a normal posture.

The suddenness of the catching action sometimes prompts a gasp from some members of the group whose own reflexive processes seem to respond to the leader's during his fall catch. Some group members might comment on the fear response they felt at the moment of the catch. They could express the fact that their heartbeat had quickened and that they felt as if adrenalin had entered their blood stream. There may be a question such as, "Weren't you afraid you were going to fall flat on your face?" or, "What made you so sure you weren't going to get hurt?" The leader can explain that he has done this many times and that he simply lets his reflexes work for him while in a sense he "gets a free ride" out of their action. At the catch point in the falling there is very little that one needs to "do" about regaining balance, just as there is little one "does" when slipping on the ice and one's legs are frantically moving about. During those occasions one has the sensation of almost watching from a distance the activity of the body in the balance-regaining process. The same is true in the fall catch when it is done properly.

The leader should see to it that the group is separated sufficiently from one another so that there is no possibility of anyone falling on anyone else and instructs the group to attempt the fall catch all together. Some members will be able to do the fall readily, some will not be able to do it at all and most will make attempts at doing it more or less successfully. Following a period of time when the group continues to try the fall catch on a mass basis, the leader can have each member attempt it individually. This way, he and the other members of the group can have the opportunity of watching individual members do the skill and determine more about the specific areas of ability and lack of it. 1499055

In some groups there have been those who cannot do the fall catch either singly or en masse. They may stand in the stance for some time and finally stand upright saying that they simply cannot relax sufficiently to do it, or that they know that they are holding back and cannot help themselves. Frequently, this same person when attempting to do emotional movement will say the same thing about that: that he cannot let himself go sufficiently to move spontaneously. Thus it can be seen that the fall catch is usable as a rough measure of spontaneity of emotional expression.

The fall catch is only successful if one can remove voluntary controls and "let" the action occur, and since this action is very forceful and violent, it is in some measure similar or reminiscent of strong emotional action and therefore, to some people, frightening. So, in some respects, there is a relationship between one's ability to "give in" to reflex and one's ability to "give in" to emotional impulses, to the extent that both require the reduction of voluntary controls and inhibitions, permitting strong forceful action. This has a learning aspect in that it is safer to give in to reflexes than it is to give in to emotions, and those who are frightened of their emotions and unwilling to act on them can learn that it is not in fact so dangerous to give in to their reflexes and that they are safer than they realized in the hands of their natural body processes.

Thus, practice in the fall catch and continued success and safety in it can lead to similar judgments and abilities in regard to emotional movement. The group member can learn that in emotional movement too one can be safe and not in such dangerous waters as one had feared, and that given the proper circumstances and environment, one can safely give in to emotions without disaster or danger to oneself or others. This is one of the aims of psychomotor training.

Group members watching others attempting the fall catch see quite clearly the difference between the reflexive catch and the voluntary catch. The voluntary catch takes place too early and without the proper body angle being achieved. There is a relationship between the amount of force of the first step forward and the angle of the body to the floor, and although one cannot say specifically what that is, there is a felt response to the difference with the voluntary step appearing spurious, both to the viewer and to the doer. There is no way to "fake" the fall catch. Either one does it or one does not; there is no mistaking it.

Sometimes a group member might do the first step in the catch and then find that he has inhibited the series of smaller steps, remaining for a moment in the first lunge, sinking slightly deeper, absorbing the force of the body's falling. These people note that they just can't seem to let go for more than the first step. Some members might take a tremendous stamp on the first step, far more than would occur reflexively. This stamp can be seen in the same light as the forceful thrusts of the arms in the torso twist, that is, as an expression of emotion that enters in this fall catch process as a "rider."

Once again I must point out that these first skills are attempts at polarizing the three-movement modalities of reflex, voluntary movement and emotional movement, and that each modality must be as free as posssible from combination with other modalities in order for the group member to gain control and freedom of his movement for use at later times in structures. If one did not "remove" the emotion from a reflexive movement, one would not have that emotion available for purer expression later. Sometimes emotion lies "hidden" in various parts of the body, disguised or "frozen" in other activities or ailments. Our aim in psychomotor training is to get all these emotions "out into the open" where they can be dealt with and processed directly and consciously, much as unconscious thoughts are brought out into the open in verbal therapy.

Regarding those individuals who find the fall catch anxiety producing, this may be caused by a variety of reasons. One member might have had a series of bad falls in real life which are forcefully brought back to memory by the fall catch exercise. Another may feel that he is extremely vulnerable and about to get hurt. One member of an experimental, all-male, hospitalized mental patient group expressed hatred for the fall catch. Conversely, he expressed distinct pleasure in doing the voluntary modality. This particular group member could actually make an attempt at doing the fall catch but not too successfully; however, his preference was clearly for the imposition of controls and not the reduction of controls, no matter how safe the circumstances might be.

One long-term member of a group of normals still has difficulty in doing the fall catch properly. He tends to include emotions in his first step by either stamping overly hard or by falling completely to the floor on his hands. This same group member is one of a small minority of individuals who cannot do direct emotional expression even though they have attempted it over a long period of time. The emotional movement that is done by these people is somewhat pantomimic, but most importantly is done without the experience of affect as reported by the group members themselves. This would tend to support the relationship between the fall catch and spontaneous emotional expression described earlier.

The speed of emotional change in those who do not satisfyingly do emotional movement can be expected to be slow, since they cannot truly change until they are willing to do or show their feelings to others as well as to themselves.

One person who had great difficulty in doing the fall catch would stand in the species stance for minutes at a time, tending to fall backward rather than forward and taking, sporadically, a small series of steps backward. This person in one session finally did successfully do the fall catch which indicated that he would be able to do emotional movement successfully too. This turned out to be the case, for future exercises in emotional movement provided no difficulty. The fear of the fall catch had little to do with fear of loss of control, for on discussing the problem it was brought out that this person had taken several severe headlong falls in childhood and it was these memories that prompted inhibition and not inhibition for its own sake. A group leader must take this type of situation into consideration before concluding that a group member is emotionally restrained or not.

As each group member attempts to do the fall catch individually, the group leader can apply his experience in assisting each member in improving his ability. He can also make assessments and expectations to himself in terms of the above. Sometimes he has merely to remind a group member to let his head fall completely down in the preparatory species stance or to let his arms hang loose at the same time. It seems that some members, particularly newer ones, upon pre-

paring for the fall catch, hold themselves more stiffly than they ordinarily would in the species stance, in anticipation of the forceful
movement to come. The group leader's corrections and criticisms are
valuable to the rest of the group watching the individual attempts
to do the fall catch. In this way they can see, perhaps, some of their
own difficulties in others and get an insight on how and why they
are having difficulty. Besides this, it provides the group with experience in assessing and watching others and sensitizing them to different qualities of motor behavior, useful in their everyday lives as
well as in the group activity.

After each person is given the opportunity of doing the fall catch
twice by having each member in turn attempt it once in two con-
secutive "go rounds" of the group, the group leader can have the
members attempt the fall catch backward and sideways. The fall
catch backward and sideways are mostly used as practice opportunities to improve the fall catch forward. It is interesting to note, however, that some group members speak of a preference in doing the
catch backward rather than forward and some speak of a greater
ease in falling to the right side rather than to the left or vice versa.
The significance of these preferences has not been looked into thor-
oughly and should prove an interesting area for study.

The fall catch done backward has a similar preparation as the fall
catch done forward. The group member begins by doing the species
stance, and then allows the center of gravity to fall back behind the
feet. The resultant is a series of short staccato steps with straight
knees going backward with the body tending to bend slightly at the
waist and the arms rising out to the side or forward of the body.

The fall catch done sideways is begun in the same manner, but
this time allowing or rather pushing (for there is little tendency to
oscillate side to side in the species stance) the center of gravity to
either the right or the left of the feet. In this exercise, the body
can be permitted to bend away from the direction of the fall or can
be kept straight in the columnar fashion described in the forward
fall catch. Either way results in an uneven rhythmical series of steps
to the side. It is harder to achieve this successfully and reflexively than
the forward fall catch, yet some group members find it safer to fall
sideways than to fall forward.

There is one other exercise in this series that I sometimes include. It is called the reflex columnar walk. This is quite difficult for most group members to do even after long periods of practice, and has therefore been discontinued as a regular feature in psychomotor training. The aims of the columnar walk are precisely those of the fall catch, and since it is so much harder to achieve and to deal with and since it offers no other value that is not contained in the fall catch, I use it only intermittently. The columnar walk can be seen as an intermediate step between the species stance and the fall catch.

You recall the instructions where one allows the center of gravity to fall slightly beyond the feet and one takes a small step forward. The reflex columnar walk is based on the continuation of the walking forward. To do this, one must step and place the weight on the leg that comes forward with a stiffened knee. The force of the landing on a stiffened leg seems to cause the muscles in the back of the legs, the hamstrings, and so on to contract, making the hip thrust more forward, creating the momentum for the next step. When the columnar walk is done properly, there is a constant angle of the trunk maintained, with the legs regularly stepping forward for as long a time as there is space to travel.

It gives the appearance, and has the sensation when done properly, of walking downhill where there is very little effort necessary to continue walking. The reflex columnar walk is fairly effortless and takes very little energy to do, but I reiterate that most group members find it difficult to do. Children, however, find it relatively easy to do.

The series of exercises that have been described fall under the category of basic motility movement; that is, movement that is mostly reflexive, based on a relaxed body posture known as the species stance, that has a minimum of voluntary control and emotional imagery and that depends for its movement on the interaction between the reflexes, gravity, inertial forces and the minimum voluntary effort that is used in the torso twist. The specific activities are: the species stance, the torso twist, the fall catch and the reflex columnar walk. At this point the leader can instruct the group members to go from one type of basic motility movement to another, gaining skill in relaxing and giving in to reflex movement. The group can practice this for approximately five minutes during which time the leader can watch the progress or lack of it in individual group members. This practice gives confidence to group members that there are other things operating besides their controls which are safe to their self-esteem and to their self-image.

The group now has something concrete to work on. There is less anxiety about the possibility of giving vent to emotions and there is much concentration on learning a specific non-threatening skill. The group is no longer facing the unknown. They are developing a skill in a new area that has been with them and which they may never have explored before or since they were children. For most group members this practice is fairly pleasurable, but for a minority, and usually the most disturbed members of the group, this may not at all be pleasant but slightly dizzying. This information, if it is forthcoming from the members, is valuable to the leader as he can make note of those with whom emotional expression should be entered into at a slow pace and with care and caution.

One member of a newly formed group could go no further than the very first session in which nothing more than what has been described to now was attempted. The reduction of even enough controls to do the species stance was far more than he could stand and he terminated his relationship with the group. In this case it was the most sensible thing to do. Such a person should find the time to work on a one-to-one basis where he might learn to relax under highly controlled circumstances. Following that he could once again attempt the activity within a group. It has been my experience that seriously disturbed patients (although the person described above was not a patient) should be approached on a one-to-one basis first until they can learn to operate within a group setting. Then the feeling of threat that arises with the dropping of controls can be minimized and safely gone through.

Following the practice period on the basic motility exercise there usually follows a moment of rest and possibly, discussion. At this time some group members may ask questions. One group member wanted to know whether at this time one was expected to be more or less tired than at the beginning of the session. When, following this question, a call of hands was asked for, it appeared that the group included those who were more relaxed than when they had begun and those who were less relaxed and positively more tense than when the group had begun. The tense ones seem to include those whose emotions have been fairly repressed and who now, after a period of time when controls have been reduced, feel headachy, fatigued and uncomfortable. It would almost seem that these people during the activity of the day might be working off their emotions in innocuous and unconscious ways and not having the opportunity to do so during the relaxed, unemotional basic motility skills, feel the backup of these emotions as discomfort, headache, fatigue, and so on. This is only speculation on my part but my experience indicates that those who are not particularly repressing emotions enjoy the freedom of the basic motility skills.

Other questions that might be asked concern the problem of getting more relaxed if one has found that one is not capable now of getting relaxed. The group leader can take this time to point out that the future sessions will deal with the expression of emotions which might be repressed, allowing the group member to be more capable of relaxing in the future. The leader might even begin to outline the future composition of structures giving that more tense member a specific goal to work toward at some future sessions. Care should be taken in this projection of the future that materials not in the group member's awareness as yet should not be aroused and brought to the surface too soon.

Although most of those group members who have enjoyed the basic motility skills may be less repressed there might be included in that number one or more individuals whose emotional expression has been so turned off as to be considered beyond physical repression. There seems to be a class of individuals whose bodies are relaxed and who respond favorably to reflexive movement but who may not be as emotionally open as they would at first appear. These people have secured a "haven" from their emotions in the relaxation of the body. For them the species stance is not a place to drop to in order to find what is exposed when the controls are off; rather, it is a haven where outside and inside stimuli are effectively turned off. This is simply one other possibility the group leader must keep in mind when contemplating the manner in which new and as yet unknown group members respond to the basic motility modality. Experience shows that some of this particular group might not perform the species stance as well at some future time when their emotions might be closer to being expressed in movement. When the conflicting or repressed material is finally expressed and resolved the species stance improves once again, and this person has the ability to use the stance in two ways rather than just one.

The basic motility skills provide a varied means of assessing the potential expression of emotional material for both the individual group members and for the group leader. They also provide the individual group member with concrete exercises which tend to improve one's ability to relax, trust one's reflexes and to trust one's fellow man. They provide the leader with some means of determining what areas to concentrate on in future meetings. This basic motility area, as so much else in psychomotor Techniques and training, is both a skill and a barometer due to its reduction and polarization away from all other elements. This reduction and polarization process underlies all that is done in psychomotor Techniques and training and provides the leader and the group with specific and clear tools with which to work.

CHAPTER

3

Following the practice of the basic motility skills for some minutes, the group is ready for the next area to be covered, voluntary movement. The leader can call the group to attention and have them sit or stand as he elaborates on what is to be done next. In psychomotor training, voluntary movement is polarized just as in the basic motility area. That is, it is separated as much as possible from all other types of movement. Voluntary movement is understood as that type of movement that has to do with conscious control of a body in space in a nonfunctional, nonexpressive way. The three types of voluntary movement that will be outlined and practiced range from the most conscious type of voluntary motion to the least conscious and most habituated and automatic. The first two types of voluntary movement are done for the sake of mastery of the body and not for the sake of function or purpose of any kind besides mastery. The third includes the function of satisfying interest and curiosity.

Reflex movement of the kind used in the species stance has the function of maintaining the balance of the body over the center of gravity. The movement I am now making with my fingers in the process of typing the manuscript for this book has the function of producing a typewritten page. Voluntary movement of the kind I am describing in psychomotor training is certainly included in the process of typing. What is sought at this time in the first two categories is the voluntary movement capacity or capability completely, or as much as possible, separated from its use within a function or purposeful or expressive act. All three types of voluntary movement include conscious predetermination of the movement to be executed.

The first category of voluntary movement is called conscious voluntary movement. This type of movement calls for maximum concentration and minimum energy expenditure. This type of movement is ordinarily called for in the most fine motor control necessitated by involvement with a new task not yet habituated. An example of this type of voluntary movement (not isolated but included in the service of some purpose) would be the movement of a person in a darkened room, who would carefully grope about so as not to injure himself or break objects in the room. That care and control would include the use of what is now being called conscious voluntary movement.

As the example shows, voluntary movement is most often used in ordinary or real life toward the end of providing the self with more perfect adaptation to external conditions. Voluntary movement can be understood as that motor system which is directed to the outside world and the body's greater congruence with that environment—the external environment of objects and others as distinguished from the internal environment of feelings and sensations. This internal environment causes what is called emotional movement in psychomotor training.

The basic motility area movements necessitate a giving in to gravity, a giving in to reflex and a giving in to centrifugal force. Voluntary movement offers the complete reverse—maximum control, maximum awareness of the process of energy expenditure, maximum awareness of the placement in space of the portions of the body. No longer is the group member to be merely a species man; he is asked to make his individual control of his body manifest, but for no purpose or function as yet. He is on the other end of the scale from the basic motility area. There is no giving up of one's sovereignty. Instead there is the development of this sovereignty, or rather the use of this sovereignty, for it should have been developed very early in life. (Note the infant's hand-eye practice as it lies on its back in its crib, slowly turning its hand this way and that as it notes and watches carefully what effect each motor impulse produces.)

The instructions the leader gives the group include the concepts described above as he prepares the group for the exploration of this skill and modality. The group is instructed to stand in a relaxed, neutral, nonexpressive manner, but not in the species stance. The group members are told to decide to move their arms to a place or angle from their body.

Although it is possible to move any part of the body in the conscious voluntary modality, it is easiest to begin practice with the arm and hand. If the leg is attempted the balance problem becomes too severe. If the head is the part of the body that is moved, the eyes tend to pick up objects in the field of vision. This focusing on external objects tends to draw concentration away from the effort. Interest directed toward the objects seen destroys the polarization that is being attempted. For this reason, it is sometimes recommended that group members attempt this for the first time with eyes closed, reducing the possibility of purposeful responses to the external world.

After the group member decides the position in space to which he wants his arm to be raised, he is instructed to concentrate on raising the arm with the minimum amount of effort possible to that position. The goal is to utilize only as much energy as is necessary to overcome gravity and not a bit more. Of course it would be perfectly simple, if one wished to raise one's arm to a particular place in space, to simply place the arm there and be done with it, but one would not have the opportunity of learning what can be learned by doing it in the way described. In this exercise, the aim is to bridge the distance between the intention and the execution of an act or movement.

In ordinary life, if one wishes to move his arm, he simply does so; however, the distance between the decision and the execution is large. The conscious self makes the intention and the execution is relegated to an automatic process that is essentially unconscious. For one cannot take the time to consciously contact the proper series of muscles in the proper order for every single act made during the day. The cost in concentration and energy would be obviously impossibly high; therefore, it is evident that much action must be relegated to automatic "systems" of the brain. It is the intention of this exercise to highlight this particular human capacity for fine motor control and consciousness, not for the purpose of using it for everyday living, but to assist in the effort of *conscious* mastery of the body. The group member is asked to make his awareness both decide and execute a particular action, minimizing, as much as possible, the automatic execution of that action, for no other reason than that he has the capacity to do it and he wishes to exercise that capacity, consciously.

Ordinarily unconscious too, is the utilization of proprioceptive feedback which informs the appropriate brain centers of the location of body parts in space. This exercise attempts to focus awareness on this proprioceptive feedback so that the group member can make the most minute actions possible, and "listen" to the most minute possible verifications of this action arriving from his kinesthetic proprioceptors. The group member is instructed to maintain this high level of concentration and awareness throughout the span of movement that is selected. All other thoughts and sensations are reduced to a minimum, all concentration being employed as much as possible in the endeavor at hand. In short, he is attempting to move at the lowest possible amplitude in terms of energy expenditure and the highest possible amplitude in terms of awareness. He is testing his own "fine tuning."

I have attempted to teach the voluntary modality to an autistic boy, age 21, but he cannot do any movement that is without function or purpose. If I ask him to place his arm out to the side he can only do so if I ask him to touch my own arm which is to the side of his. With constant passive placement of both his arms to the side and down by me, and constant verbal repetition of the spatial location of side and down I have seen him come to learn that there is such a place as side and such a place as down. In his case the nonfunctional fine tuning has yet to be developed let alone exercised. His functional fine-tuning appears quite well developed, for he can draw, cut with scissors, and handle delicate objects with great care when he wishes.

Following the instructions, the group leader can demonstrate to the group how conscious voluntary movement is done. The group leader can take the stance he has described to the group, that is, a relaxed neutral stance with the head up. The group leader must blank his mind as much as possible, turning off his response or potential response to all that is around him and decide which arm he wishes to move and to what angle and direction he wishes it to rise. That done, he proceeds to attempt to move the arm with only enough energy to overcome gravity.

It is difficult to describe the internal process that results in movement so minute but there is a constant effort to relax all muscles possible while attempting to move the smallest distance possible. At times it seems as if there is no effort at all being made and yet one can feel the slight action in the joint. To move takes so little energy that is is surprising how much excess energy is constantly being used in everyday life. The group leader may find that his mind tends to wander from the task and he must consciously refocus and concentrate his attention to the movement he has selected to do. The leader finds that as he resumes concentration that his awareness of the rest of the room and its occupants diminishes and that the activity can indeed absorb almost his entire consciousness. His eyes do not focus on anything in the room for if they do he will find that the movement of his arms tends to stop or that he tends to respond indirectly to what he has seen. If the leader is self-conscious, he will find that he will have some difficulty in maintaining his concentration. For he will be battling emotional responses to the group members staring at him. If the leader has some personally pressing problems he may find his mind darting to those topics and be unable to apply sufficient concentration to do the movement properly. In that event he may find himself depending on more automatic processes to execute the movement, or he might find that in the effort of battling his emotions he has little energy left to apply to his awareness.

If none of these negative factors are present at the time the leader is demonstrating this modality, he will find that he can control minute expenditures of energy with fine awareness of the precise placement of his arm and hand but without tension arising on any other part of his body. The arm will very slowly and somewhat unevenly be raised to the point pre-selected while his attention is focused on precisely how this feels with little or no awareness of other than that. Observing the group members during this demonstration, one would be struck by the amount of concentration that this arouses in them. There is a contagion about all kinds of movement and each kind produces more of itself. It is almost as if some of the same processes of attention and concentration were induced in the group by their observation of this being exercised. (In passing it might be said that movement done by the leader in basic motility skills produces a like kind of relaxation in the group for the same reasons.)

The group watching this demonstration becomes very still and one can almost feel a certain suspension of the normal breathing rhythm. Perhaps this occurs because heavy breathing would move the group member's own body too much and he would be less able to discriminate between his own and the group leader's minute movements.

Such slow movement seems to provide a certain fascination for the viewer. The movement is obviously not random, but purposeful, and it is so slow that one must be careful just to notice that it is moving at all. Its slowness and precision connotes concentration and the group members or other observers are made aware of the consciousness and concentration of the demonstrator. It is a combination of all these factors that makes it possible for the group leader to know when others are doing this modality properly or not.

When the group leader reaches the point he has chosen in advance, he lets his arm fall and he resumes his awareness and interest in the group. This moment of achieving one's goal, even if it is a functionless one, provides a certain measure of satisfaction, a sense of closure, a sense of completion. This is an important part of psychomotor therapy and training, for it essentially completes a very important chain of events in developing autonomy: decision, programming, implementation, verification. Some of those who are emotionally ill find it difficult to complete this chain. They may, if they can, make a decision, but find it difficult to program it. They may program it, but find it difficult to initiate it. They may implement it but be uncertain about verifying it. What I am suggesting is the beginning of the use of this exercise as a means of determining whether a given patient is growing to a point where he can complete this four-step procedure satisfactorily or note which step he is unable to complete.

Further in the book I will attempt to extend this concept to include the verification of other types of movement, with the verification coming from other members of the group. With this exercise there is not yet consideration of the group for we are still sensitizing the group member to himself and his own impulses and their successful manifestation. From this the reader can determine that systems of communication are being developed in this process: communication between one aspect of oneself with another aspect of that self; communication of that self with other selves.

Following the leader's demonstration of conscious voluntary movement, some group member might ask a question such as, "Why did you move so slowly? Couldn't you get the arm there faster if you wanted to?" The leader could take the opportunity of reiterating and reminding that the finest type of motor control and concentration was being employed as described earlier, and that faster voluntary movement would come under another category of movement, namely, habitual voluntary movement. Another group member might comment that: "It killed me to see you move so slowly; I got a terrific sense of frustration and I wanted you to get over with it." Others might say: "I was fascinated with the movement and couldn't take my eyes off it because I didn't want to miss anything." Other comments might include: "You looked like some sort of robot, it was a little frightening," or, "I'd like to try to do that now myself."

There are those who detest this type of movement and those who find it peaceful and these comments indicate possible tendencies of group members for and against doing voluntary movement. Those against doing voluntary movement tend to dislike moving their bodies without affect and purpose. Those for it tend to like inhibiting emotional expression and exercising mastery over their bodies in an abstract way.

The group has been given instructions, the rationale behind the exercise and a demonstration, and now they are ready to attempt this modality themselves. The leader can instruct them to stand, if they have been sitting, and assume the relaxed neutral stance as preparation for moving in this modality. He can briefly outline the steps to be done once again: that each group member should choose in advance a position in which he wishes his arm to be placed; concentrate on which muscles he will work with; use only enough energy to overcome gravity and no more; note by kinesthetic, proprioceptive and visual feedback where the arm is placed in space at each moment; and complete the movement as planned; all without function, purpose or emotional associations.

As the group members begin to do the movement, the group leader can watch to see what variations on the instructions some group members might make or whether the movement is done as described. Some group members will be obviously moving too fast, utilizing the habitual movement modality, others will make clear gestural or functional movements such as pointing a finger or making a fist as the arm is being raised, others may look around confused and others may do the movement just as described. The leader can make short comments in a low tone at this time, for comments might tend to break the concentration level of those who are doing it properly. He can indicate by gesture to those who are confused that this is all right and for them to wait and he will explain later what to do. Those who are moving too rapidly can be told simply, "slower," or "use even less energy" in a low tone. The group leader can walk quietly up to those group members who are using imagery unconsciously and apprise them of that fact by saying,"That movement seems to have gestural connotations, try to do it without any meaning or gesture or emotion whatsoever." In some groups the leader might not make any comment at all until everyone indicated that he had completed the exercise. The comments described might be offered in subsequent attempts at this modality. This watching of the first attempts of the group can be quite instructive to the leader, for at a glance he can tell whether an individual group member is able or inclined to do this type of concentration. Of course, with practice, almost all group members will be able to do this properly, but the group leader can begin to note which members have a natural propensity for this type of movement and which do not.

The group leader can instruct the group that whenever a member had completed an exercise to his own satisfaction he should sit quietly on the floor until the entire group has also finished the exercise. In this way the concentration of individual group members is not shattered by other members walking and talking about. Once all are seated the group leader can ascertain when to begin speaking and making comments and instructions.

When the entire group is seated or has shown that it has completed the exercise the group leader can ask individual group members to comment on how it made them feel or how well they felt they completed the exercise. Some group members may say that they decided where they wanted their arm to move but that they could not get their arm to go where they wanted it. Some group members may comment on the fact that they chose in advance to move their arms so that they would be straight out from the shoulder and that they found it difficult to raise their arms past the forty-five degree angle to the body using this method. The group leader can point out that the fine motor control method alone is insufficient in raising the arms further than that point and causes strain. Past that point the arm feels enormously heavy and the same level of concentration and minimum effort can no longer be maintained. Larger muscle groups than those used in fine control must then come into play to overcome the increased weight.

Other group members may comment that it did not feel as if they were moving their arm, but that it felt as if the arm just moved itself. This kind of response suggests that this type of person, even though exercising his own sovereignty, denies his own mastery of his own body. Comments similar to this are, "It felt something like that exercise where you press your arms against the wall or a door frame forcibly for some seconds and then when you move away from the wall or door and your arms move up without any conscious effort." This person is not saying that his arms moved up by themselves, but is noting a similarity to that, for in truth it takes so little energy to raise the arms, as noted before, that it hardly seems as if any at all is being expended to initiate the act.

Others might comment that the exercise made their arms tingle, or that they became aware of each set of muscles as they began to come into play. This type of comment illustrates the heightened level of concentration and awareness that this exercise fosters. Others might comment that the arm felt very light, illustrating the small amount of effort needed to move it. Another comment is that the arm felt terribly heavy and that it took a great deal of concentration and effort to move it even though it did not raise as high as forty-five degrees. This would attest to the amount of concentration and energy that was available to these people.

If someone were terribly weak and exhausted, even the smallest amount of effort would be tiring. These people are not so exhausted, but their energy available for concentration is exhausted and they experience this lack as strain and heaviness. Some may say that they really enjoyed doing this type of movement and that it fascinated them to see just how slowly they could move. This group includes those who find this type of movement satisfying, for it reinforces their mastery over their emotions and control over their bodies. This type experiences this modality as a haven from feeling and as a confirmation of their power over unruly forces. Generally, this type does not like to do the fall catch and can be expected to find it difficult to do emotional movement.

Another group member might comment that he found this type of movement extremely distasteful and that it made him angry to do it. This type of person, I have found, disliked the sensation of having to remove affect or feeling from his body as this exercise demands. This loss of affect is experienced as a loss of meaningfulness and can sometimes produce anxiety in some people. It also could imply that this person is carrying about in his body, unexpressed, or indirectly expressed, emotions in a "tacit" form.

Some group members may have no understanding at all of how to do this type of movement and have difficulty in doing it for some period of time. Obviously, the concentration level of these people is low and possibly will get higher following resolution of long repressed conflicting emotions. Sometimes the group leader will note that group members who are in the process of doing conscious voluntary movement will display random or irrelevant habitual movements during the period of time devoted to this exercise. For instance, they may be slowly raising the right arm, but the leader can notice that the left hand might be unconsciously raised to scratch the face, move a hair, rub the nose or eye or whatever with the group member taking no notice of the fact that he has done this. This, to me, represents a flaw in the concentration of that person, for no movement was to be initiated that was not chosen in advance and totally controlled.

Other group members might note that there was a variation in their ability to execute this movement between the right and left arms, finding it easier, perhaps, to do it on the right side than on the left. One member in one group, attempting to raise the right arm was startled to find that the left arm was the one that moved and that the right arm remained stationary. Another, choosing in advance to move the right arm, was totally unprepared for the fact that both arms moved simultaneously in opposite directions. In general, the average group member finds this modality illuminating in one way or another, for, at the very least, he is exercising his control in a way that he rarely, if ever, takes the time to do. He learns something about energy expenditure, something about control, something about awareness and concentration and something about his underlying emotional level.

When the leader has finished making comments on the manner of executing this exercise he can invite the group to attempt it once again, applying the new learning to the second effort. The leader can reiterate that the movement should be slow, unexpressive and without purpose, and remind those who showed speed, expression and purpose to attempt to eliminate those qualities this time. The leader can also suggest that if the right arm was used the first time that the group member should explore the left arm the second time, or possibly even the hand or the head. He can invite the group members to explore the possible differences in moving different parts of the body in this modality.

This second attempt gives the leader the opportunity of seeing how rapidly those who had difficulty the first time improve their performance. This would be a rough measure of educability. Most group members will inevitably show some improvement, whereas a minority may remain in the exact dilemma of the first try. Following the second attempts, the group leader can call for comment or discussion. Several members might volunteer that they now are beginning to know how to do this properly and find it interesting. Others might say, "I still don't like it," and others might simply express that they do it without any particular interest in it except that it was assigned. As was demonstrated with the basic motility area skills, the conscious voluntary movement modality is both a skill and a barometer. Those who cannot concentrate can see clearly that they do not, and yet have an opportunity for clear-cut practice in concentration. However, practice in concentration alone will not produce concentration, for energy must be made available in order that concentration may occur.

Now the group is ready to attempt the second type of voluntary movement, habitual voluntary movement. Habitual voluntary movement is similar to conscious voluntary movement in that it is movement that is preselected, without function value or expression and emotional association. It is different in that not as much concentration is utilized as in conscious voluntary movement. In habitual voluntary movement, the instructions are for the group member to choose in advance a position in space which he wants his arm to reach, to feel or imagine the limb to be in that space, to give himself the cue or order to place his arm in that position quickly and smoothly but without excess force, and to raise his arm to that position, not, however, using the same level of concentration and control as in the conscious voluntary modality. When the arm reaches the chosen spot in space the position is to be maintained with a minimum of effort. In the case of habitual voluntary movement the verification is made after the fact and not during it as in conscious voluntary movement, when each individual motion and verification of placement was done consciously. In habitual voluntary movement the action is done automatically, without the concomitant awareness and control, and the verification is made only at the moment of cessation of the movement, when the limb has reached the preselected spot.

The group leader should make it clear that each movement that is done should include the action in one direction, of only one joint at a time, eliminating complex and coordinated movements. Following the first movement, the group member is to choose in advance another placement, perhaps for his other arm, perhaps for his hand, head, torso, or any other part of his body and proceed in the same manner as for the first movement, maintaining the limb in the position selected, resulting finally in a complex placement of the body. The group is reminded that since it is so easy to move the body without awareness and without consciousness that they should be careful not to move in what is called "random mode" where the limbs move in a constantly active yet not chosen manner. This random mode breaks the chain of decision, program, implementation and verification. In "random mode," decision is removed since no conscious decision has been made; implementation is left to the same unconscious forces as are used in habitual voluntary movement; and there is no verification as there has been no decision. Obviously then, random mode does not provide the same learning opportunities as does habitual voluntary movement.

The question might be asked, "What is the purpose of going through all this difficulty for the simple reason of moving the body which can move so easily?" The answer is that we are not merely attempting to move the body easily but also attempting to gain mastery over the body and in the process learn something about ourselves. Random mode does not provide anything but exercise.

After the explanation and instruction regarding the doing of habitual voluntary movement the group leader can demonstrate it so the group can see what it looks like. The group leader takes the same relaxed, neutral, nonexpressive stance he took for the conscious voluntary movement demonstration. He then removes his interest from the group and the objects in the room, allowing his eyes to unfocus and, turning his concentration inward to his own body, is prepared to begin. He then decides to move his arm directly in front of him. He imagines the arm in that place. He gives himself an internal command to place it there. The arm is raised to that point and stops. He verifies that this is the placement he chose in advance. He then decides to turn his head to the right. He feels or imagines the head in that placement. He gives the internal command to move it there. He moves it there taking care not to focus his eyes on any object so that he does not get involved in seeing in the new direction the head is placed. He verifies that this is the placement he chose in advance. He continues on in this manner until he had achieved a complex placement of the body.

The group leader must constantly be on the alert to remove or suppress whatever associations each movement might produce, for each placement of the body must indeed have ideas and memories associated with it. One of the aims of this exercise is to remove as much as possible all expression and meaning or rather to move with as little possible expression and meaning; therefore a certain amount of attention must be paid to the suppression of the associations that would normally arise from any and all movement. The concentration necessary for the execution of habitual voluntary movement is lower than that of conscious voluntary movement as each individual energy expenditure is not processed through consciousness as is done in conscious voluntary movement. The movement has less intensity and less fascination than does conscious voluntary movement. In a sense it creates some difficulty for the doer, for he has less application or need for his concentration, and yet must not use his concentration for responding to associations that the movement can provide.

When the group leader has completed the demonstration, some group members might ask questions regarding the demonstration or ask for clarification regarding the exercise. They might inquire why the leader picked the particular placements he did and whether there was any meaning to it. The group leader can explain that the attempt was made to move as meaninglessly as possible and that if there was any meaning communicated that it was unintentional. This particular modality provides many interesting opportunities for assessing what is pertinent to the person doing it at the time he is moving in this manner. For quite frequently the resultant placement has obvious emotional and gestural meanings to the viewer that might be entirely unnoticed by the person who has been moving. Some group members end up in placements that are obviously aggressive with arms extended in front and with closed hands. Others seem to be reaching for something either in front of them or slightly above them. Not only does the external pose reflect such feelings, but the subtle involvement of the entire body and the changing expressions of the face also emphasize the emotional meanings being expressed. Of course as one becomes more familiar with this exercise one is more and more able to move without expressions but I am not at all sure that one can move entirely without some meaning in this particular modality since the actual movement is relegated to unconscious processes and each step of the way is not as controlled as in conscious voluntary movement.

The group leader can now instruct the group to attempt this exercise and he can remind them that as soon as they have completed the exercise to their satisfaction that they can sit quietly until the rest of the group has done so. The beginning group that attempts this modality makes certain predictable mistakes. Many move the body in overly complex movements that include the movement of more than one joint at a time. For instance a group member might do a movement that included a simultaneous raising of the arm and bending of the elbow. The proper execution of habitual voluntary movement should fragment the body excluding coordinated placements. By fragmented I mean that the body should not be used in a unified way, that is, with various body parts related to one another as in functional or purposeful movements.

Other group members might make very obvious and even deliberate gestural movements indicating that they have not understood the instructions or that the group leader was not clear enough in giving instructions. Among this number are those who do not know that a certain movement is obviously gestural and complex. Many look like they are moving their arms in a manner reminiscent of shaking hands or in a manner that would indicate "stop." The most common error is made in the amount of force used in this exercise. Those who have a great deal of emotional "spillover" and who showed this spillover in such exercises as the torso twist and the fall catch can be expected to do habitual voluntary movement with a good deal more force than is necessary to smoothly and quickly move the body part to the placement selected. I understand the amount of excess force to be drawn from emotional states or feelings. Those who are angry use a strong action and a sudden stopping of the arm, producing in the viewer a very clear sensation of aggressiveness. It is clear that now it is not the general look of the externals of the movement that is being expressive in this case, but the very type of nervous energy that is used to move into those external forms is being expressive. The group leader can use this opportunity of watching the group members perform this exercise to note for the future the type of emotional expression that is most predominant in each person so that he can suggest for some future time the appropriate kind of structure that would be relevant to that emotion.

Following the practice of this exercise by the members of the group, the leader can ask for comments and provide feedback to the group regarding their performance of this modality. Some will note that they found it difficult to avoid emotional associations that arose from the movement. Some will note how much more difficult it was to do a movement that they had planned than they had anticipated. They learn that to move only one joint at a time imposes difficulty in executing a complex act. This exercise provides an opportunity to explore exactly how complex movement can be broken down into its component parts. It is an education about the body but not physical education in the sense that it is customarily used. Physical education does employ habitual voluntary movement to be sure, but the movement is usually chosen in advance by others; therefore the decision is taken out of one's hands. Too often, too, physical education is done in what I call random mode; the movement is not random, but the awareness level is extremely low and the concentration level often nil. There is little that is learned in physical education of this kind as it is usually practiced.

In the exercise of using habitual voluntary movement, a person can and does learn a great deal about the body and what it can and cannot do, but most important, he is his own master and he makes his own decisions and implements them. He is not merely a puppet with someone else pulling the strings. The habitual and conscious voluntary modalities are exercises in developing mastery and control over the body that place the "strings" of his own movement possibilities into his own hands. He must take the responsibility for his own actions and he must see to it that he carries out his own decisions.

Some group members really enjoy this modality, for they can use it as an opportunity for finding what patterns they can make with their bodies. One must be sure, however, to point out to these people that the movements chosen are not to be expressive, for those who enjoy this tend to be carried away and become creative and expressive when that is not the aim of this exercise. The group leader must be sure to remind the group members that emotions are not to be included in the selection of patterns that are employed.

The third type of voluntary movement practiced and clarified in psychomotor training is called "voluntary patterns in the service of interest and curiosity." This voluntary modality includes interest and relationship to the external environment. The eyes and the sense of touch are used as the carriers of the information regarding certain segments of the environment. The other two voluntary modalities explicitly remove or ignore the environment both through sight and by touch. In this respect this final voluntary modality differs sharply from the others. The others developed movement for abstract and nonfunctional purposes, and provided a measurable index of one's ability to move without affect and meaning. This last voluntary modality includes function and purpose, but only function and purpose on the level of interest and curiosity. It does not include purpose where survival and the satisfaction of strong drives would be concerned. It is clear that we are moving into the area of "applied" voluntary movement, that is, voluntary movement for the purpose of other than mastery.

Voluntary patterns in the service of interest and curiosity share with the other voluntary modalities the same sequence of predetermination of action, program of action, execution of action, and verification of action. This modality also shares with the others the use of voluntary patterns of movement. The level of voluntary movement used in this modality differs from the other two in the direction of "automation" of the action. In the continuum stretching from least, to most automatic action, it rests in the area of most automatic. It is clearly a voluntary modality and yet it serves as a bridge toward functional movement. The addition of the environment and one's curiosity regarding elements in the environment provides us with a way of formally dealing with the environment in a somewhat measurable or evaluable way. For example, what part of the environment is selected by the group member to respond to? What does he do with that part? How much, if any, is he motivated by strong emotional imagery? These and other questions will be regarded following a description of how the exercise is taught and executed.

The group is asked to look about the room and pick out some object that is found interesting. They are to continue looking at the object until their interest or curiosity regarding that object is aroused. Following this, they are to "program" themselves, doing the movement in their minds. They can imagine rising and walking over to the selected object, touching and handling it in a way that would satisfy their curiosity or interest and then give themselves the cue to initiate and complete all this action in the way programmed, terminating the exercise.

For example, one might look at a doorknob in a room, find one's self becoming interested in its shape and texture, feel the desire to rise and walk over to said object, imagine how it would feel to touch the object and then decide to do just that which was imagined. It must be said here that curiosity in the external world is continually provoking unconscious "programs" of behaviors relevant to the dealing with, or handling of, that aspect of the external world.

What is being practised is the raising to conscious awareness of the programming that is continually and unconsciously going on during our waking hours. Each event, each object in the world provokes multiple programs relevant to the dealing with those events, and those objects. "Being startled" is to my mind being in the position of having no program available for the sudden arrival of events or stimuli. That the experience of being startled is unpleasant goes without saying and is one of the reasons why people like to be prepared beforehand for what is to be expected. This exercise highlights and brings to consciousness in a simple way this programming process while extending the programming process over time. It also highlights one's ability to become interested in the external world and then to make decisions regarding relating to that world.

Ordinarily, one is facing multiple programs overlapping and interacting with one another. This exercise demands that one limit one's awareness and interest in the external world to a single object so that clarity in awareness and execution can best be obtained. The group leader can demonstrate this fact by demonstrating the exercise and I will elaborate to the reader what might be the internal processes accompanying this exercise. The group leader stands in a neutral comfortable stance, not the species stance, and looks about the room. He selects an object or surface in the room that presents some sensation of appeal to him. It might be the doorknob, it might be a surface of a wall, it might be a spot on the floor, it might be an edge of a picture frame, it might be a chair in the room or any one of a number of points or objects in the room. For this particular demonstration, the group leader might select a spot on the floor. He then feels the wish for his curiosity regarding the spot to be satisfied.

This curiosity can be experienced or explained as an active desire to move to that spot, or it might be explained as the subjective experience of the programming process preparing for the exploration of that spot. In any event, the group leader consciously participates in this programming process. To be sure, the unconscious programming is highly rapid, complex and fluid, for it is also preparing for instantaneous adaptation to new events and balances and situations which would tend to result in revised programs, but the conscious attempt at programming is not as multi-dimensional, nor as rapid, as the unconscious one.

The conscious programming calls for an active intent on the group leader's part, slowing down or stretching out, the unconscious elements in the programming process. The group leader imagines, or programs himself standing, experiences the internal sense of walking over to the spot, imagines stooping down to the spot on the floor, and reaching his arm forward so that his hand can touch and explore the spot on the floor. Following this conscious process he makes the internal decision to implement his program and gives himself over to the automatic rendering of the program.

At this moment he becomes aware of the inadequacy of his conscious programming, for almost at once, he is forced to make other moves with his body than he had consciously prepared for, due to finding the balance of his body different than what he had imagined. He now finds functioning a kind of "on board" computer, which continues programming, as he goes along, adapting and modifying the original program in terms of what is actually being experienced in process of completing the intended action. He arrives at the point of the room he has selected to examine, notes how differently the spot looks from this angle; he stoops, finding that his body is responding slightly differently than he had expected; he reaches forward, touches and examines the spot, noting its difference from other sections of the floor and feels a satisfaction in finally completing what he had set out to do. He then returns to his place in the room.

Having completed the exercise, members of the group may now ask the group leader questions regarding the purpose or point of the exercise. For example, one might ask, "Why go through all that rigmarole when it would have been perfectly simple to walk over and do whatever you wanted to do?" The group leader can point out that, done in that way, the exercise would lose the function of bringing to awareness the unconscious programming each stimulus provokes. The group leader can spell out each section of the exercise pointing out its use and value. He can note the value, or the fact, of awareness of external objects and what kinds of responses these objects potentiate. He can explain the value of conscious participation in the programming process toward increasing awareness of thought and action processes going on unconsciously in the brain. He can point out how mastery is being developed by consciously imagining the various actions that would have to be done to gratify interest or curiosity. He can discuss the value of gaining practice and understanding in the self-initiating process that follows the programming. He can point out the value of self-discipline practice developed by maintenance of or adherence to the original plan of action, although it is somewhat modified by discovery of new elements unforeseeable in the original plan-making phase. He can elaborate on the sense of completion and satisfaction that is achievable by culminating, in actual touching and discovery, the entire plan from beginning to end.

Of course, one might say that all this was perfectly normal and going on unconsciously anyway, so why bother doing it any other way. The answer is simply that doing it in this manner gives us the added opportunity and value of clarity and distinctness about which specific questions can be raised, following an imperfectly executed program. This clarification of elements runs through the entire activity in psychomotor training and provides the leader with refined tools for making evaluations and diagnoses. It also provides the group member with a means of gauging his own efforts and evaluating his own abilities with regard to awareness, imagination, and mastery.

The group leader can now direct the members of the group to attempt this exercise. The group is instructed to look about the room until a particular object or surface attracts attention or provokes interest, and then to follow the sequences of the exercise as outlined above. The members of the group can be watched by the group leader to see in what manner the exercise is carried out, or not carried out, as described. There is usually a bit of a pause as the group looks about the room wondering what object to select, and wondering whether the exercise makes sense to them. Some group members might, at once, walk to an object and start handling it in a realistic fashion with evident interest, forgetting for the moment, to preprogram the action, and going at once toward satisfying their interest. Others might stare and strain as they look at an object, waiting for a recognizable strong "program." Others might do the exercise exactly as described and follow through with the movement after the internal programming.

The programming in this exercise is not a vivid outline of movement; it is more like a sense of the movement, and those who are waiting for something larger than this sense wait in vain, until it is made clear to them what the difference is. There might be those in the group who make a very elaborate program in their minds and who then go through the movement more in the manner of habitual voluntary movement than in the manner of voluntary patterns in the service of interest and curiosity. That is, they may go through the movement as robots or mechanical men, mistakenly assuming that this is what is intended. Indeed, it is not what is intended. The movement subsequent to the programming should be just as normal movement is, except that this movement is done with the conscious awareness that it has been consciously pre-programmed. This kind of consciousness sometimes produces self-consciousness, in the negative sense, but this is not the intent of the exercise.

Corrections can be given to those who have utilized the instructions incorrectly, or who have done the exercise incorrectly, for whatever reason, and the entire group can be given the opportunity of doing the exercise several times more, for practice. Normals who do this exercise tend to find it easily understandable after one or several trials, but those who have difficulty in concentration or in practicing sovereignty, have difficulty in finding the point of the exercise. Some hospitalized patients can make no sense whatever of this exercise, not knowing what it means to have a self in the first place. Some patients have found that they were able enough to program a series of movements toward an object, but that they had little feeling about the object in the first place, and in the second place, could not get themselves to do what they had planned or even to do anything at all. With normal group members there can be quite a bit of variation without going to the extent just described.

After a group has attempted the exercise a number of times, the group leader can ask for comments. Some group member might comment that they found they could not possibly reach the object they had selected without the use of a ladder or some other tool. My impression is, that those who pre-select objects that they later find unreachable, tend to be exactly like that in real life: constantly attempting what is beyond them, and at which effort they must inevitably fail. One group member who was highly distrustful of people, and who, although in a normal group, had some emotional difficulties, selected objects that were so high, in the balcony of a church, up high on a wall, that an attempt to reach them might result in a dangerous fall. Other group members who successfully completed this exercise might comment that it gave them a sense of pleasure and satisfaction in doing what they had set out to do and following it to the end. This is one of the purposes of this exercise: giving the group member practice in setting up a goal, programming how the goal is to be reached and then implementing the program in a satisfactory way.

It might be expected that those who had difficulty completing all aspects of this exercise would have difficulty in initiating and carrying out life goals and tasks as well. This exercise gives an opportunity to evaluate and discern just which aspect of this overall goal-attaining process is lacking. In some, it might be due to the absence of self as described earlier. In some, it might be in faulty pre-programming. In others, it might be in the selection of unattainable goals, or in the inability to execute what is planned and how it is planned. This exercise, therefore, can be utilized in making assessments of a group member's goal-finding, goal-seeking, goal-attaining process.

This exercise in itself might teach the group member how to go about such goal attainment, and it also might teach him to evaluate his own progress in such an attempt. Following successful psychomotor therapy and training in expression and resolution of conflict, he might find it perfectly easy to achieve his goals with no further practice.

The exercise of voluntary patterns in the service of interest and curiosity completes the trinity of voluntary modalities and brings the group to the point of doing work in the emotional movement skill area. Before doing emotional movement, however, it is preferable to have the group members review all the modalities done previously, to reinforce knowledge in them and refresh their minds as to the differences between them, and the purposes of doing them. By this time the group has had much practice in restraint and control in doing the voluntary modalities, and might be feeling a sense of restlessness and frustration.

This frustration may not become conscious but could be experienced and expressed indirectly. However, the group leader should be aware that anger might be focused at him for being the restrainer of feelings up to this time and that some members of the group, having anticipated that this activity will be an expressive one, might be straining at their leashes, so to speak, waiting for the opportunity to do all that pent-up feeling, and the leader could easily become the target for some of those feelings. This feeling might become expressed in some as argumentativeness, finding fault with the activity, the leader, the room, and so on. The leader should be prepared for this kind of fault-finding or annoyance and should proceed to give opportunities to the group for satisfying expression.

Sometimes a generalized stamping or shouting might be offered the group. Having the group members tense every muscle in their bodies and then letting them all relax again is useful. Sometimes having the group members simply run about the room or do any and everything they might wish to do might be appropriate. Whatever the method used, the result will be the same: the group members will appear more relaxed and ready to concentrate on what is to be done and the group leader will seem like a pretty nice fellow after all.

The dynamics of this particular situation are similar to the dynamics of a much more advanced group under certain circumstances. In the event that one of the group members arrives for the evening session with a lot of material that he wishes to express, and there is some delay in getting to his turn, he may, for want of having the opportunity to much else, vent his feelings toward the other members of the group and particularly toward the group leader. This is no different than the situation described above. The leader in this event, however, would be able to provide a more direct release by having the "worked-up" group member have an earlier turn than might be the case and following that, point out possibly that the anger directed toward the group and the leader were spillovers from his yet to be done structure. It should be pointed out, however, that those who do such "acting out" out of turn, tend to be the ones with the greatest problems, and such overt expressions of annoyance in the early sessions points out to the group leader such persons who will require help in this respect.

Following the tension releasing exercise, if it has been needed, the group can go on to reviewing the modalities from the beginning, starting with the species stance, going on to the torso twist and the fall catch to complete the reflex relaxation area, then going on to conscious voluntary movement, habitual voluntary movement, and finally, voluntary patterns in the service of interest or curiosity. The group leader can take this time to review the purposes of each exercise and to note if there is any improvement in each exercise. Now we go on to emotional movement.

CHAPTER

4

Emotional movement, as it is done in psychomotor techniques and training, is not the same as emotional behavior in real life. Emotional behavior in real life tends to be a compromise between what is felt as an emotional impulse and what one learns one can do in a given situation in a given society. The attempt, in psychomotor training, is to polarize and release for expression the emotional impulse itself, separated from the restraining situation and the restraining society. It might be said that the restraining situation and the restraining society are represented by what is called the voluntary modality area in psychomotor techniques and training. Hence, the voluntary skill area is useful to a person in the service of greater conformity to the external environment. Clearly in practicing the voluntary skills, one is practicing restraint of the emotional impulses, thus giving the body over to the nonaffective motor processes which tend to produce congruence with the world, not congruence with what is felt.

The reflex area skills tend to relate to a single constant external reality, gravity; the voluntary skills tend to relate to what the senses tell us about the external world and the emotional area skills tend to relate to the internal world of what is felt or sensed, regarding one's affective state. If a group member is exceptionally skillful in the reflex area, one might expect that this person was well sensitized to gravity and to his proprioceptors which responded to gravity. If a group member performed well in the voluntary modalities, one could conclude that he was sensitive to the visual sense and to the restraints of society. If a group member performed readily in the emotional modality he might be quite aware of his own internal feelings and willing to have these have precedence over what society prescribes.

Most people show preference for one area of motor skill over another and this preference makes it relatively easy to predict certain general attitudes and behaviors in advance of specific situations. That is, a person doing only reflex movement relatively freely will tend to be relaxed and go the way strong forces indicate rather than fight against it; a person doing only voluntary movement as a preference will tend to restrain the expression of his own feelings or convert them into other than behaviors (i.e., headaches, stomach-aches, etc.), and that he will tend to try to conform to what is expected of him; that a person accustomed to moving directly in terms of feeling only, will tend to be spontaneous, unpredictable, and hard to restrain in terms of social forces and other people in general.

A goal sought for in psychomotor training is a balance between all these forms of motor skills and not a rigid preference for one over the other. In a given situation, one type of action or attitude might be called for as most appropriate and in another situation another attitude and behavior might be most appropriate. The aim of psychomotor therapy and training is to enlarge the range of possible behaviors and attitudes, giving each person a larger fund of skills, feelings, controls, and experiences to call forth in coping with given situations. It is the same as saying that one's personality is expanded as one's senses and potential behaviors are expanded.

Given the fact that each culture or society imposes certain restrictions on the motor expression of emotions, it becomes clear that psychomotor training has a large task in releasing those emotions which society frowns upon. One factor that makes the task easier is that psychomotor techniques and training does not expect, train, or permit group members to exhibit this spontaneous emotional behavior in social settings but only in the highly proscribed and controlled setting of a psychomotor structure. Therefore, the very real restrictions and inhibitions that one would impose on oneself in reality are substantially lessened when the realistic retaliation, humiliation, shame, and so on are suspended from operating in a psychomotor setting. Clearly, the reduction of controls and inhibitions can be a frightening process, and it is up to the group leader to assist in this endeavor by developing a group situation that is safe for each group member

to explore the step-by-step expansion of emotional freedom and reduction of inhibition.

The personality of the group leader must inevitably be a factor in
this most important process. If the leader's emotions are obviously
hidden and he is patently uncomfortable with the group, it is certain
that few of the group members will feel free enough to expose their
own very tender and sensitive feelings in such an atmosphere. A group
leader who permits one member of the group to comment unfavor-
ably or to react humorously to another group member's expression
of feeling cannot expect much further expression of emotions from
that first group member, or from any other group member who
identifies with that group member. The group leader must permit
freedom and yet have control of the group for the protection of the
individual who is exposed at the moment of expression. This control
becomes less necessary as the group progresses, as invariably, the group
assumes the same attitudes as the leader in this protective effort, and
the group leader's role has other emphases covering other responsibilities to be discussed later.

The ease of the group leader cannot come from an intellectual
knowledge of the processes involved; he must have experienced and
expressed his most powerful emotions himself. Only that experience
can produce the individual who can contain and absorb the strong
emotions of others with equanimity.

Emotional movement in psychomotor is a physical manifestation
of the emotional impulses that man is heir to, with a minimum of
restraints and inhibitions. The specific setting developed in psychomotor training is designed to remove responsibility toward the environment of the one expressing the emotion, and to so control the environment that it does not retaliate toward hostile expressions, but
provides the doer of emotions with appropriate evidences of his efficacy as well as provides the doer with whatever positive input he
desires. In other words, the setting adjusts to the condition when a
group member drops his voluntary controls and inhibitions, so that
maximum polarization of emotional movement can be achieved. The
consciously constructed response of the group is called accommodation,
and will be explained at length in chapter seven. At the early stage

of the group, accommodation is not practiced, but is implied in the behavior, bearing and control of the group leader.

In the same spirit that a psychiatrist tells a patient to "free-associate" and say whatever enters his patient's mind regardless of its seeming irrelevance, the group leader can explain to the group the premises on which emotional expression in psychomotor training rest and he can elaborate by saying that ultimately, all emotional impulses, no matter how seemingly foolish or irrelevant, can be acted upon. It might seem that emotional movement in psychomotor techniques is similar to free association in psychiatry and, generally speaking, this is so, but it is even closer to the actual state of dreaming, but acted in a more concrete and less symbolic form. Dreams are an arena for the uninhibited expression of emotions without regard to others, and society in general. The psyche seems to require the satisfying discharge of emotions whether it be through fantasy, as in dreams or daydreams, or in action, as art and sports. Psychomotor training attempts to provide another more controllable discharge. Emotions that are not discharged tend to become dreams, and if they are inhibited from being dreams, then symptoms of one psychosomatic kind or another can be expected to appear. The goal in psychomotor training is to provide a controllable movement arena for the clear and satisfying expression of emotions. Though this is easily said, it is not so easy to achieve, for there is much history and investment in restraint, and personalities are not easily changed. The satisfying expression of emotions does not mean play-acting, role-playing or pantomime; it means maximum congruence between the emotional impulse and the emotional behavior with a minimum of inhibition and modification imposed from within or without. This includes the essential point, that the possessor of the emotion in psychomotor never loses awareness that he is in a structure and not in reality. This is clearly a large order and the following will be an attempt to demonstrate how it is to be carried out.

It is possible to move at once into the area of emotional movement, ignoring all the preceding steps, as is sometimes necessary in a short-term workshop. With a long-term group, it is preferable to work at a slower pace, providing greater comfort for those few individuals in the group who might experience anxiety from a too-rapid exploration of this area. The breathing exercise is a good bridging step from voluntary movement to emotional movement which highlights the subjective difference between the two modalities.

To initiate this exercise, the group leader invites the group members to sit or stand comfortably, for the group will be concentrating on relaxed breathing. When the group is confortably settled, the group leader tells the group to turn their attention to their breathing without overly affecting the manner in which they breathe. The group is instructed to breathe normally for a series of breaths and then to refrain from inhaling following a normal exhalation. They are instructed to refrain from inhaling for a sufficient period of time to experience keenly the reflexive efforts to inhale during this time, then to resume breathing normally once again. The point of this aspect of the exercise is to highlight the subjective state experienced during the restraint of breathing.

Following the time of resumption of normal breathing the group leader can ask for comments on how it felt to refrain from breathing in this manner. Some might respond that they did not feel a thing and that they were calm. Some will say that they felt as if their body were growing cold and that they were frightened. Others might say that they felt suddenly very anxious and found the experience very unpleasant and distasteful. I have found it significant that the individual responses to this experience are related to feelings about holding down strong emotional impulses. That is, those who are calm tend to be able to repress their emotions without too much difficulty or discomfort and those who are frightened tend to experience fear when strong emotional impulses are rising. Those who find it unpleasant are those who prefer not to hold down strong emotional impulses.

The group leader can characterize the impulse to breathe as similar to the impulse to move in response to emotional impulses. The impulse to breathe is direct and clear, and very specific sets of muscles are involved. Very specific sets of muscles are potentiated by emotional states, and the coordination of these sets of muscles is not voluntary; it is directly related to behaviors relevant to those emotional states. Just as the impulse to breathe can be inhibited, so the impulse to behave emotionally can be inhibited. However, the impulse to breathe is so immediately of survival value that it cannot be postponed for an indefinite period of time as emotional impulses can. Certainly one does not die if emotional impulses are inhibited, as one would die if the impulse to breathe were indefinitely inhibited, but a kind of psychic death *does* occur from overlong inhibition of emotional impulses. It is assumed that the very same type of inhibitory processes are at work in both, restraining the impulse to breathe and restraining the impulse to behave emotionally. It is felt that the first order of inhibition is neural and the second order of inhibition is muscular. That is, the first inhibition takes place in the seat of the nervous stimulation; it results in no noticeable muscular response. The second inhibition takes place in the muscles antagonistic to the action being stimulated by the reflexes or the emotions, resulting in what is commonly called "tension."

A tense individual, who undergoes psychomotor training, comes to a point in the activity when he is about ready to directly experience emotional movement. When he does the species stance and removes, as much as he can, conscious voluntary controls of his musculature, certain portions of his body may tremble. This trembling can be understood as the expression of the conflict between the impulse and its inhibition. When this person does take an action that is sufficiently similar to the desired repressed impulse, it is noticed that the trembling either stops or is reduced considerably with the concomitant statement from the individual that he feels less tense.

Looking into this situation, something further can be gleaned which is quite interesting. It was stated that the inhibition arises out of the use of antagonistic muscles to the muscles potentiated by the emotional impulses. Those antagonistic muscles must be innervated by what we have called the voluntary modalities. These three voluntary modalities are similar in that they are shown to be effected consciously. The individual who is tense has attempted to remove his conscious control from his body, and yet the trembling occurs, which we have described as an expression of the conflict between the emotional impulse and the conscious inhibition. Now how can this inhibition be conscious if the individual has consciously removed his control of his muscles? It can be speculated that what is ordinarily a conscious process of control and inhibition, under the stress of psychic survival and threatening emotional impulses, becomes utilized by unconscious processes for psychic-protective reasons. Thus, one can hypothesize that under sufficient emotional threat, conscious rational processes are taken over by unconscious irrational processes for other than conscious, rational ends. This might be referred to as voluntary movement in the service of the unconscious.

Humor notwithstanding, there is some basis in this for the lessening of intellectual, rational, voluntary abilities in those who have become mentally ill. Is it not possible that these rational, voluntary faculties are no longer in the hands of the conscious part of the individual but more "in the hands" of unconscious but survival-based factors? They might therefore become distorted and appear as delusions, hallucinations, and so on, and no longer be in their normal position of providing congruency with the external environment, but rather congruency with the internal environment. Let us put these speculations aside for the time being and return to the breathing exercise which seemed so small but which prompted this outburst of hypotheses.

The group members have focused on the subjective feelings aroused by the conscious restraint of the breathing reflex; now they are ready for the next step in the exercise. The group is instructed to repeat the first part of the exercise whereby they breathe normally for several breaths and then neglect to inhale following a normal exhalation, but this time they are to focus on the moment when they decide to breathe again. The moment of the resumption of breathing provides a choice of either a "letting" or a "doing." The group is instructed to permit themselves to resume breathing rather than to "take a breath." They are instructed to focus their attention on the sensation and manner of breathing following a fairly long restraint of breathing. When they have completed this section of the exercise the group leader can ask for comments on how it felt and what was experienced.

The comments can vary considerably. Some group members might say that they took a huge breath, others that they found themselves gasping uncontrollably, others that they simply resumed breathing. Most group members tend to comment on the relief they experienced when breathing was resumed. What can be pointed out to the group is that when the breathing is permitted to resume there is no need to take a breath; the reflexes, if allowed, take care of it. Naturally,

people do not normally take conscious breaths; but when they pay
attention to the fact that they are breathing they tend to modify
the normal reflex pattern by the inclusion of conscious voluntary
effort.

This exercise attempts to prepare the group members for the separation between awareness and inhibition mentioned earlier in the
chapter on reflex movement. In this particular exercise we are focusing
our awareness on the breathing reflex without imposing control and
inhibition. Voluntary control is needed to simply say "yes" to the
reflex and step out of its way. The reflex "breathes" and satisfaction
or relief is felt or experienced. The group leader can point out the
similarity between this exercise and the reflex exercise and carry the
simile further by comparing emotional expression and letting the
emotions "go" physically with letting the reflex to breathe "go."

The sensation of relief or pleasure that so regularly follows the
giving in to a physiological process such as breathing is called "function
pleasure" in psychomotor training. This breathing exercise can be
used as an example of function pleasure. It points to the possibility
of experiencing the same thing when emotions are permitted their
unhampered expression in a psychomotor setting. While function
pleasure is experienced when the normal physiological and emotional
processes are permitted physical actualization, the reverse is true when
such actualization is stifled or blocked. This negative condition is
characterized by the term "function frustration."

While focusing on breathing one can note that the moment "yes" is
said to the reflex, the reflex (to speak anthropomorphically) "knows"
exactly how to go about breathing. It immediately finds the correct
pathways for the satisfying act of breathing. One can marvel how
nicely it breathes without one's knowing how it does it. One can conclude again that one can trust one's reflexes.

Consider what happens in the next segment of the breathing exercise. The group is instructed to repeat the same beginning part of
the exercise—breathing normally for several breaths and then refrain-
ing from inhaling following a normal exhalation. The attention is
now shifted to the moment when not inhaling becomes intolerable.
Instead of saying "yes" to the reflex to breathe the group members
are instructed to take several voluntary and conscious breaths inhaling

and exhaling, utilizing the habitual voluntary modality. When the group has completed this exercise and is asked to compare the subjective quality of breathing voluntarily to the subjective quality of breathing reflexively, the bulk of the comments show preference for the reflexive breathing which is more satisfying and less tiring. Breathing in a voluntary fashion provides most people with function frustration, which is of a type that is not due to simple restraint but due to improper neural stimulus. That is, what should have been brought about neurally through reflexive action was reproduced neurally via that flexible auxiliary system which is characterized as the voluntary modality. The group members were asked to utilize a neuromuscular system related to congruence with the external environment to attempt congruence with the internal environment. Naturally it could not be as successful as the neuromuscular system which was created, so to speak, for that purpose.

Although most group members show obvious preference for the reflexive breathing and the function pleasure it produces, there are always some group members who prefer the emotional response they receive from voluntary breathing. They comment that that manner of breathing gives them a sense of power and mastery, that they find enjoyable. It should be apparent to the reader that such group members will show the same marked preference for voluntary movement over emotional movement and that their sense of control and mastery has primacy over their sense of spontaneity and emotional freedom. The group leader can make mental note of those individuals in order to assist them in the process of "letting go" whenever such opportunities arise in future sessions.

The purpose of the breathing exercise should now be coming clear. First it provides an opportunity for intensifying and extending over a period of time the moment prior to the physicalization of an impulse. The impulse in this case has strong survival value and thus its postponement results in rapid amplification of its intensity. There are few opportunities for observing an impulse of such magnitude on the emotional level unless one were extremely mentally ill and were receiving powerful impulses to do any action during the time when emotions had super-potency. This exercise serves the normal by providing an intense motor impulse which can be examined in terms of the discomfort its postponement causes and the satisfaction its expression provides. This exercise can be used as a model for what occurs when emotional impulses are postponed overly long and when emotional impulses are given satisfying (through direct physical expression) release.

Second, the exercise points out the possibility of providing the impulse with an alternate route to the body by way of the voluntary motor system. Although this route provides a reasonable facsimile of the preferred action, it provides little of the easy relief and long-term satisfaction of giving in to the demands of the impulse in its own "style" and route. Even those group members who found a sense of control and mastery in breathing consciously would not be apt to breathe that way all day long. It would be too fatiguing and would call for too much concentration.

The third value of the exercise points out that awareness or concentration can be used to "look" with and not necessarily to "act" with. This develops the concept of awareness as supervisor and not as executor. Consciousness and awareness cannot possibly do the job of unconscious motor systems. It would be wrong to use it for a job that would overtax its abilities and yet make little use of its primary function, which seems to be supervisory and decision-making.

In summary, the exercise provides a safe example of the process that will be involved in giving an emotional impulse access to the musculature. It gives the group members reason to expect that emotional expression can and will be satisfying and not necessarily dangerous as they might fear. It gives them practice in giving in to and letting go of impulses that are other than voluntary. For this reason the group leader can suggest that the group attempt once again to experience each step in the process and note the different results when alternate routes for expression are chosen. Alternate routes are not only available to the act of breathing but are naturally available for controlled expression or modification of any emotional motor act. One of the aims of psychomotor training is to reduce the amount of unnecessary or damaging modification and to reroute pathological modifications and restraints by first finding them in tension and then giving vent to their primary and primitive emotional expression, much as the young infant and child move in primary emotional and reflexive manners previous to the process of acculturation.

Certainly, the intent of psychomotor training is not to provoke regression, but if essential behavior is to be affected, the component parts of behavior must be brought to be manifest, under the scrutiny of the individual's awareness. Primary emotional behavior, manifested without the individual's consciousness and deliberate intention, would be a regression of another order, not the type noted above. Emotional behavior without awareness would be acting out, and acting out is not the aim of psychomotor training.

The capacity for repression in the human is great. The capacity for modification of emotional behavior is equally great. These two facts attest to the strength and weakness of the human psyche. The modifiability of the human personality and behavior systems permits great adaptation to varying environmental and social conditions making man the unique and constantly changing and developing creature he is. It also provides man with the possibility for conflict and it is at this conflict, in an increasingly emotion-provoking world that psychomotor training is directed. As the world grows ever more complex, as social pressures and responsibilities grow greater and as fear-provoking world situations grow ever more numerous, man's capacity for repression and inhibition remains the same. Our present society offers fewer and fewer opportunities for emotional release while making ever greater demands for the control and restraint required for technological and industrial ends.

Man's emotions, though restrained and inhibited, are nonetheless sending impulses or pre-impulses to his body, which he generally suppresses. Suppressed or not, emotions are sending messages which are intended to be acted upon. Emotions are messages to the body to be responded to as action or behavior. Since we are man and not animal we hear those messages as whispers and not as commands. The breathing exercise highlights the message "to breathe' as a command. Psychomotor attempts to give all physiological and emotional messages to the body the restraint-free use of the body in a sort of "bill of rights" for the internal needs.

Psychomotor training structures the right time and place so that all emotions and all physiological processes that we are heir to can have an arena where a "yes" can be said to their insistence on the use of the body. Practice in the breathing exercise and subsequent practice in emotional movement strives toward the amplification of the whispered emotional impulses so that they may be responded to in their primal force once again, this time with an adult's awareness and understanding watching and participating, not repeating the child's awareness and understanding as occurred in our acculturation processes.

In psychomotor, it is not sufficient to merely speak of the emotions that one is repressing. It is felt that since the emotion is considered to be an impulse to behave in certain ways that the behavior itself is the clearest form the impulse can take. Translation of impulses into words can cause semantic confusion, ambiguity, transformation of meaning, sometimes resulting in the camouflage of the original intent as many psychoanalysts and psychiatrists will attest. This method of concretizing the impulse is an attempt to cut through the verbal foliage that sometimes surrounds repressed feelings. While finding what one wished to do, one has the opportunity of experiencing the satisfaction of doing it in a safely structured yet relatively unmodified way. I do not believe that words should not be used in the therapeutic process, but the emphasis in psychomotor is on the use of words as focusing agents, on selecting the appropriate behavioral circumstances, events, and populations for the satisfying and pertinent expression of the emotions engendered by those circumstances, events, and populations. Clear words before and after the expressive act are an important element. Clarity for the assembling of the appropriate constellations surrounding feelings and clarity following the act of emotional expression of those feelings put the entire event in the proper perspective.

Following the practice of the breathing exercise the group leader can instruct the group members to rise in preparation for the first emotional exercise. The group by now could be on its second meeting or third depending on the length of each meeting and the speed with which the group leader is working. Throughout the entire book the exercises will be dealt with one by one as if the group were a constantly ongoing one, so that the repetition and review that would normally go into the development of each individual session will not have to be discussed. It is taken for granted that psychomotor group leaders will bring each individual session to a satisfying end, with a sense of continuity and goal for each meeting. It is not expected that a group leader will follow a specific set of exercises without regard to the individual composition of the group or stop at some allotted time without having developed any exercise to a satisfying conclusion.

The group leader can tell the group that in a moment he will ask them to assume the species stance at which time he will give them a specific emotional image. The group is instructed to note for themselves what changes take place in their subjective states and particularly what changes take place in the species stance. They are asked to note if and where tension arises in the body and to question whether this tension might suggest any action.

There are four basic emotions focused on in this exercise: fear, anger, love and joy, in that order. When the group members have assumed the species stance for sufficient time to allow maximum relaxation and reduction of affect, the group leader can tell them to recall a time in their lives or invent a time when they were terribly frightened. (The cue includes inventing a frightening time as some group members cannot recall a real life frightening situation.) They are instructed to focus on their internal impulses without acting on them and to sit quietly when they are through.

Soon some members of the group may have clenched hands and others might show raised shoulders. Others might show no overt signs of their response to this imagery but show a lessening of the oscillation in the species stance. Some might show an increase of oscillation in the stance. Some might show nothing at all. Some group members might look up and glance quickly about the room to see what other groups members are doing. This external interest highlights that individual's greater concern for the appearance emotions give, over and above interest in his own subjective state. Some group member might rise abruptly out of the species stance, walk to the side of the room, and light up a cigarette.

After a fair length of time, individual group members will terminate the exercise, some looking uncomfortable and some, possibly with their arms clutched around their own shoulders or waists. During this period of waiting it is important that the group leader does not make any moves or sounds that would interrupt the imagery process. Should any one of the group members make a sudden move or loud sound, the group leader should gesture to that individual to wait comment or action until the entire group has completed the exercise.

During the species stance the individual is attempting a "zero" state. The stance provides a blank slate upon which imagery can sketch an outline. The silence of the "zero" point of the species stance serves as a field of silence against which the "whispers" of impulses can be internally apprehended. First the species stance acts as a blank slate and with imagery added, as a focusing agent. This is the reason for silence in the room. Each sound can become part of the image-stimulating process. Each sound can get woven into the response of each individual, distorting the internal stimulus.

When all the group members have completed the exercise the group leader can ask for comments. Some group members might comment that they found their hearts beating faster and their breathing quickened as they recalled a specific event in their past but that no tension reached any particular part of their musculature that they could recognize. Others might comment that they found their hands getting tense as if they wanted to push away something. This individual might elaborate that he recalled the moment in an automobile accident when he had the impulse to push away the oncoming automobile before the impact. Others might comment that they felt a strong sensation at the backs of their necks as if there were someone or something behind them which was threatening them. Others might comment that they felt like running and hiding under an object in the room. Others might comment that they felt a quivering behind their knees and in their legs. The group member who went to light up a cigarette might comment that the feelings of discomfort he aroused were too unpleasant and that he would prefer not to do this exercise. Some might comment that they could not ever remember a time when they were extremely frightened and might wonder if everyone were simply making up all those statements about hearts beating faster, and so on.

The comments and responses are as variable as the people in each group, yet there are certain constants underlying the variations. Fear tends to produce a strong physical action in direct relationship to the stimulus, the most common being fight or flight; however, the fight reaction is more pertinent to anger than to fear. The flight can take active form and result in a desire to run (consider the shaky tense legs of one group member), or the passive form of trying to hide (consider the individual who wished to climb under an object). Avoidance approaches would include the raising of the shoulders, protecting the neck or pushing out arms to ward off the oncoming threatening object. Another reaction to fear might be capitulation and despair as evidenced by the individual who wished to crumple to the floor. Fear might be so overwhelming and devastating to some that they prefer to cut short the imagery or some psychic mechanism cuts short their affective response. There are those whose avoidance is unconscious. They tend to find it difficult to work in the realm of the physicalization of the emotions, as their emotions never reach their conscious minds or their bodies.

The group leader can ask whether the group feels comfortable or uncomfortable. It can be expected that the bulk of the group members feel uncomfortable with the few who could not recall any strong emotion feeling unchanged. The group leader can point out that once an image which provokes strong impulses is brought to the threshold of action by this exercise, movement is necessitated in order to dispel the disquieting sensations the imagery arouses. This is a good example of function frustration. The disquieting sensations might be the resultant of the impulses to behave being restrained from making themselves manifest. We carry about with us many emotional responses to events of the past which are not potentiated. Once the image reaches this action threshold, however, action must be done in a relatively unmodified manner, unless discomfort is to be experienced. If nothing is done, then something must be said. If nothing is said, our perceptions change or our body gets affected in a nonactive somatic fashion. To hypothesize for a moment regarding changed perceptions due to repressed emotions, it may not be the perceptions themselves that are modified, but the translation or interpretation of the mechanical perceptions that is modified. The eye may see as well, but the brain may translate the message differently when function frustration is being experienced.

Following the comments by the group, the group leader can instruct the group members to resume the species stance. The group leader can instruct the group to recall a frightening incident but then to move as directly as possible to the whispered muscular messages the image provokes. Once again they focus on the fear-stimulating imagery of their own making. What is the result this time? Some might begin to move directly in terms of their emotions. One individual, perhaps the one who wished to hide under something, might suddenly run across the floor and dive under a piece of furniture, huddled in a ball with arms circled around the head. This precipitous action might startle another individual into agitated attention, hands to throat and chest. It might produce laughter in some, anger in others. Both responses to and defenses against, emotion. When the room settles once again, others might make self-conscious attempts with eyes closed, at recapitulation of whatever occurred in the original setting surrounding the emotional event.

When all in the group have finally attempted to move in terms of their emotion or have given up in annoyance with themselves and the exercise, they are invited to make comment on how they felt. The most comfortable individual might be the one who moved at once in terms of feeling. Many might be angry and less comfortable than they had been before in the activity. There will be those who have very strong feelings surrounding fear and who will now be in the grip of that fear, not having had an opportunity to dispel, deal or act on it in an efficacious manner. Their discomfort will be voiced and self-evident. There will be those who have attempted to recapitulate whatever movement they did in the past situation that provoked the fear. That is a mistake, because they may not have allowed themselves to move directly in terms of their impulses at that original time. Naturally the recapitulation of a voluntary act, which in reality substituted for a restrained emotional act will not now provide function pleasure. This can be mentioned to that individual so that he can move as he would have liked to move (could he have had the opportunity to move directly, emotionally at that time) the next time he repeats this exercise. There will be those who recapitulated on an emotional base what it was they did in the past who, nonetheless, are still experiencing displeasure. The real-life past behavior that these people have chosen to "re-enact" was not successful in real life, but provided them with a miserable result. That result is now being re-experienced and they may be quite unhappy. Those that had difficulty feeling, experiencing or remembering a fearful situation will very likely be in the dark regarding the others' behavior. They might have attempted to do voluntary movement in a pantomimic way that would pass for fear and are feeling very little.

Following the comments, the group leader can suggest these "hints" in the psychomotor expression of emotion. Whenever an emotional expression is attempted in psychomotor training the individual should see to it that the emotion turns out to be successful. That is, if one were to express the emotion of fear, one should see to it that one successfully escaped the threat. For example, one might recall a time when one was beaten by another and one, in the actual past, merely covered one's face while the beating took place, that person could so structure his expression of fear that escape takes place and the beating is avoided. In another situation, one might remember being in an automobile that was moments from being crashed into by another automobile. Possibly one had the impulse to push the automobile out of one's path. In this exercise that gesture should mentally be provided with superhuman strength that literally could push the onrushing machine out of the way. Another could have imagined jumping out of the car and rolling to safety before the impact. Another example could be remembering being terrified as a child and having no one to run to, running in this exercise to another individual as if to an ideal parent figure who would provide the needed protection. That would be the beginning of a structure, because it would include another individual who would provide the needed protection that was lacking in the past. But one could run to a corner of the room in this early exercise and imagine a satisfying escape.

The group leader can point out that it is difficult to get emotions to become fully expressed unless one is certain that one's emotional expression is going to be provided the appropriate results in the environment. Accommodation by the environment, or, in psychomotor techniques, by other members of the group, facilitates greatly the satisfying expression of emotions. Since this is too early for the group to practice accommodation the not entirely gratifying second best of imagined and nonaccommodated emotional expression can be sufficient reward.

If one had expressed strong emotions when one was quite young and those strong expressions of emotions received negative reactions from one's parents it can be expected that that individual would soon learn to inhibit *all* kinds of emotional expression. It is too painful to have emotions rejected. Psychomotor training can be seen as providing a safe haven for the expression of emotions. If emotions can be seen as a baby that is very tender and sensitive, psychomotor training can be understood as providing a crib for that baby, so that its tender skin would not be injured. This attitude toward the development of a "crib" does much to reassure those who have good reason to suppress their feelings that their needs and feelings will be respected in this arena without possibility of embarrassment, restraint, humiliation or retaliation.

The formula or architecture for this crib should be evident in the behavior of the group leader. It is by his example and explanation that this attitude becomes developed in the group as a whole. Even as individual members might look up and wonder what the rest of the group is doing in response to emotional stimulus, they note the demeanor and response of the leader. Consider how disastrous it would be for future spontaneity of the group if the leader were to be observed frowning in displeasure at a particular response or laughing in ridicule at another. Rather than being impassive, it is best that his face be expressing concern for and acceptance of the individual, not concern in the sense that the group leader is worried over what is being expressed and that he may not know how to handle it, but concern in the sense of unspoken sympathy for what has been shown. An impassive face might show unconcern and this would provoke anger in some group members who might project the unfeeling response of parental figures on the group leader. Most important, the group leader cannot show fear or inability to cope with what is being expressed. No group member would dare to expose himself or even to look deeply into his feelings in an atmosphere where weakness or inability was being manifest by the group leader. It is often noted by group members in early sessions of the group that they would not have dared to express certain feelings unless they were certain that the group leader could handle them and not be thrown by them. Soon this trust spreads to the entire group and in later sessions the same comment is directed toward the group. This trust, first of the leader and then of the entire group is an important step and task toward the development of a successful ongoing psychomotor training group.

The group can be given another opportunity for the expression of fear following the clarification of how to structure the situation allowing for the satisfactory ending and release of the undone emotions. (This is also important training in preparing to find alternate responses to painful situations. It is essential in doing future structures and essential in the development of new responses to old patterns of relationship to the environment.) Once again the people in the group are instructed to assume the species stance and to recall or invent a time when they were extremely frightened. This time a larger number of group members should get a satisfying response to the newly expanded possibilities for action. It is important that each group member move directly as the feeling demands and not in some predetermined fashion, decreed by someone else. Some group members, however, having pulled up a strong memory and not having been able to respond satisfyingly to it previously, may attempt to impose an action on themselves suggested by the possibilities put forth by the group leader. This imitated action will provide little relief or pleasure.

Other group members, feeling on the verge of acting in response to their feelings in the previous attempt, might now find that the emotional image is without force and that they are completely blocked from feeling it once again, perhaps since the first attempt was so unsuccessful and so unsatisfying. It might also be that this particular group might have found so much force behind the imagery the first time, that they were frightened away from so much as experiencing it again this second time. Less than the entire group will have successfully reached a state of equilibrium at this point and those who have not, will be experiencing function frustration and annoyance at themselves and at the activity. The group leader might suggest to that blocked group that they attempt running in place, hiding, or an averting type of action. Then those who have remained immobile in the face of their own stimulus of fear might experience a generalized release. However, this type of instruction can be an imposition or a distortion of what is felt to at least one member of this immobilized group and can provide added frustration and annoyance. It is at the maximum a weakly satisfying action to some in that group.

Most people at this point in the progress of the group have taken reasonable small steps toward the process of spontaneous and uninhibited emotional expression. However, there are those individuals whose controls are loosened and whose impulses are near the expression stage. These individuals come quickly to a point of doing structures in psychomotor training. Once their inhibitions or defenses are lowered they may find stronger feelings than they expected. The group leader should be prepared to accommodate those feelings alone or with the aid of other members of the group who would seem prepared to be good accommodators. These breakthroughs, far from being destructive to the functioning of the group, offer an opportunity for the group to look ahead toward the future when structures will be accomplished by all.

They may be so overwhelmed by their feelings of fear that they are unable to "turn them off" at the end of the exercise. When this person's fear becomes evident, either by his actions or his words, the group leader can indicate to another member of the group to go over to that person and put his or her arm around that person's shoulder. The group leader can instruct the fear-experiencing member to respond to the supportive or positive accommodating member as if he or she were a person who in fact could be a protector at this moment of fear, and to accept the comfort. Ordinarily, the person receiving this attention is visibly relieved at the contact he receives and this might be enlightening to him. That is, the power of contact and touch during fear might become evident to him and make him wonder at its absence in his past.

Occasionally there will be a group member who will move somewhat spontaneously to a fear stimulus who will nonetheless be left shaken and miserable at the end of that expression. When explored it becomes apparent that this person could not imagine a positive resolution to that experience. He might have found that he could not find any person in his imagination to whom he could run with security.

This person's experience with security-giving individuals is so meagre that such a being cannot even be imagined. It becomes evident that such an individual must first learn to believe that others do really care and are capable of protecting and offering security, capable regardless of the extent of fear felt by that individual and regardless of the circumstances under which it is being experienced. This is a large order but one that can be successfully met in time. Experience shows that such an individual must test the group many times in its positive accommodation before he is willing to finally give in and trust that others will care for him. Such an individual reacts to not having been cared for as evidence of his worthlessness, and subsequent permission on his part allowing the group to care for him is an expression of his feeling of self-worth and a reinforcement of that feeling.

Anger is most appropriate to explore next, as fear quite often turns into anger. Even if it did not, it would still provide an outlet for the frustration of those who have not yet been able to express themselves in the fear situation. The exercise in the expression of anger is initiated in the same manner as was the exercise in the expression of fear. The group is asked to assume the species stance and to remove all imagery. When it is apparent that the group is at a maximally relaxed point, the group leader can ask the group to recall or invent a time when they felt very angry. The group is instructed to note if and where there are tension changes within the species stance and not to move directly in terms of the imagery.

The group leader gives ample time for the response to take place. Some members of the group show overt changes in posture almost at once. There is a stiffening or clenching of the fingers and hands in some, a locking of the elbows in others. Some might show a tensing around the mouth as a result of clenching the teeth. One might hear a quick, audible intake of breath indicating that strong emotions were being felt. Some might show no external changes whatever, yet later comment that very powerful feelings were being experienced. The oscillation normal in the species stance might show variation in some by either increasing or decreasing depending on the individual's response to the internal imagery. Group members complete the exercise and slowly sit or stand. They may watch the remaining group members as they continue or they may consider their own subjective reactions to their internal stimulus.

When all of the group members have completed as much as they can in this phase of the exercise, the group leader can ask for comments on how the imagery affected the species stance and their emotional responses to the imagery. Once again there will be comments regarding increased respiration and heartbeat. Some will say they found a tension in their arms as if they wanted to push someone away or to hit out at someone. Some might have felt tension in their hands and when asked what movement the tension might suggest they might reply, "slapping or scratching someone." Some might comment that they felt a tingling sensation at the back of their neck, much like fur raising on an angry cat. Some might say that they felt their mouth tightening as if they were going to bite, or as if they were holding back an angry shout. Some might say that they didn't feel angry but that they felt frightened and that it gave them a funny feeling in their stomach. Some might say that it made them feel nauseous and that they were truly concerned that they would throw up. Some might say they felt like turning their backs on whoever was making them angry and that if they could have they would have spun on their heels and walked away. Some might say that their eyes felt the increased tension and that most awareness was focused there. Some might say that they could not recall any time that they *ever* felt angry and wonder at the diverse comments of the rest of the group. Others might feel the onset of a headache and comment that they felt anxious and uncomfortable, without noting tension anywhere. Others might feel a tension in their legs and feet and when asked for possible action might wonder out loud if they wished to kick or to grind their heel into someone's face. These comments show the individuality and the range of possible responses within the group. Naturally one would expect these selfsame differences to show up more directly when the movement was permitted direct expression beyond tension.

With the knowledge of the potential overstepping that is possible at this point the group leader can invite the group members to assume the species stance and this time to allow themselves to move directly following the concentration on the anger imagery stimulus. The group can be in a rough semicircle or random placement around the group leader, and the group leader should see to it that he is in a position to observe every member clearly. Following a buildup of the imagery by the members one individual might suddenly give a huge shout and simultaneously forcefully swing both arms to the floor while landing in a stamping jump on both feet. If this is the case the entire group would respond at once in a startled fashion perhaps resulting in laughter. Some heart-pounding reactions are offered, given as responses by some frightened individuals in the group. The laughter provides generalized relief to the feelings that have been building up in some individuals. Some group members might understand that outburst as a provocation and find that their anger has become real, directed at that shouting person in the group and not merely remembered, directed at an imagined target.

Although the foregoing has occasionally occurred the usual first response to the opportunity to express anger is more suppressed, modified and uncomfortably manifested. Some group members can be seen in the grip of a real conflict. The impulse to strike or to strangle is clearly showing on their arms and hands, while the counter desire to control those impulses is graphically shown by the alternate slow raising and slow lowering of the arms. In some the conflict literally takes place via both sides of the body; one arm raising with the other hand pulling the raising arm down; the rest of the body writhing with impulse and counteraction. Some may literally strike at the space in front of them once and then, seemingly unrelated to the first movement, slap themselves on the thighs—guilt concretized. Others might get as far as raising both arms overhead and be precipitiously ready to bring them smashing down on some imagined target when the next movement suddenly becomes a literal holding down of the head, as if to contain the very origin of those forbidden impulses. Others might make small but successful pushing movements with their arms and, partially satisfied, look up and semi-contentedly stop the exercise. Others might make well-integrated and coordinated, forceful, and complete punching movements with their arms and body and these individuals seem relieved compared to the conflict-ridden battlefield of the majority of the group at this time. Others might be seen literally holding down their entire selves with their arms tightly wrapped around them, swinging from side to side, punching armlessly, and miserably. Clearly, the response to anger is tremendously varied, with almost each individual and each group presenting different norms.

Some groups leap at once into overt and comfortable expressions of anger, screaming, stamping and swinging like mad. Occasionally, a group can contain an individual who does not get any imagery regarding angry feelings and who will stand throughout the exercise in a species stance, unchanging and ostensibly, unmoved.

When the entire group has completed what they are able and have sat down, the group leader can ask for comments on how they experienced this exercise—specifically, whether comfort or discomfort was a result. The individuals who moved somewhat directly to their feelings are easily seen as the most comfortable in the group and this is verified by their immediate and pleased response, reinforced by happy smiles. This is in marked contrast to those other members in the group who are wretched and who report that they have developed a headache and now feel tense and anxious.

What can the group leader do to alleviate the self-evident discomfort that he has precipitated? He can offer a generalized expression of emotion as was offered in the case of fear. The difference is that a generalized expression of anger is more satisfying than is a generalized expression of fear, since fear is more specific to a situation. The group leader can take this opportunity to demonstrate to the group what a generalized expression of anger looks like, and do a temper tantrum type of action which would include stamping, punching, and shouting with a global use of the body. This demonstration serves several purposes. One, it gives a license to the group members to behave in like manner. Two, it gives an example to emulate for those who have not developed patterns of overt expression of anger. Three, it gives a small measure of vicarious release and relief to the viewers. It also demonstrates that the group leader is not afraid of his own strong, violent feelings.

Not the least of the values of this demonstration is that it concretely shows that the group leader is not afraid of looking foolish, for there is an element of childishness in such global expression. Indeed, psychomotor training has been described with good reason by some as an opportunity for coming in contact with the child within ourselves. The demonstration can result in some laughter by the group which might include several members who might feel compelled to announce that it looked like fun and could they do it too, please? The group leader can offer this opportunity to the group, but experience shows that if the explosion into a temper tantrum is permitted to be randomly initiated, the group will tend to dissolve into self-consciousness with one or two feeble efforts at imitation and little satisfaction. A preferable way to pursue this exercise is to instruct the group to resume the species stance, instruct them to conjure up that anger-provoking image, and then, when the group leader counts to three, the entire group simultaneously is to burst into action and sound in the temper tantrum.

The usual reaction and response at this time is tumultuous. First, the screams and shouts and stampings and then unrestrained laughter are a surprised experience of childlike function pleasure. Then there is obvious reduction of tension in the group with instantaneous requests for repetition: "can we do it again please?"

Once again the preparation is repeated, the count of three reached, and the mad shouting and stamping and swinging ensues, followed by unrestrained laughter and real delight. "Boy, this is fun!" might be a typical comment at this time. All this pleasant function pleasure and satisfaction of pent-up feelings notwithstanding, this is the time for the group leader to look for the individual who may easily, by the force of the group concerted stimulation and action, have gone further than he was prepared to or intended. He may easily go unnoticed for a moment but as soon as the mirth settles down and the noise ceases his discomfort and worried face draw attention to his situation. He may then complain that he feels strange and that he has never behaved that way before in his life. He may be frightened at the strangeness and frightened that he may have or already has "lost control." This type of individual might not appear in every group but his reaction is always possible and therefore worth preparing for. It is the extreme case that tells us about limits. One should not assume that only the healthy individual will be encountered in psychomotor training groups.

The group leader can give verbal reassurance to that individual that it is certainly all right for him to behave in that manner in a psychomotor training group, that this type of expression is actually being encouraged. The rest of the group can bring immediate weight to this statement and usually does by chiming in with the group leader that it is fun and all right and that nobody has gotten hurt by this type of angry expression. If this is not sufficient, once again, as in the expression of fear, the group leader can offer contact and closeness to the upset individual either with the help of one of the other members of the group or by himself if none in the group is so prepared. Usually that individual is visibly relieved by the concrete acceptance that an arm around the shoulder demonstrates and several moments of this type of physical contact accompanied by verbal reassurance is all that is necessary to return that individual to comfortable feelings. (Ultimately that individual must find the earliest patterns of anger inhibition and successfully change them. Parent and authority figures ordinarily demand anger restraint and now parent figures must be set up to countermand the original orders.)

In some cases the entire group can be invited to do a group hug following an outburst of this sort, allowing the entire group to touch simultaneously. A group hug is a circular formation with all the members of the group, the leader included, doing a type of species stance with arms around each other's shoulders. It is much like a football huddle, except no excuse or reason for being close is made other than the desire to be close. A group hug at this time is surprisingly acceptable to the group as closeness is always more desirable and attainable following satisfying expression of anger.

To return to our overstimulated and overexpressive group member, he may be included in the center of the group hug, if the group is small enough to come in contact with him. He may be invited to be in the center of a nucleus group of two or three who then are surrounded by the rest of the group. The group hug may last for one or several minutes with the group oscillating in a circular manner.

An interesting development might appear at this time from our frightened individual. He might find that he cannot accept or tolerate closeness following his outburst. It is often found that an individual who has suddenly come across large amounts of anger for the first time in the concretized form of movement, will feel a great deal of guilt and unworthiness which does not permit him to receive the closeness and comfort of others. This guilt may appear indirectly in a statement that he just doesn't like people that much and would prefer not to be included in the group hug. This might be an indication that this individual is still extremely angry and further opportunities for anger expression might be offered to lessen the force of his undone anger so that he can accept or tolerate group closeness. Within the range of "normals," however, one can expect relatively easy resolution of this dilemma, for such excessive guilt and intolerance of touch is rare.

The group leader cannot offer contact either individually or en masse without thought and understanding of the personalities in the group confronting him. Simply to know that contact following angry expression is pleasant and ordinarily acceptable does not permit the group leader to indiscriminately say "all right let's do the group hug now." Albeit the expression of anger is largely inhibited in our society, so is its counterpart or antidote, the expression of physical proximity. It can be almost as shocking to an individual to be close as it is for him to express his anger. The group leader must have assessed the group carefully and noted the progress of the group in experiencing unity before suggesting the group hug. In a patient group one would move extremely slowly in the dimensions of emotional expression and physical proximity. However, normal groups contain individuals who are near illness in some aspects of their personalities. Precautions must and should be observed in all new groups. Whenever the first group hug is attempted, possibly at the time just noted, following the temper tantrum exercise or further in the course of the group's progress, the group leader should note carefully if there are one or more individuals who appear uncomfortable in this endeavor. Their presence can be determined from several signs. They may simply announce that they don't like to do this. They may be the first to raise their head in the hug and look about the group. They may shuffle their feet. If their arm is about the group leader's shoulder he may indirectly announce tension by the amount of forceful pressure or by the relative lack of pressure on that shoulder. (It is interesting that people who are uncomfortable in closeness may show either of two extremes in their handling of this discomfort. They may try to overcome their dislike by holding much more firmly than they wish, causing pain and discomfort to the person receiving this pressure. They may partially withdraw from contact evinced by the light touch of their arm and hand.) They may begin to laugh or giggle uncontrollably, which is a combination of displeasure and relief at contact long sought. They may stand rigidly in the group hug, in contrast to the total group's relaxed oscillation.

The oscillation of the group sometimes is circular or wavelike, with the movement traveling almost from person to person. When there is an unrelaxed individual the oscillation process becomes disturbed in his area and it is easy to note the source. When the oscillation process reaches that individual, he may not use his reflexes and control to support the action but may continue totally relaxed and pull the entire group off balance, thus breaking up the group hug. Proximity tolerance is slowly built up in future exercises in psychomotor training and this first attempt at the group hug can serve as a preparation for that time.

The relationship between expression of anger and the desire and willingness for proximity is an interesting one. It can be seen in the classical situation of fighting mates, who, following the fight "kiss and make up." It can be seen all braided and woven together in the sex act itself which can be a simultaneous expression of anger and proximity wishes. It can be seen in the angry mother who smacks her child who has incautiously crossed a street and narrowly escaped being hit by a car. The smack is followed by a more passionate loving hug. One sees it regularly in psychomotor training groups. The prime example is the grateful hugging of one's negative accommodator after one has figuratively torn that person to bits. The hugging and warmth one feels toward one's accommodator is very real and very satisfying to express.

It makes one wonder whether all this overrestraint of anger expression in our society does not also result in the byproduct of inability or unwillingness to be close. Surely compared to our Latin neighbors we are a cold bunch. One can speculate that our overemphasis on sex in movies and books in this culture might be caused by our inability to attain such satisfactions in reality due to overrestraint of our anger. Certainly the present style of dancing shows a lack of closeness, perhaps because of the tightly restrained anger our living style produces.

This speculation highlights the fact that once a group has reached the point of expression of hostility and the concomitant expression of proximity, they are changed as a group and as individuals. They have achieved basic, primitive satisfactions that are organically meaningful and satisfying. They have tapped the roots of their own being and come closer to others. They have transcended their society and have begun the first step of developing the society of the group which will permit them to discover even more of themselves and to permit even more of themselves to be acted on in a satisfying way.

As a landmark it might also have negative aspects. It may prove the point of no return for those individuals who find that it is more than they can take. Recall those individuals who felt nothing during the expression of fear and anger. Those individuals are now at the crossroad. They have seen some of the group members produce strong actions as a result of inner sensations and they have seen those members relishing the satisfaction that this action has produced. They have seen the outburst of anger and the first exploration of proximity and they may still feel nothing, or possibly they may be experiencing displeasure at such overt expressions and a real desire to leave the group. They might possibly feel concerned as their relative lack of feeling and expression marks them as somewhat different than others. They might wonder if something is wrong with them. Some might decide to terminate their relation with the activity following this meeting and others might opt to inquire further into their inability to feel and apply themselves to the longterm task of change. The group leader might be asked by that individual whether he or she should continue and the group leader should give assistance in coming to a decision by offering clarification of the processes to be followed without deciding for the individual. Sometimes the individual might be indirectly asking the group leader whether he or she has hope of feeling and whether he or she is worth the effort. Sometimes this individual shows concern that they might be slowing up the group, and so on. In this case the leader can demonstrate his concern for the individual and reassure him that the activity is for him as much as for anyone else. His capacity for change is not known in advance and he can be given the opportunity of finding out for himself. Others might feel that the expression of emotion is too overwhelming and for this reason wish to terminate. Whatever the cause, the group leader should assist the individual in either staying or leaving depending on whether that appears to be the most desired end on the part of the individual.

The group now has become a bit more defined. There will be those who will find it relatively easy to accept both fear and anger and who move easily in regard to both. There will be those who have made the first efforts toward experiencing and expressing their emotions physically and who made "soundings" of their state of being, and those who are wondering and looking forward to exploring the further depths of their emotions. There are those who might think that this kind of activity is "far out" and who have begun defending themselves against it by slight aloofness and disdain, and there are those who have definitely "turned off" and will not return.

The overall patterns in regard to the other modalities will have come a bit clearer too. Those that do a relaxed species stance and easy fall catch can generally be expected to be among those who can express themselves easily. Those who are tense in the species stance and who have enjoyed the voluntary modalities will find this emotional area difficult and a little upsetting. However, all groups are different and this is merely a sketch of a "typical" group. It is of paramount importance that the group leader make it easy for each individual to do as his feelings bid him and not to impose his own viewpoint on any individual.

The next emotion to explore is that of love. The group hug has taken a step in that direction, and the expression of anger has also facilitated the experiencing of that emotion. After the group hug, the group members are now quite relaxed for the most part, and may have resumed their original placements or have found new placements as a result of their new experiences. The group leader can instruct the group members to resume the species stance and to respond to new imagery. When the group has appeared to be at a point of maximal relaxation, the group leader can instruct the group to recall a time when they felt very loving to a person, a pet, or an object and to let the image affect their feelings without allowing themselves to move directly in terms of the feeling. Invariably the comments following this experience attest to the calming effect that the consideration of tender feelings produces. There is no commentary regarding increased heartbeat or quickened breathing (although sexual imagery might produce that state); there are, rather, reports regarding the desire to touch, to fondle, and to bring close.

If one were to inquire whether the species stance felt different before the imagery was attempted, one would be told that it seemed much more relaxed than at the beginning of the activity, attesting to the relaxation value of angry expression. There is not the same force or flood of feeling regarding love as there is with anger. Tenderness is not that much repressed. It appears that the undone or unexpressed emotions are the powerful ones. If one has not succeeded in either expressing or being offered love it is not the love repression that seems to cause the discomfort but rather the frustration at the lack of love satisfactions and the rage that this produces that builds up the reservoir of repressed impulses.

Following the first exercise in the evoking of the love imagery without action, the group leader instructs the group to repeat the beginning of the exercise but this time permit the imagery to produce the action that it would seem to. The responses to the imagery are now put into motion and the variation, as can be expected, is great. Some find it difficult to be overly expressive of tenderness. Others find this emotion more acceptable than any of the others. Some may seem to be reaching toward some object or person in the space in front of them, a poignant gathering of sensitivity around the front of the body becoming apparent. The surfaces of the chest and stomach are made available to touch or be touched and there is an observable difference in the way the torso is held and carried. The movement of the torso toward the object suggests an offering to be touched and a subtle concavity of the torso suggests a potential surrounding of the loved object. The tonus of the muscles of the face appears relaxed and the fingers and hands although reaching are relaxed. The head is often tilted to one side as if to proffer a cheek rather than held straight on. Some group members tend to encircle their arms either about some object directly in front of them or about themselves, in a combination of wanting to love and to be loved, even if only by themselves. Some tend to stroke an imaginary held object; that is, one arm and hand appear to be holding some small object, either a child or pet in size, and the other hand tends to be caressing the held object.

The laxity of the muscles in some results in literally sinking to the floor with the body once again being offered for touch or to envelop and to touch another. This enveloping action seems to be mostly feminine and the word "curling" of the body seems to be the appropriate description for some. Some female group members may be seen sitting on the floor with the arms reaching forward and the legs outstretched. Some female group members appear to be in conflict at this time, evincing first the feminine receptive posture described above and then an almost fetal position with the knees drawn in to the chest and the head covered with the hands. It is the covering of the head and face that seems to suggest shame at the openness of the previous position, but it may be that the fetal aspect of the posture is the more significant one, for in the structure of an advanced female group member, the fetal posture seemed extremely appealing and necessary to do (not consciously described as the fetal position) following a conscious wish for a baby.

An interesting contrast between male and female responses to the love image developed in a dance class consisting of five females and one male, who were practicing responding to emotional imagery of love. At one point in the exercise the male suddenly looked about him and exclaimed, "I don't understand it, all the girls are curled up on the floor and all I feel is that I want to reach to the ceiling and grow taller and taller." He wondered if there was anything wrong with him since everyone else was differently moving than he. Although this example does point toward a basic difference between male and female responses to the image of love, based on sexual roles, both males and females shared the impulse to move toward the love object and to come in tender and sensitive contact with it.

Some group members comment that they cannot respond physically to a love image because they cannot find such an image within themselves. One male member of a hospitalized patient group found that he experienced anger when he attempted to think of loving someone, but that he could experience the desire of being loved by someone else. The someone else in this case was not exactly another human. It was described by him as warm bright sunshine coming from above, which bathed him in its light as he reached upwards toward it. Some group members reach for a love object and then fall despairingly to their knees or drop their arms. When giving comment later they note that their love object seemed unattainable and therefore, they found themselves giving up wishing for it. Other group members can be seen having an ecstatic expression on their faces attesting to the fact that they are capable of imagining loving or being loved, with concomitant satisfaction. The questions that a group leader can keep in mind as he watches a group responding to the love imagery are: Can the individual conjure up a love image? Can the individual allow himself to move directly in terms of that image? Can the individual allow himself to be successful, loving or loved?

Other points to be looked for and stored for future use in structures are: Does the individual choose, as an object, another human being? If so is it an adult or a child? If an adult, is the individual doing the imagining seeing himself as an adult or a child? In the love interaction is the individual giving or receiving? Or both? Is the individual responding to a pet or a loved toy or blanket? Some individuals who profess that they are imagining loving a child can be seen to be almost smothering that child and more receiving from it than giving to it. This kind of loving is most apparent in those individuals' attempts at positive accommodation where they are supposed to be giving nurturance to the individual whose structure it is. Indeed they appear to be taking far more than they are capable of giving. This is shown by that individual's face, sometimes buried in the neck of those who are intended to be the recipient of their care, for all the world suckling at the neck. It is sometimes shown by the individual's reluctance to terminate the embracing of the individual who is supposed to be receiving nurturance, making that individual feel suffocated by the embrace. The line between giving and receiving love and the line between nurturance and sexuality is a fuzzy one and this fact is clearly demonstrated by the many responses to this exercise. It was noted earlier that it was the lack of being loved that caused frustration and subsequent rage, but experience shows that the experience of not being permitted to demonstrate love to a loved object is equally frustrating although a particular individual's manner of loving may be more honestly called a mode of receiving love as described above. Clearly, the group leader can ascertain much that would be useful in setting up future structures based on observations in this exercise. It would seem, in psychomotor techniques, that all roads lead to a return to the basic relationship between the child and his mother or mother surrogate. It is the re-experiencing of this relationship that tells us much regarding the extent of the individual's capacity to give or receive love. If there has been a deficit in this area one can be certain to encounter much rage in either a passive or active form and much overconcern with inability regarding the giving of love, and much confusion between sexuality and nurturance.

Maslow's concepts of "D" love and "B" love seem to be relevant in the context of psychomotor techniques. "D" love is the type of love that wants and desires to be given. "B" love is the type of love that is unconditionally given and seeks nothing in return. Psychomotor training offers an arena where one can finally return to the infancy stage and receive as a child receives, with a sense of endlessness, eternity and total satisfaction. An individual who has lived through a nurturance deficit subsequently becomes a much more giving person in a "B" sense after having received love from his positive accommodators in a "D" sense in his structures. This person then can practice giving in a "B" sense to other members in the group when it is his turn to be a positive accommodator. This kind of giving is really only possible after one has received in that manner.

The confusion in some people between sexuality and nurturance is an interesting one and raises some interesting speculation regarding its dynamics. A female member of a mental hospital patient group showed very clearly this confusion and its subsequent developments. She showed a strong compulsion to seek male company with an eye toward eventual intercourse or opportunities for performing fellatio on them. Her need for proximity to males was at a parasitic level and and one attempting termination of a conversation with her had almost to pry loose from her presence.

Her motor expression of love imagery invariably included a wrapping of arms about the love object and herself, with a professed lack of a sense of gratification. Pursuing her fantasied wish for a child to love demonstrated markedly the confusion noted above. The accommodator playing the part of the loved infant found his fingers the center of attention. The patient showed strong interest in massaging the fingers of the "child." The massage resembled the milking of an udder. It is almost as if the child's hand had indeed become an udder to her. The motion was one of pushing and squeezing the finger beginning with the thumb being pressed on the base of the finger and pressed upwards to the tip of the finger, the rest of the hand wrapped around the finger. The group leader commented that it would appear that something was being squeezed out of the finger and that if the tip of the finger had an opening something would certainly come out of it. The patient promptly placed the finger into her mouth and began sucking on it. The sucking continued for some minutes resulting in comments indicating strong feelings of comfort and gratification were being experienced.

Subsequent commentary by the patient included the fact that, indeed, the fingers were being imagined as penises and the fluid imagined was not milk but semen. In a subsequent meeting, pursuing the fantasy of having an adult man at her disposal to behave in any way she pleased, she imagined wanting intercourse with him several times a day in an innocent wish for the same rhythm a nursing baby would have. Pursuing the fantasy of being with her father all day long, which father she had strong conscious incestuous desires for, she wished to see him urinate and wondered about letting all that urine be flushed away, once again confusing another body fluid with milk.

Given the opportunity for a positive accommodator in the role of a nurturing mother she expressed distaste for feminine company and particularly showed strong hatred for "the old ladies" on her particular ward. Given the opportunity of venting through movement the hatred for these older women on a negative accommodator, she produced strong violent actions resulting in their "death." Following the negative expression she found that she could accept a younger female figure as a positive mother image and discovered the gratification of being held in a suckling manner in the accommodator's arms that she did when sucking on the fingers of her own imagined child.

Regarding the feelings toward the "old ladies" it was interesting to note that her own mother conceived her some twenty years following the conception of her older siblings and that said mother left the patient in the care of surrogate figures during her infancy and early childhood. Following the positive feelings of gratification experienced with the positive mother figure this patient wondered about the possible homosexual implications of this relationship, once again making (albeit perverted) sexual, what was patently nurturant. By satisfying directly some of the original oral needs this patient's pathological sexual acting out was somewhat reduced. One is led to wonder and speculate why for some people it is preferable to act out endlessly on a sexual level resulting in only temporary satisfactions when it is really nurturant needs that are pressing for satisfaction. It is easier to see oneself as a nymphomaniac than as an unsatisfied and frightened infant.

The group leader should keep in mind the many possibilities for expression there are to nurturance and love and with the above confusions in mind attempt to direct the group toward opportunities for the less distorted gratification of these needs. One can see that sensitive observation of the group through the early modalities for action and particularly through the emotion modalities can produce elaborate sets of expectations regarding different individuals. A rough profile even at this early date in the history of the group can be sketched with some accuracy using these skills as a barometer and a diagnostic tool.

The final emotion to be explored is joy. Psychomotor training attempts to bring to sharp focus or polarization all of the emotions and their expression as well as all the ways that the body can move, including the reflex and voluntary modalities discussed earlier. A pretty solid case for fear and rage can be made in terms of calling them distinct emotional processes, but it is perfectly evident that the love is anything but clear, and that confusion, distortion and ambiguity abound in the expression of love, particularly the early expression of love in the progress of developing a group. Of course there are some simple common denominators in the expression of love, such as the desire to move toward the loved object whether it be sexual or nurturant love, and the desire to come into tactile contact with the loved object whether it be sexual love or nurturance. The acceptance and incorporation qualities, either in their distorted form or more direct form still show basic similarities. The most distinct and specific expression of love as a basic physiological human expression might be in the inclusion and use of the mouth as an organ for contact and incorporation of the loved object; note kissing and suckling similarities.

Joy shares with love the ambiguous and fuzzy outlines perceived in the attempt to clarify just what is meant by the motor expression of joy. Specifically the group leader approaches the expression of joy in the following manner. He instructs the group to resume the species stance. Now the group is more truly a group, since it has a history of experiencing and expressing some emotions together and is becoming familiar with the terminology and skills of the activity. The group quickly achieves the stance and the group leader instructs them to recall or invent a time when they wished very much for a specific desire to become realized and particularly concentrate on how it felt when it did become realized. In other words, joy is being looked at as the joy of gratification, of wish fulfillment. The joy of successful closure, of success of the happiness of things coming out all right. Not the more internally felt joy of looking at nature, contemplating one's children and other joys of that more sedate strain. This is the simpler joy of childhood when school is over, when the wished gift is received, when the shocked surprise of gratification is experienced whole.

The group is instructed to concentrate on the feeling and see in what manner it affects the species stance without allowing it to become overtly acted upon. The group leader can observe what effect the concentration on the imagery has on the members of the group. In some there is the obvious birth of a smile on delighted faces, in others, the flicker of sudden movement. In some there is little or no external show of the emotion.

When the group is asked to comment, some will say that there was an irresistible desire to laugh and jump up and down. Some will say they wished to clap their hands. Others will comment that they felt lighter and younger in their bodies. Others will comment that they felt energy in their legs.

When the group is instructed to resume the species stance and this time to allow the emotion full expression in action, the result is as can be expected. There are those who will suddenly burst into delighted laughter and spin about hugging themselves. There are those who jump up and down shouting. There are those who will skip and run about the room. There are those who throw their arms above them and lift their faces upwards smiling. There are those who tumble to the floor hugging their knees, rock or roll from side to side on their backs. There are also those who look in wonder at the outbursts of those around them and are puzzled that they are experiencing nothing of the kind.

These individuals may very well be puzzled as they may never have experienced such unadulterated, childish joys in their lifetimes. Joy seems to be a shot of energy, useful for no utilitarian ends but for shouting and jumping and kicking and hugging. It seems to be just a "good" feeling. Some groups have found themselves laughing almost uncontrollably at this time, much like children whose laughter provokes one another to even higher mirth.

Some groups may be more self-conscious and restrained than others when not a single member may move in a joyful manner. At such a time the group leader, using the same technique described earlier in the expression of fear and anger, can tell the group to concentrate on an image and at the count of three the entire group is instructed to jump up and down clapping hands. Inevitably the entire group, either from the feeling of exuberance such jumping creates or from a feeling of being silly, or from a combination of both, bursts into laughter. At one such instance one group member who did not take the opportunities for generalized expression and was not able to move in terms of anger and fear, suddenly commented following jumping up and down during the generalized expression of joy, that he now felt frightened and angry. It is almost as if the imagery he had brought into the "ready room" took the opportunity to come out as a "rider" on the generalized movement he made in the expression of joy. Evidently this person had strong inhibitions regarding the expression of fear and anger, but was not as strongly inhibited when expressing joy. However his "joy" was far from being joyful! It is an interesting commentary on the confusing and distorting results inherent in over-repression. Suddenly the emotion "had" this individual rather than the individual having the emotion. It lends weight to the theory that action must be involved if the emotion is to be felt. Certainly he did not experience the fear and anger until he moved in what he was fully expecting to be joy. Certainly the group that purposefully jumps up and down experiences some semblance of joy even though no joy was experienced until that point.

Now the group has explored four basic emotions and has learned something about themselves individually and as a group. They have learned that, when emotional images are responded to with the direct action of the body in a spontaneous, primitive fashion, one of the results is the experience of function pleasure. They have discovered that each one of them has a different sense of emotion and a different way of responding to emotion. They have learned that anger can be a frightening emotion as well as a violent one and possibly some have learned that by moving in an angry way they are increasing and not diminishing their angry feelings because of the extent of the reservoir of undone angry feelings. They have learned that touch is an important element in the guilt-reducing reassurance that one's strong angry feelings are tolerated and accepted. They have learned that touch can also be frightening if one is not ready for it. They have learned that touch is easier and more welcome following a discharge of angry feelings. They have learned that love is a complex emotion that produces markedly different muscular responses and internal states than either of the two negative emotions, anger and fear. They have learned that joy can be a return to childish delight and a source of energy. If they have noted the responses of others to all these emotions they will have noticed the wide variation that has been exhibited and begin to realize that although we are basically similar, we each are undeniably individual.

This is the time for the group leader to instruct the group members to systematically go through the four emotions doing the species stance in between and examine which emotions are the easiest to express and which the hardest. Which emotions have the most force behind them and which the least. Which the most satisfying to express and which the least. This method of self-exploration and self-examination is one of the ways that more advanced groups discover what to work on in structures. They notice that there is a variation in responses from meeting to meeting, and when certain emotions seem to have predominance, a structure can be developed that permits satisfying expression of that emotion related to past manners of expressing or not expressing that emotion. This exercise takes a fair amount of time, and the group leader should see to it that he does not interrupt the complete inventory of all the emotions dealt with.

It sometimes happens that one person's emotions are loud and active enough to cause another member of the group to react to him rather than to his own emotions. Some sensitive members of the group may find this kind of stimulus extremely disturbing and anger-provoking. One answer to this problem is to suggest to that person that he use the anger stimulus to produce the internal state which would result in doing his own angry movement. However, there is not a complete answer to this problem, since everyone will undoubtedly work at his own speed and no two people will be moving through the emotional categories simultaneously. This points up what is true in everyday life: so often we are in the midst of having an emotion or attempting to express that emotion when the environment interrupts and in one way or another does not permit us satisfying expression of that emotion. This verifies the value and need of structures and accommodation.

If each individual did not have his own turn in a structure where everything was controlled to result in a satisfying expression and resolution of his own emotions, all would be expressing at once, resulting in chaos and frustration. No one would be prepared to exhibit his feelings and all would tend to restrain and inhibit what was really felt—the usual condition of everyday life. This would be and is perfectly acceptable so long as the reservoir of early undone emotions was relatively small. However, given the kind of upbringing that all of us have had, it is no wonder that there is so much that we would like to do over again and make come out right.

When we first experienced those strong feelings, it was concomitant with the understanding and awareness of a young child. In a psychomotor training structure, we re-do those emotions with the understanding and awareness of an adult, and very important new reorganizations of feelings, thoughts, and behaviors take place as a result. It is felt that it is not sufficient to merely recapitulate in thought and word the feelings of our infancy and childhood, but to once again experience the powerful forces of the impulses in the most direct and uninhibited fashion, touching once again the raw forces of our being and learning once again with an adult's mind to control and channel those impulses and energies in more suitable and satisfying ways. Before this can be done, the individual must learn anew how to find those impulses and to discriminate them from his impulses toward control, inhibition, and modification, and from his reflex impulses. This is the reason for the sensitivity training in the polarization of those three motor modalities.

It is now time for the group to go through each modality from the beginning and learn to turn himself and them on and off as he wishes and to bring up whatever images he wishes. He will gain articulateness and control in this motor sphere. This practice completes all the elements in the motor sensitization aspect of psychomotor training and will be repeated over and over again as a regular feature of each group session. This practice results in fine discrimination and sensitivity and allows advanced students to be aware of subtle motor impulses while having the capacity to move directly and uninhibitedly in terms of them. It also permits greater relaxation and control of the body for a more efficient use of the body.

Another use of the skills is one that has been noted throughout the descriptions, that of a diagnostic value. Through exploring each one of the movement exercises described, a group member can determine for and by himself if and where he is unable to relax his body and see whether or not he can concentrate successfully on voluntary movement, and so on. This information can lead him toward finding the appropriate structure that could eventually resolve the emotion that is being suppressed or over-experienced. Although each one of the modalities has its separate style of subjective feeling and manner of moving, there is a similarity in how each is handled. In each modality there is never the loss of awareness. In each modality there is an attempt at successful closure or completion of the exercise in a satisfying manner. In other words, species stance if properly done results in relaxation and a resultant posture that is enjoyable—a closure is effected.

Voluntary movements result in a masterful use of the body as is predetermined by each individual. Emotional movement results in function pleasure and the ability to successfully express what is felt. Each of these when successfully completed conditions the group member with expectation of satisfaction and successful completion, which is often transferred to everyday life. One becomes accustomed to not giving in and to not losing. One becomes accustomed to finding ways, thus alternate ways to effect closure. This is moving far ahead to structures, a topic that will be examined later. What we shall now inquire into is the other side of the coin of "inner-outer." We now will look into how the outer placement of people and things makes us feel subjectively.

CHAPTER

5

It is well understood that each position in a room of either objects or people has different meanings to the viewer. The differences are not only internal and relevant to the state of mind of the viewer, but also inherent in the objects themselves. When a man views a chair, he not only sees the chair as a perception, but he experiences unconscious and conscious programs of action relevant to that chair. These programs of action are termed the *effector* image in contrast to the *perceptor* image of the purely visual pattern that the chair makes in the eye. The unconscious programming process was examined in the exercise using voluntary patterns in the service of interest and curiosity. The patterns are brought to consciousness to determine what the physical impulses relevant to those objects and persons might be. The aim in this chapter and in this segment of the progress of the group is to manipulate the objects and the persons in the room in such a way that programs, projections and anticipations relevant to the purely spatial elements can be isolated and examined.

When the group leader introduces this new skill area to the group, the members can be sitting comfortably on the floor or standing in whatever places they have been accustomed to standing or sitting. The placement of each person in the room is no accident and is an expression of each person's total relationship to everyone else in the room including the group leader. Further, as the taking of that specific place is repeated over a period of time, there develops a stronger and stronger investment of interest and value in that placement. The place becomes an anchor and a location in space, a point of reference which has become stabilized and which gives security to the occupier of that space, not the space in abstract, but the space in relationship to all the other spaces and places in the room. A person's perceptions are relevant to his space. He becomes accustomed to seeing the room from a particular angle and presents one side of his body to one person and another side of his body to another.

It is always interesting to note the reactions of people when they are asked to exchange places with one another. At the moment of transition when both persons are walking past each other toward their new locations, the group leader can ask them to stop and have them comment on how they feel about themselves and each other. If they are sensitive, the usual comments are that one is resentful toward the group leader for asking them to leave their comfortable location, that they have become self-conscious for having been singled out and now are caught standing out from everyone else, that they do not like the other person potentially occupying their space. That they feel uneasy, that they feel they have lost something. When they are permitted to continue on to their new locations and are asked what they feel now, they comment that the room looks different from this new angle, that they feel unfamiliar with the people immediately around them, that they find themselves looking around more to orient themselves to this new location, that they are not for the moment as comfortable as they were, that they do not like to see the other person occupying their space, that they find themselves seeing the new people around them differently than when they were at a distance from them, that things do not feel as friendly as before, that they are angry with the group leader for making them change.

A number of people contend that they do not feel anything at all, that it doesn't make a bit of difference to them where they sit in the room, and that one place is the same as another for them. This last group might very well include those who have found it difficult to conjure up any emotion strong enough for them to act upon. They now are in the same position as before in that they are unable to ascertain their emotional states. Another comment that seems to be offered regularly is that the new space does not feel as warm as the old space and this is often literally true, for it is not entirely likely that the new person would occupy the precise location of the other person's seat on the floor. But it is easy to see the possibility of other values attributed to the hot and cold relativity.

After the people who have changed places have spent a minute in their new locations the group leader can ask them to return to their old places, and an interesting phenomenon appears. Given sufficient time to orient to the new place, a group member begins to invest values to that place by virtue of having prepared programs of action relevant to the new people and the new orientation and location. This is manifested when the group members exclaim that they were just getting "used" to the new space and now did not feel particularly like moving again. One should not overlook the negative reaction to the fact of being manipulated from space to space regardless of whether one has invested in that space or not. This is a relevant point of annoyance in itself. Some members, however, are obviously anxious or cheerful about returning to their own space. When they do return to that location they fall at once into a recognizable posture that they have developed over a period of time in that space and seem literally to settle into it.

This recognizable posture might include a leaning back on the hands or a sitting forward with the legs crossed and the hands on the chin. The posture that they return to is not a single one that is rigidly adhered to at all times, but the particular manner and style of the postures that one assumes over a period of time become recognizable and are not random and accidental. When the members who have returned to their new spaces are asked how it feels, the common responses include that it is much better and usually accompany this statement with a smile of genuine satisfaction. They are not as busy in their old locations looking about and checking their relationships with everyone else. This has been accomplished long before in previous sessions and in many different instances. They seem a little less alert in that respect, for they seem to immediately blend back into the group where in their new spaces they still seemed to stand out.

It is interesting that although they appear to blend into the group, the subjective feeling is that they feel more like themselves again. Evidently feeling like ourselves includes the function of fitting in with others in very subtle and unconscious ways. The room looks "right" once again to those who have returned to their original spaces and it is interesting to speculate how perception is affected by our point of reference. What is seen is still the same room, but one's evaluation of the room varies in terms of one's comfort or discomfort, familiarity and unfamiliarity. One can wonder whether a backlog of programs relevant to a familiar situation is what produces the sensation of comfort.

When one is caught without a program of action that is relevant and pertinent to a given situation, one is "startled," and that produces discomfort and lack of ease. Perhaps what one is really perceiving is a paucity of programmed action, and that is what produces the unease rather than unfamiliarity of the room from this new location. Yet, it is experienced as if the room does not "seem" as nice, when it is not the room but our unprogrammed reaction to that aspect of the room and its people that we are perceiving.

It is well known that old locations and old familiar things produce the most comfort, and it is not surprising, for the programmed behavior relevant to those things is tried and true, and there is little need to awaken into conscious awareness. Anxiety includes an intensification of awareness in the attempt to construct in a short span of time a new and workable program relevant to the situation one is in.

Once the program is complete and tested, a certain part of awareness can be dropped or lessened and one can be less conscious of one's surroundings. Constant anxiety must include the possibility that one's programs are deemed unsuitable and unworkable in the given situation and one is therefore left exposed and unprepared and startleable over considerable periods of time.

To leap ahead in this speculation, a program can include the action of others. When others are expected in a specific program and they are not present, this too can produce anxiety. It would seem that when a person is an infant and a child, he includes in one's program, mostly unconsciously, his parents and protectors. As he matures, he hopefully diminishes the extent to which he depends on another to fulfill his programs of action which will produce satisfactions. In psychomotor therapy and training a person is permitted to regress to the point of having others help him to re-experience the comfort of completion of program and security the "other" person affords until he can slowly mature through succeeding structures to the point of greater self-reliance.

To return to the moved group members, there are those who evince a greater liking for the new space than for the old space, and this presents the possibility that that individual had not selected for himself a place in the room that was entirely suited to him. The balance of the group watching this process has learned from the watching, and the group leader can select another two members to have them experience this change of location. Of course, one could not have the entire group change places simultaneously, since this would destroy the stability of the group, and there would no longer be points of reference.

The new couple would be prepared to undergo the same experience as those they watched, and one would expect it to dull the edge of the experience. However, the difference between the intellectual understanding of a change and the experiential sensation of that change is quite large. More than likely, the expectation of surprise reinforces the sensation of surprise, because the newly-changing group members experience the same sensations that the watched members experienced. The second couple have the advantage of comparing the different sensations relevant to watching and knowing and doing and experiencing.

Having heightened the group's interest in the area of sensitivity spatial location, the group leader can offer the following exercise. After each person in the group has exchanged places and then returned to his original place, the group leader can ask the group to rise and form a circle. Before the circle has actually been formed and while the group is in the process of rising and walking toward one another to form a circle, the group leader can ask the group to stop and to assess what this group action has created in terms of feeling. The comments might be that they did not like leaving the space they were in, that they were looking forward to being closer, that they did not like the idea of coming closer, that they were comfortable where they were.

The group can be instructed to continue moving and to complete the circle formation. When the circle is complete, the group leader can once again ask for comments. It could be commented that the circle is conforming, that now they resent the restrictions that the formation imposes, that they feel less free and less able to move their arms as they wish. After standing in the circle for a moment, the positive comments begin to be reported, including the fact that the circle gives security and group support, that the circle develops a sense of unity or togetherness, and that the circle feels warm.

It is interesting to note that it takes a moment for the positive reactions to be developed since new programs must be developed first. The new programs at once grasp the fact that there are others available to do for one what one may not be able to do for oneself. The group formation evidently gives one a sense of protection beyond what one could reasonably create for oneself in isolation. It is also interesting to note that some group members appear entirely uncomfortable in this formation and are clearly agitated and unhappy about it. Their feet are further out from the circle than others and they can be seen looking elsewhere than at the other group members.

Often these group members will verbalize their discomfort and let the group know in no uncertain terms that they just do not care for this at all. Other group members can be seen with their arms folded across their chests or with their arms behind their backs, making it clear that they feel their arm movements are restricted by this formation as they are indeed, for the circle usually forms with each group member's shoulders approximately two feet from one another. The clasped arms also indicate that one is restraining oneself. This restraint might be relative to one's desire to put one's arms about one's neighbor's shoulders, for this location might very well trigger a social, tender reaction to place one's arms around the shoulders of one's neighbors, an act that is difficult in our distance-demanding culture.

When all the comments have been made and the group has become adjusted to the circle formation, the group leader can instruct the group to return to their original places. When this process is approximately half-completed, the group leader can ask the group to halt and to comment on the responses they have to terminating the circle. Some may comment that they experience a feeling of loss, some that they are experiencing a sense of relief. Some may comment that the room feels colder. Some may say they feel freer and happier. Some may feel that something is missing or that they have lost something. Each comment reflects the individual's feelings regarding individuality and need or lack of need for others, and the particular feelings relative to this particular group.

When these comments have been completed, the group leader can instruct the group to resume the return to their original spaces. When the group has settled in, and it is remarkable how *inevitable* the process of falling in to one's space appears to be, the group leader can ask for commentary regarding the return. The comments are as can be expected: that this feels right, this feels better, that they feel freer now, that they miss the security of the group, that they feel more individual. Freedom surely is a state of mind, for the group appears anything but free. The formation that is made is so regular that one is led to consider that one has become free to do as one must do without being imposed on to do other than one feels internally compelled to do.

Following the completion of the commentary, the group leader can ask the group to form a circle and, without stopping them this time, note that by and large, the circle will form as it did the first time. A precedent has been set, programs have been made. If one person is in another place than before, it is very likely that one member of the group, probably the one most proximal to the changed placement, will comment that that person is in so and so's place, or that that person is in the wrong place. The circle placements have not been a random selection. The choice of neighbors has been a subtle and partially unconscious one demonstrated by the preference shown for the return of the original neighbor. This can also be considered a wish for repetition rather than preference but one should note that preference was made in the very first formation of the circle.

Now, when the group leader asks for comments, the responses can be faster, for they know what to expect. There is greater security and unity, there is a loss of individuality and freedom. The advantages and disadvantages of formal relationships between groups of people, circles for example, have been demarcated. The process of returning to original places and then reforming the circle can be repeated several times for the benefit of the group. During this they are in a position to explore their immediate responses and are able to compare their feelings in their own spaces more poignantly to their feelings when the circle is formed.

When the learning process involved above is somewhat diminished and the group has accustomed itself to being formed in a circle, the group leader can draw the attention of the group to several dimensions the circle develops. The group leader can ask the group to concentrate for the time being on how the front of the body feels while the group is in the circle formation. At first the group might not be able to respond intelligently to this, but when asked to compare the difference between the way the front of themselves feels compared to the back of themselves, the associations begin to flow. They become aware of the eyes of everyone in the circle and that all are looking toward the center of the circle. They note that the front of their bodies seems far more sensitive than the back of their bodies. They note that their arms tend to reach more in front of themselves than they would tend to reach behind themselves. They note that the fronts of their bodies seem warmer than the backs of their bodies. They note that they are not terribly aware or concerned with what is going on behind them whereas they are most concerned and aware with what goes on in front of them.

Many of the dimensions expressed above relate to an individual's sensitivity regardless of whether or not he is in a circle formation, but the circle formation tends to emphasize them since all are experiencing the same dimensions simultaneously. If the group were in random placement and were asked to consider the differences between front, side and back, one would have to take into account that some group members would have others behind them and at different angles to the side of them, which would distort the clear picture that evolves when all are facing the same way. All are facing the same way in a line formation but the end individuals would not feel the same about their sides as the middle individuals and so on; so even though the dimensions elaborated on above relate to the individual in isolation, they are particularly evident in the circle formation with a group. This is because of the specific nature of intensification that occurs with a circle.

When the group is asked to consider how the sides of their bodies feel, they become aware of the limitations of the arms to the sides, and this is a frequent comment. In comparison to the front and back, the side seems less important than the front and more important than the back. The side people are closer to one than the front people and the side gives the sensation of being with people whereas the front gives the sensation of being opposite people. It is interesting to note that the sense of group is intensified when group members look about to see if all the spaces between people are equal. If they are not, some group member is bound to comment that he would like to see all the people equidistant so that there are no holes in the group. This demonstrates that no one is missing and that all the people in the group are the same and equal. If a space surrounding any individual is larger than most, that individual seems to stand out from the group, and the sense of group equality and totality is disturbed. If the openings in a group were on either side of an individual several spaces from him, the circle would no longer seem like a circle but more like two lines opposing one another. Side feelings demonstrate or produce the sense of togetherness and equality of spaces. They connect the people opposite with the self, maintaining the sense of group and preventing the sense of opposing lines.

Once the group becomes sensitized to these dimensions, there are always interesting new comments produced by them as they search for their own individual responses to these dimensions. People who are short suddenly note the difference of equality surrounding the taller person who is either opposite or directly beside him. People who are tall feel as if they are above the group and see a dimension that others do not see, that is, the group circular shape from above. They also feel more separate from the group, indicating that the point of reference resides in the head and not in the feet. When these people are asked to bend their knees so that their heads are the same level as the majority of the group they may either feel more secure and more part of the group or feel as if they have lost power and are now like everyone else.

The group becomes aware of the space they have created and how different that space is from the rest of the room. There is an intensification of perception regarding that space, and the feeling about the rest of the room is mild compared with the feeling toward the center of the circle. The temperature of the space in the center seems (and very likely is, due to body warmth) warmer than the space immediately behind and in the rest of the room. The group is asked to place their arms toward the center of the circle and to consider the feelings that this engenders. The usual comment is that it feels warm and is almost like placing one's hands over a campfire. The commentary reflects the culture's way of dealing with a circle, football huddles, campfires, children's games, and so on. Once the hands are all in the center, there is a sense of the group doing something together, something purposeful and somewhat powerful, for the presence of other hands gives force to one's own gesture. When the arms are placed behind, the comments are that it feels considerably cooler behind, and that the hands seem to become meaningless and almost disappear although they had so much power when placed where they could all be seen.

When the group is asked to place their hands sideways and touch the arms or shoulders of those beside them, the sensation that the group has become even more close is usually expressed. Those who dislike the group in the first place find this closing of the group even more distressing than the simple circle and find that they have strong desires to drop their arms and to leave the group entirely. This highlights the fact that indeed the visible and tactile perception of closing the group does reinforce the sense of solidity and security that the group affords and negatively imposes even more conformity on the individuals' separate and free actions. The group clasping hands is similar in effect to the group touching each other's shoulders, but is rendered more personal. The hand holding makes a friend of the person and a more intimate feeling is created. This type of hand holding was experienced during childhood school games and this type of reminiscence is often spoken of. Some group members feel this so strongly that they suggest that the group all skip to one side or the other and the group leader can comply in this and permit the group to experience this together. This can be a little moment of joyous regression to childhood days for some and for others a miserable and stupid action that only produces embarrassment and annoyance.

This desire to skip points out the power of group and individual placement to arouse strong emotional impulses related to those movements. The gaining of this knowledge is one of the purposes of sensitizing the group to the language of action and placement so necessary for the effective organization of structures. There are many kinds of learning that can be gleaned from the varied placement of the arms, and the group leader can offer the group the opportunity to explore or suggest movements that all can do simultaneously. Each group inevitably produces actions and sensations that are interesting and have not been explored by previous groups.

Following the satisfactory culmination of the exploratory phase, the group leader can ask the group to face in a clockwise fashion and note what happens to the dimensions of front, side and back. The immediate difference is that now everyone is facing another individual's back and has his back to some other individual. For some, the individual in front can become a leader or a loved or hated authority figure. For others, the back may take supreme importance and the member behind can be imagined to be a loyal follower or if one is of a suspicious nature, an incipient back stabber.

They may note that the arm toward the center of the circle seems warmer longer, and more important than the arm toward the outside of the circle. The thought may be offered by a member that because the right arm is toward the center of the circle it would seem more important than the left. When it is suggested that the entire group face counterclockwise surprisingly the left arm takes on the characteristics ascribed to the right. Another feature of this change of direction is that the individual who in front became the archetype of the leader and authority figure, now becomes the lackey or the distrusted who is waiting eagerly to stab one in the back.

It is not only the person but also the position of the person which determines the response to him. Those who do not like leaders comment that they feel a compulsion to push the person in front aside and take over his place. Those that like leaders comment that they feel safe with the person in front in control. If a woman is in front of a man, his attitudes toward having a female in a position of power come forcefully to mind. If a man is in front of a woman, her ability or willingness to be a follower of a man are made readily apparent to her, not because of the comments of the group leader or others but by the immediate and undeniable feelings the placement arouses in her. The group can be asked to turn and return clockwise and counterclockwise several times followed by a period during which sensations can be evaluated. The extent to which placement changes subjective feelings may be a revelation to the group. One is ordinarily certain that one's feelings are based in fact and reality, relevant to experience with individuals. This exercise points up the discrepancy between what we call our knowledge of the person and our response to his placement. It lends weight to the proposition that our role is relevant to our position and not only to our personalities. Such controlled exercises make it clear that projection and anticipation is a function in our estimation of those around us. It makes us more willing to look into our attitudes and expectations regarding others.

The group leader can instruct the group members to turn and face the outside and consider what happens to the dimensions front, side and back. The comments point out that the sense of the circle has dropped completely away. When the persons beside one and those across from one are no longer seen, the circle is no longer experienced. One *knows* intellectually that the circle still arches out around from one and circles back behind one, but one has to turn and look to be experientially certain that it does in fact exist. This points out the difference between the concept of a circle and the experience of a circle. The concept of a circle is an abstraction whereas the perception of one is an experience. The contrast between these two ways of perceiving reality is powerful in this exercise. All that is meaningful about the circle, the proximity to one's neighbors, the equality of spaces between each member, the visibility of those opposite one become memories but not an immediate experience.

Turning back to the center of the circle produces at once all the sensations on the front of one's body that were there before. The front of the body, while facing away from the center, is much less reactive, much emptier of feeling. The act of facing the center of the circle produces a program whose incipiency is experienced as a heightened feeling felt on the front of the body. Those who imagined a threatening individual behind in the clockwise and counterclockwise facings find a similar response when facing the outside of the circle. Now it is compounded by the larger numbers of people who can be potentially threatening. In this case the imagined or internal reality is stronger than the experiential reality.

The majority loses interest in the group when it is no longer seen. The circle and the group disappear for them when they face the outside. In the outfacing, the back feels warmer and the front of the body cooler, with the sides feeling freer. The dimensions just described represent the average in a typical group but individual reactions can vary considerably. Some group members' imaginings can be more powerful than real experiences. The lack of visible evidence of people, rather than reducing associations, acts as a blank screen onto which these individuals can project anything, much as radio was a more dramatic medium to some who could populate and costume the stories far more effectively than any TV producer could. These individuals have a rich inner life that may be more real than what is seen, heard, and felt. The group leader can outline the next phase to be explored following some time spent on the above exercise. The group is instructed to maintain the circle, and each group member is individually given the opportunity to change the circle size from the smallest possible diameter to the largest possible diameter several times. The individual group member can ascertain for himself which distance settings are the most pleasant, and which are the most unpleasant for him. When it is his turn to control the size of the circle, the group member indicates with his hands to move the group to either toward or away from the center of the circle. He can indicate to the group to stop at any point as he explores the feelings each setting offers him. He is not asked to divulge which setting is the most or least satisfying to him as that would tend to influence his selection and experience of the dimension. If the group member is expected to let everyone know his preferences he tends to demonstrate those preferences toward which the group seems inclined. Once the group member knows that his choices will be private, he can allow his sensitivity full receptivity to the changing dimensions.

Although no group member intentionally demonstrates his preferences, the speed with which some members shoo back the group as it gets smaller and the obvious pleasure which some have on their faces as the group gets smaller are clear evidences of two extreme points of view regarding proximity. Some group members desire such closeness that the group is forced to turn sideways in order to make the diameter as small as possible. Some group members keep the group moving backward until they are unable to take another step without climbing backward up the wall.

The exercise is complete when each member in turn has changed the circle dimensions enough times to satisfy his curiosity. This process takes place in complete silence. The transition from one group member to another is done automatically without intervention from the group leader with the termination of a turn left to each individual. Many insights can be gained by self-observant group members through this exercise. This information can be applied to other circumstances, such as parties or groups of various kinds which afford opportunities for observation of oneself and others in terms of this dimension.

The next exercise is designed to emphasize the difference between the concept of a gesture and the experiencing of a gesture. The group is shown four arm placements which they will exhibit, on order or on signals from the group leader.

The gestures are: One, each member holds his arms out to his side approximately at rib height without touching the arms of the person on either side of him. Two, each member clasps the hands of the individuals beside him. Three, each member extends his arms straight forward toward the center of the circle, both arms parallel to each other and the floor, with the palms of the hands facing the person in the center. Four, each member opens his arms with his hands extended straight and slightly upward, the arms open approximately 60 degrees.

One by one, each member in clockwise or counterclockwise sequence steps into the center of the circle. The circle then adjusts so that no gap is left from that person's leaving. The four gestures are directed at the individual in the center. When they are completed the individual resumes his place in the circle. The next individual steps into the center and so on until each person has a turn. From seeing the gestures demonstrated by the leader and from doing the gestures himself each member becomes conscious and aware of what gestures will be forthcoming when he is in the center of the circle. The group is instructed to remain neutral in facial expression throughout the gestures (but in actual fact the room becomes quite lively with feeling as the center individual very obviously reacts to the different gestures). Comments are not called for until the end of this exercise.

The first placement can elicit the feeling that one is being penned in, that they are "it" or that the group is going to harm them or come after them. The eyes of the individual can be seen scanning the openings between people and some comment that they were looking for a way out. This particular spatial pattern sometimes provokes programs of escape procedures and group members have commented that they had passing thoughts of diving out of the center under the arms of the group.

When the hands are clasped it intensifies the feelings of being trapped for some. Others respond as if the clasping demonstrates a friendly group as they like to hold hands. Many note that the group would be harder to get out of with the hands held. That is the most significant difference between gesture one and gesture two. The individual in the middle may sometimes try to avoid seeing the entire group by focusing on a single individual in an attempt to avoid the full impact of the gesture. Others may look about the group noting the regularity of the gesture and checking for variations. Some group members can become uncomfortable by merely being in the center. They might tend to giggle or try to talk to the group members to establish channels of communication in order to avoid experiencing the unpleasant sensations. Some members may express the feeling that they are controlling the group from the center and not feel at all uncomfortable.

The third gesture can give the individual in the center a visible shock. This gesture can sometimes precipitate crying even though the group member knows that the group is simply going through a series that they have seen and done themselves. The group leader can provide a safety area for that individual to run to for protection, by providing "ideal parents" who are separate from the circle and to whom that individual can run for support. For some groups, it is necessary to state beforehand that any individual who does not wish to experience this exercise can pass his turn. However, most groups suffer this relatively mild shock without difficulty although the expressions on individuals' faces as the arms raise up in that rejecting gesture are clear and expressive.

Some individuals may comment that even though they knew that that gesture was coming and had previously decided it was not particularly pertinent to them, wondered what they had done wrong to warrant the rejection, finding themselves believing in the validity of the rejection. Others may comment on a desire to shrink away from the gesture. Some said that it really hurt their feelings. Some group members may find it difficult to proffer such a gesture and comment that they temper it by smiling or turning their heads to one side as if to dissociate themselves from their own hands.

The final gesture can produce instantaneous affective changes accompanied by smiles. Some may note that now the group loves them. They may feel a flood of relief and other sensations across their bodies. Gestures provoke many potential programmed responses in each individual. These responses are largely irrational and nonintellectual. It is these responses that produce the waves of feelings that the gestures elicit. This exercise emphasizes the power of nonverbal messages even if they are contradictory to verbal ones. Emotions respond to spatial placements, and verbal denials will not eliminate these responses.

When all the group members have had their turn in the center and all comments have been made, the group leader can move on to the next exercise. Each group member in turn is instructed to step into the center of the circle. The group member is given the option to stand in the center with or without any action directed toward him by the group. He can then examine what responses this placement and the gestures he requests produce in him. Some individuals direct the group to do protective gestures and others hostile gestures.

Some report that the center placement increases a sense of vulnerability and that the group seems to have power over them. Members on the outside may verify that they feel that they *do* have power over the individual in the center. Some in the center feel as if *they* are controlling the group and indeed some on the outside may say they respond as if the individual in the center is the leader of the group and is about to tell them what to do. Thus power can flow from the group toward the center or from the center toward the group. Many cultures have rituals utilizing the circle. In some the god figure is in the center at which time power flows out. In others the victim is in the center at which time the power flows in.

Many group members experience fear and discomfort as they face the group from the center and one might think that this would be universal, yet some group members express that a marvelous sense of security flows over them for they feel protected by all the people around them. Some group members have asked the group to extend their arms diagonally upwards and make the circle quite small. Then they have sat on the floor and asked the group to meet hands in the center and form a kind of roof over them. They report that this gives them the feeling that they are in a little house and they feel quite content. Other group members may ask the group to point fingers at them, and they may squirm with contradictory pleasure at this gesture.

The values of this exercise are that it gives the center individual an opportunity to explore, in a controlled manner, what certain gestures mean to him. In real life one may receive gestures toward oneself that are truly or not truly felt by the sender. This exercise gives one a clear circumstance when the directed gesture is *not* felt by the doer of the gesture and one which the recipient of the gesture has asked for. It is evident that this is what the center individual either wants to receive from groups or feels he should receive from groups, for in this case the group is patently neutral and feels nothing specific about any individual as yet. Clearly some individuals' request for hostile gestures bespeaks a desire to be punished by the group and by extension the world. Some individuals' request for a little house bespeaks a desire to be nurtured by the world and a willingness to accept this nurturance.

The exercise also develops trust in the group as the group demonstrates its willingness to do precisely what the center individual requests. This gives the group practice in accommodation, which is the act of doing for the other what is wished for. Accommodation rather than being unpleasant becomes a satisfying way of giving to others in the group. Accommodators in advanced groups report that it makes them feel good to help produce a satisfied reaction in others by assisting in the expression of emotion. Individuals to whom the accommodation is demonstrated express a strong gratitude toward the group members who are accommodating for them. Accommodation does indeed develop strong group feeling and trust.

This exercise also gives the group leader an opportunity to note how the individual sees the group and by extension the world, whether he sees it as benign and protecting or hateful and vindictive. The individual's use of the circle is a direct and obvious expression of those possibilities. This knowledge regarding an individual's group orientation can be useful in assisting that group member in solving future group relationship problems in structures.

When most of the values of the exercise have been exhausted, the group leader can move on to the next exploration. This particular sequence of exercises should be allowed to proceed at its own speed. It is unlikely that they will be completed in one session. The group leader can use his own discretion in providing relief from the monotonous maintenance of the circle formation by having the group do some free or emotional movement of some kind to break the tension. When the group has resumed the circle and they are relaxed enough to continue (for if they are not relaxed their perception of what is going on will be dulled), the group leader can set up the next exercise.

This time each member in turn is instructed to step *out* of the circle and into the room at large. The individual is instructed to wander at will within the circle or around the room to explore the different responses each location offers him. He is asked to focus on how it feels to step away from the group. The group focuses on how that individual appears to them as he steps out of the circle and how he appears to them when he is in different locations in the room. The goals of this exercise are for the individual and the group to determine the meanings inherent in the act of separation and the kinds of motor responses it generates. When the individual has ascertained all he wishes from outside the group, he is instructed to focus on how he feels when he returns to the group. The group is instructed to focus on how they feel as he resumes his place in the group.

The responses and comments that this exercise elicits are infinitely varied, but there are several more common ones that I will describe. Some individuals note that when they leave the group they feel that the group has rejected them and that they have been isolated. Some say that they feel as if they are now free and that it is a relief to step away from the group. Some comment that the group seems hostile to them when they leave and others feel that the group feels friendly and that they don't want to leave. Some note that the group appears more solidified when they leave and that now it is a real group in their absence.

The basic modes are those of feeling rejecting or rejected as one leaves the group. When the individuals are walking around the circle, the comments vary from feeling powerful and able to injure the group, to feeling powerless and about to be injured by the group. Some members comment that they feel like pushing the group over and that they look like a silly bunch just standing there. Others comment that the group looks strong and unified and meaningful.

When the individual steps back into the group he may either feel relief in joining the group or a return of feeling stifled by the group. Some may feel that the group does not want them back and others feel that the group does indeed want them back as demonstrated by the fact that the group left a place for them. Most feel less self-conscious as they step back into their spaces in the circle, for when outside of the group they feel that everyone is looking at them. Some note that it is much warmer in the group than it is on the outside. Most feel safer within the group than separate from it, although an important minority strongly prefer the individual feeling of importance that separation from the group provides them. That minority might comment that the group is stupid and unmoving and now they are free to do as they please.

On the side of the group the comments vary from feeling rejecting to feeling rejected as the individual leaves. Some comment that they feel as if the group has thrown out that individual and that they feel sorry for him and wish he could be brought back. Others may feel that this person is rejecting the group and this gives them the feeling that the group is bad and that they should leave too. Some feel that the group has power over the individual and that they can all walk over and kill the individual who has left. Others feel that the individual who has left is freer and stronger than the group and that now the group is at the mercy of that individual. Some group members feel that since that person left, his place should be taken away for with the space open the group feels broken. Other group members comment that the space is left for that person to return, that it is his space and it would be unfair to take it away, that he is free to resume it when he comes back.

This exercise provides a screen which highlights basic attitudes regarding the group and the individual. It develops sensitivity to what an act of leaving a group means to a person, and what actions one is prepared to make relevant to that leaving.

The next step in this exercise is to have the group focus on the gap that the individual makes in his leaving and how they respond to this gap. Each individual successively leaves the circle to give each member the opportunity of being on either side of the gap and opposite the gap, because these locations are particularly pertinent to the gap sensations. The gap provides a break in the sense of unity with the group. It is most poignantly felt by those who are directly opposite the gap and who can see it most clearly. The leaving may provoke a programming of a desire for one to leave also. This is experienced as a wave of feeling or a force field sucking or drawing one toward and through the space that is left. This sensation is most markedly felt by those who are opposite the gap. The individuals on either side of the gap generally feel either of two extremes. One, the desire to reach for the person as he leaves. Two, the wish to reach for the arm of the person on the opposite side of the gap to effect closure. When the individual returns to close the gap there is an experience of strong relief from those most opposite and most close to the gap.

A variation on this exercise is to instruct the individuals most apposite the gap to move closer together and close the gap. The attention should then be focused on the responses in the individual who has left and in the group remaining. The individual who has left may feel as if he were dead, as if he were thrown out, as if the group no longer wanted him and as if there were no longer any place for him. If his attitude toward the group were negative he may feel that they have no more power over him, that it is finished and that he has no more obligation to them, that he can stay away for good.

On the side of the group the sensations may be that they have killed the individual who has left; they may feel sorrow or anger at the group for having done so, and sympathy for the locked-out individual. If their feeling toward the individual leaving is negative, they may feel relief that without him the group is whole again. They may feel that now the group can function, since that person was a bad egg anyway. They may totally lose interest in the individual who has left and be prepared to treat him as if he did not exist. These responses highlight the importance of children's games which utilize these formations. These games can and do have remarkable power and meaning to the individuals who are participating in them. Teachers and group leaders should analyze each game carefully in light of the above, to be certain that each one is not giving negative reinforcement and traumatic experiences to some sensitive children. Obviously there is no single true or right response to any formation. It is a very individual thing, but certain elements remain constant, and one should know the possibilities of responses that are inherent in each formation before utilizing these games in a creative situation.

Another factor reported by the individuals who were separate from the group is that the room looked different from the different locations and particularly different from the outside of the circle. This reinforces the hypothesis made earlier that one's perceptions and one's programmed responses were relevant to one's location. Generally one's feelings of power were increased when within the group and one's feelings of powerlessness were increased by being absent from the group. One tended to see the room as a comfortable place when within the group and as a hostile place outside the group. One's original place in the group provides the most security, as one has the greatest history of behaving from that particular place.

Following this series the leader can have the group explore the qualities of feeling aroused by holding the hands of or placing the arms around the shoulders of one's neighbors in a circle. This exercise tends to neutralize the feelings of disunity that the gap exercises engender, and reunifies the group. Standing holding hands vividly revives children's games and provides feelings similar to those in a civil rights rally.

Hands on the shoulders intensifies familiarity. Diminishing the circumference of the circle by this act increases proximity, giving those who project positively on the group a feeling of warmth and satisfaction. Those who project negatively on the group may get a sense of being suffocated and restrained. Some individuals may be unable to tolerate a tightly closed group such as this and demand to be let out of the circle. This is not a frequent occurrence, since the normal individual finds group proximity generally tolerable and most likable. If there is a group member who does have strong reactions to closeness, the group leader should be certain to structure the activity to minimize the discomfort. A possibility would be the inclusion of that individual in a slower-moving group that would include some others whose feelings were similar.

The exercise possibilities surrounding group formations and variations are endless. A creative group leader can develop his own or utilize the many and infinitely varied suggestions that members of his groups will provide. It should be noted, however, that the exercises should not be permitted to get out of hand to the point of loss of focus and specific value. One should structure each exercise so that only limited changes occur, the better to determine whether what one is experiencing is a projection or a real message from the group or individual. With this in mind, the learning from these exercises will be maintained. Yet one should not look askance at the real pleasure and fun that such manipulations in themselves provide without looking too deeply into their use as learning tools.

The final exercise that will be described in this chapter breaks the circle dimension and focuses on the individual in a less structured group formation, created by each individual in turn. The group can be sitting about in a relaxed way following some tension-breaking opportunities that the group leader can have offered the group. The group leader can describe the exercise and the purpose of it while the group members lounge comfortably. Each member can tell the other members precisely what he wishes them to do until he has created either a static group formation or an active one that satisfies whatever he wishes to see. The group can be used as a blank canvas on which each individual group member can create a world, a formation or whatever meaning he wishes. It is a way of concretely expressing how one sees the world, and following that a way of looking at the world one has created and contemplate it for whatever it is worth. It gives the individual group member a sense of power and control, and this in itself can be of value, particularly to those who have lost their sense of mastery and power.

At the outset of this exercise, individual group members might tend to be conservative and tentative in what they ask the group to do, but as soon as it becomes apparent that the group will tolerate anything, they come closer to acting out their fantasies using the group as the figures in their fantasies. This exercise can provide a lot of fun as well as learning, and the humor in this situation should not be suppressed or repressed by the group leader.

Some group members first begin to explore how they wish people to look or behave relevant to them and then begin to note the different responses they receive toward each individual in his assigned placement. Some group members make the other members act as their slaves and do all kinds of menial things to and for them. Some act as if they are the ruler of the world. Some have the group do something negative toward them. Some have the people choose what movement they are to make, defaulting their opportunity for sovereignty over the group. Some try to make the group look ridiculous. Some make the group turn their backs so that the individual will no longer be looked at.

A group of male hospitalized mental patients showed some interesting variations on this exercise. In that instance one had each member turn constantly around and around themselves in their own little spaces. Another asked each group member to walk in a different direction until they ultimately walked into the walls and he instructed them to try and keep on walking. Another had each group member stand in corners as if, as he said, they were bad children. Another had the group leader and his assistant turn their backs and effected a mock escape from the room. Clearly, each group use reflects important attitudes.

In normal groups it is interesting to watch the development of a group formation. Following giving the group a ridiculous task to accomplish or a ridiculous series of gestures to maintain, the individual may be convulsed in laughter and then feel more benign to the group. If one is free to do one's negative feelings in such playful ways, the positive feelings may possibly make subsequent appearances; experience indicates that this is so. It is important in the supervision of this exercise that the group members easily comply to all that is asked of them so that each individual will get maximum gratification from the satisfaction of his images. This compliance, as noted earlier, assists in the development of group trust and group helpfulness that is so important in future sessions. When one is certain that one is in control and that all that happens is truly of one's own making, one is in a less ambiguous situation than in real life. One is in a better position to measure the difference between what one thinks the world is saying to one and how one structures the world to say certain things to one. This is the theme of this chapter: The clarification of the process of projection.

When all elements are controlled and then only one or two are permitted freedom or change, one can examine what effect those changes have on one's anticipations, feelings and programs of behavior. This type of practice strips away ambiguity and gives opportunities for exploration and concretization of one's feelings. The creative group leader can invent other exercises that result in the same or similar learning. Profitable areas to explore would be the relationships that occur when two lines face one another, with mixed sexes in the opposing lines, with all males in both lines, with all females in both lines, or with males facing a line of females. Distance factors can be explored and the factors of placement on the end or in the middle of the line can be looked into. Also worth examination is the response of the viewer to the diminishing space between lines approaching one another in respect to the sexual composition of the lines. This chapter is not intended as a complete exploration of the learning process in this dimension but more as an outline of how this exploration can be approached and certain ranges of response inherent in the kind of formations discussed.

CHAPTER

6

This chapter will concern itself with the exploration of one to one dimensions in contrast to the one to group dimensions in the previous chapters. As noted earlier, each situation produces an internal program of potential behavior or behaviors. The program range depends on what opportunities the spatial dimensions permit and on which of one's attitudes or histories are relevent to the objects or persons seen. In addition to the programs one has relevant to situations, one has relatively constant ongoing programs that are relevant to one's self-image or to one's own body parts.

From long experience with one's body, one knows approximately to what extent in front, side or back of him one can be effective with one's own limbs. One has made unconscious estimates of the amount of force one has in each segment, that is, he knows how hard he can hit or how softly he can touch with each hand. He knows how high he can kick and where his foot would extend in front, side or back of him. He knows where his mouth is without touching it and how hard he can bite and how large an object he can sink his teeth into. Through this long experience one builds up an infinitely variable series of programs that reflect one's history and one's anticipations in the use of the limbs and all the movable structures of the body. The range of the possible movements described can be understood as a field surrounding the body.

The purpose of the next exercise is to explore the extent of the field and the nature of the programs inherent in the field. It is called the controlled approach and the exercise is implied in the name. One group member, designated as the controller, indicates by gestures the directions in which he wishes another group member, designated as the controllee, to move. The controller remains stationary while the controllee is directed to move only as indicated by the controller. The controller explores all the dimensions of the field surrounding him by placing the controllee in all dimensions, changing the controllee's speed of approach or retreat, the direction, and the level.

The idea is not simply to manipulate the controllee, although that in itself is a value, but to savor the varying response and changes in the field or program that one experiences relevant to each placement. Therefore, the activity should not be hasty with a great deal of constant moving about by the controllee. If it were, it would not give the controller time to examine his subjective states relevant to each placement. It is important that the controllee remain neutral in expression so that facial expression will not have too great an effect on the controller's responses. Sometimes, controllers request that there be eye contact during the manipulation process, and some maintain that eye contact destroys the purity of response to the purely spatial features of the relationship.

The group leader can demonstrate the exercise by choosing a member of the group to act as controllee while he acts as controller. The group leader can place himself in a section of the room that permits approach from all directions and begin by having the controllee stand as far away from him as possible, so that the group leader's field can be first experienced as relatively neutral as regards the controllee. The group leader can indicate, by making circular motions with his hand, that the controllee should move toward him. At intervals, the group leader can hold his hand toward the controllee, indicating that the controllee should stop where he is. As the controllee comes closer, the group leader can feel the changes of feeling across the front of his body as waves of feeling dependent on the distance begin to be experienced. The group leader can explore at what distance these waves occur by alternating the distance of the controllee several feet or inches in either direction to note when the feelings change. The group leader can have the controllee come even closer, noting if and where a feeling of discomfort is included in the waves of feeling. He can again increase the distance of the controllee to ascertain what distance produces this change. The group leader can have the controllee stand as closely to him as possible and note what reactions this produces.

The group leader can have the controllee step back several feet and then have him move to one side to explore how it feels to have the controllee approach from the left or the right and note if there is any difference in response between either side. The group leader can have the controllee walk around him in a circle slowly, stopping the controllee at intervals to note if there is a variation in feeling between times when the controllee can be seen directly in front, can only be seen from the side of one's eyes, or cannot be seen at all. The group leader can have the controllee approach from behind him and note if the sound of footsteps coming closer and closer from behind produces any effect. He can have the controllee walk from directly behind him until the controllee bumps into the group leader. The group leader can do all of the same sequences but vary the speed with which he had the controllee move toward or away from him to note if the controllee's speed is a factor in the response pattern. He can do all of the same sequences including the factor of changing the level of the controllee's approach or retreat to note if there is a variation in response due to the changed head level of the controllee. He can kneel and repeat the same sequences and note if there is a change in response relevant to that. He can have the controllee lie down on the floor in various locations and note if that has any effect on his responses. In other words, the group leader demonstrates all the possible dimensions of the exercise and notes for himself the changes in feeling and program each change produces.

Following the demonstration, the group leader can have the group pair off with one group member acting as a controller and the other a controllee after which the roles will be reversed. The entire group can attempt this exercise simultaneously and this has both advantages and disadvantages. The advantages are that no individual can feel on display while he explores his feelings when there is no audience. The group leader, incidentally, makes it clear that no group member is required to divulge his feelings during this exercise. If any group member does feel the compulsion to talk about the variation of his feelings that is his prerogative, but his feelings can remain private if he wishes.

The disadvantages are that most rooms are not large enough to permit full use of the room for each couple in this exercise. Often,
someone else's controllee will be to one side of another couple's controller, which overlapping can diminish the purity of the response.
This can be pointed out at the outset. Steps can be taken to utilize
selective inattention to all but one's own controllee. The entire group
can attempt the exercise at once and this point in the session is similar
to the point when the group tested one another in the species stance.
The same type of informality develops with the concomitant laughter,
talk, and so on, before the group settles down to the process.

The group leader can take this opportunity to relax and watch the
ensuing exploratory activity. Usually some member of the group
will have some question to raise regarding the implementation of
the exercise, and the group leader can make himself available for this
end. He should not divorce his attention from the group, for this
would be consciously or unconsciously felt by the group. The answer-
ing of questions would not be noted as disinterest by the group but
it should be done quietly so as not to disturb the group concentration. The full exploration in this exercise can vary in time from
group to group. Some groups will complete the exercise in a very
short time which it is fair to say is not entirely productive. It indicates that the exploration was cursory and without depth. No matter
how long it takes, the group should sit quietly until the final couple
has completed the survey. Sometimes the remaining couple or couples
suddenly note that they are the only ones who are continuing and occasionally they abruptly terminate the exercise. The group leader can
tell them that there is no need to cut off the learning process and
that they may continue as long as they wish. For some this is sufficient
license to continue but others may not be able to work effectively
with the group watching them.

Many group members have commented on the variations of feelings
they experience during this exercise and they cover a wide gamut
indeed. The following is a sampling or a reduction to common denominators of the significant findings. As can be expected, there
is great intensification as the controller comes forward. Some find
that they cannot tolerate a proximity of less than several feet. Some
find that they enjoy the proximity at its closest point. This would cor-

respond to those individuals who showed a dislike and a liking of proximity in the previous chapter. Most noted differences between right and left and suggested that they minded proximity less on what they felt was their strongest side. Those who had fantasies regarding vulnerability from the rear found the controllee behind them to be highly disturbing. The changes in speed produced feelings of being pursued or approached with danger or approached with affection, depending on one's past history with speedy approaches.

The changes in level produced feelings of being in power if one were taller than one's controllee. Coupled with the power issue is the association of being a parent or a child depending on the height of the controllee. The parental or child factors produced intense feelings and programs and are useful for discovering essential factors to be used in future structures. Most group members report highly specific motor responses to certain dimensions. If the controllee, due to height, sex, distance, and so on, represented someone who was hated in one's real life, one might report feelings about striking or strangling the controllee. These feelings would vary when the controllee was made to take another placement.

The discovery that certain placements are that potent is surprising to some group members. They might wonder if some responses to the outside world were irrationally provided by these selfsame spatial determinants. By exploration, group members discover those placements which provoke the strongest feelings of a positive or a negative nature. This learning is obviously helpful in application to real-life situations.

As can be expected, intensified and subtle responses can be elicited by including the element of gestures to spatial placements. That is the goal of the next step. The group is instructed to repeat the exercise with the incorporation of gestures, and to note which gestures coming from which angle and which speed and height elicit the most responses. The group can utilize the same couplings as before and explore this new dimension. The group leader can be as relaxed and attentive as before. Once again, he is available for questions and comments. This process may take more time than the previous one since the group is now more familiar with the elements of this exercise and more able to be proficient in gleaning values from it.

This type of exploration is essential for the group members' future work in the course, since it gives him the material with which he must instruct his accommodators. Through this type of exercise, he begins to know which placements and which gestures are important to him, and can tell both his negative and positive accommodators precisely what he wants them to do for the desired effect. It is possible that at this time one member of the group will be so affected by the gestures and the placements of his controllees that he might ask the group leader for permission to move directly in terms of the emotional impulses he is experiencing. If the group leader deems it appropriate he can allow a structure to proceed. A structure at this point can provide a clear example of the organic qualities of emotional action as distinguished from pantomimed acts and prepare the rest of the group for doing structures.

The group leader can instruct the controller to proceed with his movement while the group watches. He might ask his controllee to do the provoking gesture once again and, finding the same response as before, express the actions that this engenders in him directly and emotionally. If he is successful and his controllee responds appropriately to whatever movements the controllee directs to him, the controller will show obvious evidence of function pleasure. If the sequence is repeated several times, it might be found that the force of the gesture and action of the controllee is diminishing and that it loses its power to provoke the controller. This sequence can be valuable in preparing the group for the rhythms and qualities of future structures, and in showing how to utilize this exercise for their own ends. The diminishment of the reaction to the provocation tends to render the provocation meaningless. The satisfactory response to the provocation is an element in reducing the provocative nature of the action of the controllee.

The group leader can have the group resume their explorations following this demonstration. The return at this time can be more avid since the group has seen an example of what might very well occur with themselves. Following the completion of the entire exercise for the group, the group leader should offer some opportunity for the release of the pent-up emotions that this exercise might have developed. This release can take many forms. One can be the opportunity to do the temper tantrum described earlier. Another can be the license given to the group to do whatever it pleases for a limited period of time. Whatever the form of emotional release used, the group hug can follow it since it is an effective group unifier and tranquilizer following emotional outbursts.

These exercises are developed with an eye to providing insight to the controller relevant to what produces strong emotional reactions in himself. To learn this it is necessary to control as many factors as possible so that ambiguity is reduced to a minimum. That is the purpose of having the controller be immobile while the controllee is mobile. If both were active simultaneously and if both were moving independently, it would be difficult to ascertain what was real and what was projection, and what action provoked what response. The compliance of the accommodator is an important fact in this and other exercises, for without it, the controller would not know whether it was the controllee personally who was provocative or whether it was the movements he told the controllee to do that were the causative factors in the evocation of feeling.

The following exercise utilizes the same factors as the first except that the controllee is now kept immobile while the controller is mobile. The group leader can demonstrate this exercise to the group in the following manner: he selects a place in the room to have the controllee stand immobile. He then moves toward the controllee in all the dimensions in which he had the controllee move toward him previously, noting all the while the variations in feelings that this creates in him. He notes to himself how it feels to walk slowly toward the controllee from straight ahead. He notes how different it feels to walk toward him from the side and from the back. He notes how it feels to walk toward the controllee with the controllee either taller or shorter than he, with the controllee kneeling, standing or standing on a chair. When he has completed the demonstration using every dimension, he instructs the group to couple once again and to explore the new element.

The group by now has learned to utilize this type of activity and goes promptly to work. The group leader can observe and see to it that the exercise is properly carried out while being available for questions as before. Couples may find different features to emphasize and learn from, and the group leader can learn new facets of this exercise from their attempts, since each person has his own way of perceiving the response to the reality he creates. The mobility of the controller permits him to bring his field to his controllee rather than the reverse in the first exercise. The controllee can ascertain which direction elicits the greatest desire to move toward the controllee, and from which direction it is the most difficult to approach the controllee.

The comments the group members offer reflect the obvious relationship dimensions. If the controllee is stationary and taller than the controller, he might appear to be a parental figure whom one is approaching, and comments will reflect the controller's attitudes and programs relative to parental figures. Some group members might feel that they had done something wrong and that the parental-seeming figure was angry; therefore they felt it difficult to approach from the front. Some might perceive the parental controllee as a benign figure, and find themselves running toward him in memory of running toward the parent as he returned from work in the evening. Some might comment that when they came up behind the controllee, they felt an impulse to hurt, injure, or surprise him. If the controllee were kneeling or very much shorter than the controller, the comments might include responses that one would have toward one's child, and the essence of the emotion would reflect the real life condition. Although these variations seem obvious from their description, the force and reality of the feeling is directly related to the experience of the placement and not to the contemplation of the idea of the placement.

The exercise can be repeated a second time to include the addition of gestures as was done in the first exercise. The inclusion of gestures tends to intensify the responses by making the stimulus even more specific. The learning that takes place in the controlled approach exercise and its variations cannot be minimized. This exercise can be repeated over and over again in many sessions, since the responses do not remain the same following appropriate expression and resolution of feelings. Future sessions, when structures have already been accomplished, can use the controlled approach exercises to produce the material for the evening's structures, much as the example given earlier. It is important that the group leader point out how best to make use of the exercise and its variations, since some group members might get overly absorbed in the more superficial aspects of the situation, forgetting to focus attention on their own subjective reactions. The group leader can elaborate on the different values to be found between the exercise where the controller is immobile and where the controller is mobile. In the first instance, the controller's orientation will reflect the passivity of his role, and in the second, the orientation will reflect the active nature of his role. In both instances, the most important feature is that the controller is always in control and therefore is in a position to test the source of his subjective changes.

Hospitalized patients show interesting variations in reacting to this series of exercises. A group of male mental patients who were offered a demonstration of the controlled approach in the process of several sessions repeated almost identically the series of placement instructions that the group leader indicated to his controllee. This was understood as over-compliance on the part of these mental patients and reflected their inability to be self-initiating. It also reflected the caution they felt in venturing into the area of proximity, since every order to the controller to move had been given the license by the group leader's example. Practice of the controlled approach by this group over a short period of time evinced little change in their style of utilizing it, whereas practice with a normal group produced much change and variation during comparable periods of time. The hospitalized group tended to keep their controllees relatively distant from themselves, never once exploring responses with their controllees touching or nearly touching themselves.

The rigidity of pattern demonstrated by this group was also reflected in their handling of the voluntary modality which became for most of them a standard set of placements done very much the same each time. Paradoxically, the patients did not demonstrate their compliancy in the controllee role, for accommodation was difficult for these patients. This group of hospitalized patients did poorly on the species stance test, demonstrating compliance on the arm raise. They did poorly on the voluntary modality by repeating over and over again the original types of pathways demonstrated by the group leader. They demonstrated compliance in the controlled approach by following the group leader's example in the manner of exploration to an unusual degree. Yet, where compliance would have produced satisfactions and gratifications, as in the controllee role in the controlled approach, they invariably made mistakes and did not at once understand the directions their controller was indicating. This lack of ability to accommodate and produce gratification and satisfaction for others was noted in other mental patients also.

The controlled approach completes, for now, the exploration of responses dependent on the visual placement of others, begun with the circle exercises in chapter five. This chapter is devoted to one-to-one dimensions; however, it will transcend the visual in one-to-one dimensions and explore the tactile. This exploration is the subject of this next section. The visual and the tactile are the only two sensory modalities that are inquired into in this writing. Future developments might indicate the need to expand this sensory list, but practice and experience through this time have only pointed toward the immediate value of the visual and tactile in the application of psychomotor therapy and training. Visual sensitization, relative to spatial placement of others, is not in a real sense visual sensitization. This process is more truly a sensitization of one's own responses to visual patterns. True visual sensitization would include sensitization to all acts of seeing. In the same manner, tactile sensitization as practiced in psychomotor training does not have direct relevance to learning to "touch" better, since the visual sensitization was not relative to learning to "see" better. The aims of the tactile exercises are: to arouse awareness of the sense of touch; to produce tolerance for the act of touching; to neutralize or de-eroticize touch (for touch has been overly eroticized in our culture); to develop one's sensitivity to one's feelings regarding the touched object and being touched; and to make it easier for one to be touched and accept the satisfactions of being touched.

The sense of touch is the most personal sense. One cannot touch an object that is a great distance from oneself or any distance from one's skin surfaces, whereas one can see objects that are great distances from oneself. One sees with one's eyes but one touches with oneself. Touching is always local. Touching is the closest and most real sense to us. The infant first apprehends reality with his tactile sense, his mouth being the most alert receptor of tactile stimuli. It is only much later that seeing produces responses comparable to touching. As adults when we discover a new object we look at it closely and then pick it up in our hands and explore it simultaneously with touch and sight. When we see an object we understand that it exists but when we touch it we have verified its existence as no other sensory modality can with such certainty. With the importance of touch so seemingly self-evident it is surprising to consider the relatively small use of and emphasis on touch in our culture.

There is something embarrassing about touching and being touched. Perhaps it arouses too much that has been held down. Its restriction is a testimony to its strength. To touch is to be near and to be near, as we have discovered in previous exercises, is to experience strong movement programs relative to that proximity. Better to stay away if one cannot express those programs satisfactorily. This statement seems to reflect sexual connotations but that is not my intent. Our culture seems to imply that the natural culmination of a touching experience is sex. In reality this is patently not so, but in the reality of our culture it *is* so. Truly, sex is the most notable way to touch in our culture and if one wished to touch for any other reason one would have to gain that end as a byproduct of sex. Surely sex can be a natural outcome of touch or proximity, but so can aggression and so can nurturance and so can socialization. What has happened to the other three possibilities in our culture?

Aggression is certainly to be frowned upon and contained, for the most part, but where is the outlet for our aggression in our culture? In sports to some extent, but what proportion of the population is utilizing that outlet? Therefore there is a great backup of aggressive energies that touch and proximity arouses. Nurturance is an interesting word and an interesting behavior mode. It seems most appropriate to offer this to children, but what about adult needs to comfort and be comforted, or to put it in Eric Berne's verbal terms to "stroke and to be stroked"? Must we "stroke" in a verbal sense in this culture? The answer has been yes and that provides the population with backed up nurturance energies that are provoked by proximity and touch.

Socialization is a word that would seem divorced from the consideration of touch in our society, yet touch is a perfect way to express that socialization. Touch verifies the fact that one intends to be friendly, to be accepting, to be helpful. Yet, in our culture the touch of socialization ends with the handshake. Anything further would be looked at askance, and at once askance becomes a sexual word. Hence the socialization elements that would include touch are inhibited in our culture. Surely, considering all that is to be held down, touch would seem to be highly explosive to our culture's residents and it is. The outcome is a half-empty bus peopled with strangers, no two who dare or choose to sit beside one another, leaving equidistant spaces between each individual. Is this what we mean by individuality, or is it isolation? If proximity and touch provokes intolerable and inexpressible programs, call it individuality; at least that word has status.

Psychomotor training deals with the expression of all emotional feelings, and certainly sexuality, aggression, nurturance and socialization would have to be considered and naturally we would have to come across the need and value of touch. Specifically, it was found that touch was a necessary element following the expression of strong negative emotions. After an angry explosion in action the proximity and touch of the group verified the group's acceptance and continued friendliness. It indicated the group's willingness to continue to be nurturant. In order to be able to include the element of touch without having it received with a predominantly sexual emphasis, the following series of exercises was developed.

The group leader can outline the aims of the exercises to be done in the tactile area noting much of what was described above, setting the stage for the discovery of more-than-sexuality in the sensuousness of touch. The group members can either be sitting or standing depending on their choice, and the group leader can suggest that they focus their attention on their touching surfaces. This attention can be elicited by rubbing the hands together or the hands over the body parts that will be utilized in the touching process. The touching exercise has three parts: first, the tactile exploration of the surroundings; second, the tactile exploration of oneself; third, the tactile exploration of others. The three stages are of an intensifying sequence with the first being most neutral and the final the most charged.

When the group has sufficiently intensified attention and response to tactile stimuli the group leader can give a short demonstration of the first step in exploration. The group leader can rub his hands over the walls and floor of the room with his hands and face noting the differences in shape and texture. He can have his hands and fingers follow the outlines of furniture and objects in the room. He can rub his face over the different surfaces and see how differently the same surface feels when touched by the front of the hands, the back of the hands, and the face. In other words, the group leader uses to maximum the tactile equipment available to him in the exploration of the room. Following his demonstration, the group leader can suggest that the group members explore the room to their own satisfaction.

The purpose of the demonstration is to give license to the sensuality of this exercise. The group leader by virtue of his authority lends credence to the idea that touching is permissible, at least in psychomotor training sessions. Some group members might get embarrassed or comment that they are embarrassed not only by the prospect of going about the room touching things, but by having watched the group leader do this. The group leader can reassure those members, and reassurance is what they want, that the group leader is not embarrassed by touch and that it is fun and that they can take the opportunity to enjoy it too. Most group members, however, tend to go straight to the assignment with interest and energy. The variation of approaches to the act of touch exploration is marked. Some touch as from a distance with their hands held far from their bodies. Some touch with their eyes closed and their bodies curled like a radar dish over the object being touched. Some touch with their whole hands in contact with the surfaces being explored. Some touch with the barest of fingertips. Some touch with one or two fingers extended, as if probing and touching were the same. Some touch mostly with the backs of their hands and only occasionally with the palms. Some seem to be curious to find how it feels to touch with all parts of the body and are touching with their toes, their feet and any part of the body they possibly can. Some group members remain standing all the while they explore, while some can be seen prone on the floor with their arms and legs outstretched, feeling with all that is in contact with the floor. Some climb on top of whatever objects of furniture are in the room. Some creep under all surfaces and feel the undersides of tables and chairs.

In contrast with such activity noted above is the restraint shown in this type of exercise by many hospitalized mental patients. Watching them one gets the distinct impression that they do not want to be affected by what they touch. The touching is tentative and cursory with the fingers extended as if poking away the object being touched. The length of time doing the exercise in a group of that composition, is short as compared with a normal group. The hospitalized mental patient group simply went through the motions of this exercise and stopped as soon as possible. Possibly the associations aroused by proximity and touch, even if only to inert surfaces, were more than they were willing to expose themselves to. It also seemed to say that they were going to keep the world at a distance, as if they did not trust it to come close enough to feel it. This would indicate that these patients' openness to change, growth and learning was severely limited. It shows a lack of fondness for the world, as one would avoid that which one did not like. It is a concrete example of the narrowing of the horizons and the avoidance of all but internal stimuli.

One particular female hospitalized mental patient showed active distaste for all that was touched in this exercise. Of course it is a generalization to say that all mental patients avoid touch, but the majority certainly do. Another particular female mental patient, noted earlier in this book, showed obvious desires for touch as shown by the example of milking the fingers of her fantasied little child; however, when doing the tactile exercise simply as an exploration of the surroundings she showed the same dilatory, disinterested behavior common to most patient groups. Apparently, for her, touch had to be sexual, or more truthfully, nurturant before she would show any interest in it.

The normal group takes a fair amount of time in this type of exploration and the group leader should see to it that he offers this exercise at a time in the session when there is ample time to complete it and the "tactile exploration of the self" exercise. The range shown within the group, extending from those who appear relatively like the hospitalized group in their inability and unwillingness to touch, to those who are open and eager in their exploration of the surroundings, bespeaks the variability categorized under the term normal.

The group members who tend to touch at a distance are generally those who prefer the voluntary movement modalities and who have difficulty with emotional movement spontaneity. The group members who touch with relish and childlike enthusiasm and curiosity are those who dislike the constraints inherent in voluntary movement and who explode easily into emotional movement and childlike, spontaneous behavior. There are those within the group who are taking sensual and possibly sexual delight in this touch process and those who are evidently making a tactile inventory of the room in a businesslike manner.

There are those who are self-conscious in this endeavor and who, fairly frequently, look about the room to see what others are doing and noting whether anybody is watching them. The group leader should resume his relaxed but available posture and attitude without focusing attention on a specific individual, for this might provide self-consciousness and therefore inhibition. Some group members might use this time to ask a question of the group leader or to regain reassurance that it is all right to do this exercise.

During a psychomotor training session, an individual who was doing this exercise came over to the group leader in great fear and, practically whispering, said, "Please tell me that it is all right to touch the radiator, it makes me feel as if I am masturbating to touch it." The group leader can reassure that individual that indeed, it is perfectly proper to tactilely examine a radiator and that it was not in truth masturbating to do so, even if it reminded one of masturbating. This is an extreme example of the eroticization of the sense of touch.

In subsequent tactile exploration of the self, this individual, during a time of exploration of the neck exclaimed in shocked tones that touching the neck produced a sensation of impending death. Apparently the guilt of sensual self-exploration produces in some the feeling that one is going to die. Reassurance at this time that it was proper to touch oneself on the neck sufficed to permit this individual to continue. Following an extended program of psychomotor

training within a normal group, this individual's capacity to touch
and indeed to respond to all senses increased markedly with a concomitant drop and total loss of a sense of guilt. Interestingly, this individual reported that the sense of location within the city and the sense
of color when looking at art had increased substantially. This is not
to say that simple exercises in tactile exploration can produce such results, but tactile exploration in conjunction with an entire psychomotor training experience appears to promote such growth in sensory response.

At the completion of the first tactile exploration exercise there is
generally little comment offered by group members. What their associations were can only be inferred but it is safe to say that a fair
amount of it would tend to be sexual, which would explain the reti-
cence in offering comments. Needless to say, the group leader does not
inquire into the nature of the feelings this exercise engenders so as to
provide the element of acceptance and nonexposure to all that is felt
and done.

When the group is once again relaxed and receptive to new material the group leader can describe the second phase and provide a
demonstration of how it can be carried out. The group leader can tell
the group to explore every part of their bodies that they can touch
with their hands and to note changes in shape and texture of flesh,
bones, hair, clothing and so on, so that they would get to truly
"know" themselves in this sense modality for no other reason than to
know. The only time the average individual explores and touches
his body to any extent is when he is bathing and then he touches it ostensibly for the purpose of cleansing himself. This exercise emphasizes
the purposelessness of touching except in the interest of knowledge.
Most other such manual exploration to those who are unaccustomed to
this type of knowledge would tend to connote vanity, perverted
self-love, search for palpable tumors, or any other such negative ends.

The group leader, in demonstrating the exploration of self-ex-
ercise can sit or stand comfortably, as he chooses, and tacitly explore
every surface of his body. He can begin with his head and face and
feel the changing topography of his brow, rubbing his fingers across
the faint ridges surrounding his eyes, note the transition from hairless
brow to hairline to fullness of hair, notice the sensation as the hair is

moved from one side to another, note how it feels on the hand to touch and on the face and scalp to be touched, run fingers across the bridge of his nose, feel the variation from rigid bone to softer cartilage, feel across his cheek bones the pressed skin of his cheeks, note the hollows beneath the cheek bones, and so on.

It should be noted that before demonstrating this exercise, the group leader places in perspective the exploration of the sexual or genital areas of the body, for no doubt the reader is wondering just how far the group leader will go in exploring himself in such minute detail. The group leader, having attempted to place the touching of oneself in a more neutral and uneroticized light should include the notion that one must not exclude the sexual factor in self-exploration but should recommend that group members attempt this exploration at their discretion in other instances than at a group session, for no other reason than that sexual arousal would lead to expectation of sexual gratification and such gratification is not offered in this context.

One group member in a recent group took issue with the group leader on this question and felt that it was his right to explore his entire body, including his genitals during this exercise. He further maintained that psychomotor training was weakened to the extent that it did not encourage, permit and structure sexual gratification within its context. Suffice it to say that this group member found it too restricting to function under the limitations described and elected to leave the group. Let it be clearly stated that, hopefully, one of the many byproducts of participation in a psychomotor training group be increased sexual pleasure and gratification. Nevertheless, it does not seem feasible to include in the activity these desired ends under the present cultural and social limits.

Following the group leader's demonstration, the group can be invited to partake of this personal, tactile inventory. The purpose of the demonstration is, once again, to provide a license as well as an example in an area that is quite charged. The majority of the group members tend to find the exercise within their capability to do with a minimum of concern but a minority will evidently discover that their inhibitions and restraints are difficult to overcome and that these produce some measure of self-consciousness and embarrassment. The group leader can attempt to assuage this embarrassment by reassuring them not only of the permissibility of such exploration, but also by pointing out the complete necessity for touch in the process of fulfilling depth structures. During most members' time in psychomotor training, they will choose to do some structure which will include nurturant factors, such as being held by a parent, being protected by a parent, and so on. At that time they must have overcome their timidity regarding touch, since there is no way to express this nurturance other than to embrace, fondle, and caress that individual.

If, by the time such structures are attempted, one has not yet placed the sexual and embarrassment questions in the proper perspective, one will be unable to resolve the emotions that the structure has brought forth, or one will be experiencing a flood of sexual responses out of proportion to the nurturant attitudes expressed by the positive accommodators. It is accepted that nurturance touching includes sexual factors, but the proportions can be put out of balance by the incomplete development of tactile acceptance of other-than-sexual factors.

During the group attempts at this exercise, the group leader can observe the group without focusing attention on any one individual, while making it clear that he is not divorcing himself from the group by his lack of attention. It should be stated that groups vary in their capacity to tolerate this type of activity, and the group leader should be sensitive to this factor and pace the activity accordingly. Some sophisticated groups would find the shyness elaborated above to be laughable, and would proceed at once to explore their bodies with interest, enthusiasm, curiosity and energy. Indeed, such groups would already have initiated such inventories individually in their own lives. However there are many more individuals and groups who would feel the concern expressed above, and the group leader should be prepared to meet successfully with both types. Mental patients, once again, are notoriously oversensitive in this area, and one would hesitate to move with haste or any lack of sensitivity when exploring this area.

The male hospitalized patient group noted earlier was totally unable to perform this exercise and the tentative suggestion that it be done was quickly retracted. It aroused instant feelings of perversion and guilt, and pursuance of the exercise would have produced far more feelings than could have been dealt with at that stage of the group. It should be a maxim that a group leader should never develop exercises or procedures that produce more feelings than can be expressed by a given individual or group. There are no criteria to follow in this respect separate from those that each individual and each group evinces. If a group leader is insensitive to such guidelines as individuals or groups manifest, he and the group will experience difficulties that could be painful and uncomfortable.

The group variations in the execution of this exercise are wide. There are those who will sit on the floor and, energetically though not hastily, examine with great care and interest every available inch of their bodies. Some tend to linger over one part of the anatomy more than other parts, some tend to move rapidly and insensitively over their bodies and then wait for the rest of the group to complete the exercise. The range will reflect the constituency of the group and the difficulties or lack of difficulties one has with this area of sensation.

When this exercise has been completed, the group leader can go on to the next step in the tactile trilogy—the exploration of others. It is not necessary that all three steps in the tactile exploration be contained in a single session, for each session usually includes the review of all that had gone on previously from the species stance on through, and this review takes time. It is also wise to slowly acclimate the average group to the area, and to give them time to build up confidence and tolerance. It should be understood that the direct progression from one step to another as outlined in this book is not indicative of how an actual group proceeds. The elements of speed, review, and group readiness are constantly being considered by the group leader in his selection of what is to be completed in a given session. However, for the purposes of the book and brevity, the steps will be described as if they were laid out in a straight line.

Returning to the next process, the group leader can select an individual from the group to demonstrate the tactile exploration of another. Either the group leader can explore the group member, or the group member can explore the group leader in this demonstration. It is probably most effective if the group leader demonstrates touching first and then demonstrates being touched, in that order. In that case the group leader can have the selected group member sit or stand on the floor and the group leader can systematically feel that person's entire body excluding the aforementioned sexual areas. This restriction can be noted to the group if it seems necessary to do so. The group leader should be careful that he demonstrates his concern and respect for the individual in the manner he effects his exploration. The individual should not be treated as a patient undergoing a physical examination or as an inanimate object. Simple care and courtesy should be evident without calling attention to itself in the manner in which this is effected.

It is optional whether the individual who is being touched should keep the eyes open or closed. Although the emphasis is on the person doing the touching at this time, the individual who is being touched is experiencing strongly too. Those feelings can perhaps best be felt with the eyes closed. When it is the group leader's turn to be explored, he has the option of either closing or opening his eyes as he sees fit. It can be expressed to the group that either is permissible in the event that a group member might feel constrained to ask. The group should be instructed that the goal of touching others in this exercise is to know the other and not to arouse or stimulate the other.

Following the demonstration the group leader can instruct the group members to pair off and decide which group member should be the first to do the exploration. This exercise is not completed until each member in the group has tactilely explored every other member of the group, male and female; thus those concerned with their initial partner's sex or appeal can be assured that this is not the one and only turn they will have. This point in the session is usually marked with conversation, laughter and general disturbance until the group members settle down in the selection process and decision process of who is to go first. The group leader can settle himself comfortably as this process takes a considerable amount of time to complete.

Some group members will find this exercise titillating and go to it with relish; others find it exciting but do not express this excitement directly. Instead they may overcontrol their exploration so that it would appear that they were examining a cadaver in an anatomy class, palpating all the surfaces they are supposed to remember for the examination. Some group members take at once to being touched and appear like cats being petted by a loving master. Some find this embarrassing and can be seen sitting tensely and uncomfortably, their bodies held stiffly. Some group members tend to find one area of the body which merits minute attention while scarcely paying attention to others. Some group members tend to touch each part once over and then indicate that they are through and wait for their turn to be touched. Some pairs of two males or two females seem to experience some embarrassment at exploring someone of their own sex. Some such groups manifest no concern. The room stays generally quiet during this time but often there are discussions as to how it feels to touch or be touched in one manner or another or in one part of the anatomy or other. It is clearly a learning situation for it is noted by many that this is the very first time in their lives that they have ever taken the time to do such an exploration.

Many comments reflect the attitude that it is very satisfying to be touched in that manner, that the only memory of having been touched in similar fashion was when one was very small. There is surprise at finding the touch so soothing and caressing without being directed toward a sexual end. There is surprise at finding that someone whom one does not know extremely well, as few in the group do know each other previous to being in the group, can provide such pleasant feelings.

There is commentary on how different it is to be touched by others in contrast to being touched by oneself. However, some comment that when touching themselves in the previous exercise it gave them the sensation that they were being touched by another. Apparently the stimulation from being touched on the surface of the hand and the stimulation of being touched on the face, neck or wherever this individual was touching himself did not get apprehended by that individual as coming from the same essential source. It almost appears as if it represents some neural misconnection; yet it is not entirely unusual to receive this type of comment. It is almost as if these individuals literally did not know themselves.

As soon as the first few couples have completed the exercise, the group leader can suggest that they pair off with new partners for the experience of doing this with another person. Ultimately the entire group is paired off with every other individual in the group. If there were ever ways for a group to "know" one another quickly this is certainly one of the ways. If the group has been adequately prepared and if the members of the group are sufficiently normal in the area of proximity and touch, the end result of this exercise (coupled with the history of the group in exploring emotions, and so on) is that the group feels considerably closer than before. Yet, some of the comments at the end of this exercise reflect the fact that some individuals are more careful in their touch than others and that some people experienced a sense of distaste in being touched by one person that they did not experience when being touched by another.

Some people speak of being reminded of when they were very little and others note that when touching another it was similar to giving their child a bath. Evidently, the touching experience, as does the proximity experience, produces powerful feelings and memories. Most important, when those people reported that they enjoyed being touched, the touch signified to them that they were liked and being cared for. This last is the essential factor to be used in structures to provide new sensations in the place of past deprivations in the area of nurturance and security. It goes without saying that at this time, one of the sensations while being touched for some is sexual in content.

A variation on the touch exploration that incorporates the child-parent elements is the face-telling exercise. This is an exercise where one figure plays the child, sitting on its knees, facing another who plays the parent figure, sitting on a chair. The parent figure touches the child figure's face, lovingly telling the child figure the names of the various features of the face and giving approval to that part of the face that is being touched. The group leader can select a member of the group, preferably a different person than he selected in the earlier demonstration, and show the group how the exercise is to be carried out.

The point of the exercise is to provide a simultaneous aural and tactile confirmation that one's face is there, and is liked and approved of by a parental figure. It is surprising to many how pleasurable this can be. The essential features of this exercise are similar to that game one plays with one's infant saying, "Where is your nose?" and so on. The added dimension is that here the parent is doing the naming and simultaneously saying that it is a good nose and if it is a girl a beautiful nose, and so on. One really does not know what one looks like except for what important parental figures say about one's looks and how others tend to respond to one's looks. The picture is built up from the outside. Even when one is physically beautiful but has not been told that one is physically beautiful there is difficulty in believing the mirror. The tactile and verbal learning in childhood concerning one's face is more real than any later visual perception of oneself.

The group leader can have the group member who is to play the child figure kneeling or sitting on the floor in front of him, while he describes the essential features of the exercise listed above. The group leader can begin by touching the child figure's hair caressingly and saying, "This is your hair, your nice soft hair," while the child figure invariably assumes an innocent upward looking expression, smiling at this description. Then he can go on to say, "This is your forehead, nice and smooth and behind that are your brains where all those nice thoughts and feelings are," while stroking the forehead.

The group leader can go on for the entire face-telling exercise describing each feature approvingly, and if he wishes, inventively. The tone tends to be affectionate with some element of humor without the type of humor that would tell a child, "Here is your nose your funny little nose that keeps running all the time." Many parents do just that type of casual kidding, so called, with their children, providing the child with a somewhat mixed picture of himself. When the group leader gives his demonstration he can include the comment that this type of kidding although funny, is not to be utilized in this exercise. The group can pair off once again following the demonstration and description of the attitudes to be used and the group leader can be relaxedly observant while they make their first attempt at this exercise. The group leader should be careful to see to it that the tenor of the exercise does not descend into horseplay without damping the essentially humorous element that is bound to arise from this circumstance.

The commentary that arises as a result of this exercise attests to the touch deprivation prevalent in our society, for it is full of expressions of distinct pleasure and increased awareness and sensitivity to one's face. If there was not this type of sensory deprivation our faces would not soak in the touch with such thirst. Many group members announce that they are going to do this exercise with their children when they get home and subsequent reports regarding this relate to their children's strong pleasure at this "game." Many children request this game over and over again, finding no diminishment in its delight.

Some of the group members report that they felt silly playing the child and found it hard to believe that anybody could say nice things about their faces. It takes little imagination to construct the kind of affection that was extended to this individual when he was a child. Some found that they did not like to be saying nice things to someone else but that it made them angry since they were the ones who should be receiving. Those individuals reporting that appear to have had insufficient satisfactions, hence are unprepared to offer those satisfactions to others.

Following the first child-parent face-telling, the group leader can instruct the couples to switch roles. This switching enables both members to experience both aspects of this exercise and eliminates the possibility that any one single individual might see himself as only a child or as only a parent in this activity. To leap ahead for a bit, it is so structured by the constant rotation of roles in a structure, that no one figure, including the group leader, will be crystallized into the giving or receiving role. Ultimately, in a psychomotor techniques and training group there is no split between givers and receivers, since all play both parts. In this way no single individual, including the group leader, receives undue emphasis as an all-important figure in the present or past of an individual, and all have the opportunity of giving and helping others as well as receiving from others.

A further extension of the tactile exploration exercise is the body-telling exercise which carries the attitudes and behavior utilized in the face-telling to the rest of the body. The sensations that are experienced in the body-telling are not as meaningful as in the face-telling, since one identifies more with one's face than with the rest of the body; however, this exercise is a natural extension of the first and offers the group member a further verification and extension of his worth as a physical entity.

At the termination of the tactile exercise the group can be in a tense or in a relaxed state, depending on the individual reactions and responses to this experience. The group leader can offer the group an opportunity to move freely, in any manner, to dispel whatever emotions were aroused. If the emotions were specifically sexual there is not much that one could do to dispel it, but if the emotions were diffuse and unspecifically sensual, one could move his body in a way expressive of that feeling. If one developed anger at the lack of complete gratification, one could at the very least express that anger.

Following the first tactile explorations exercise series, some group members have commented that this left them distinctly "horny," a condition which is uncomfortable if one were unmarried and without an available sex partner. How these group members solved this dilemma has not been reported but the condition must have lessened as later tactile exploratory exercises did not produce the same response.

The group at this point is quite close to the final stage before takeoff into structures. They have been carefully led to become more sensitive to their motor impulses and have been given opportunities for practice in moving in response to those impulses in a relatively free and spontaneous manner. They have been given skills in apprehending how the spatial arrangements of others affects their anticipations and preparations for action. Most recently, they have explored their reactions relative to touching and being touched. They have been prepared to be expressive in what has developed into a tolerant and permissive group. All that is lacking for the doing of structures is the control of the response to that expression, which is the topic of the next chapter.

CHAPTER

7

The structured response of the group, individually and en masse, is called accommodation. Accommodation is the last step in the communication loop that provides the necessary feedback information that an action is or has been successfully and effectively carried out. The first germ of the concept of accommodation occurs in the voluntary modality. In the process of doing that exercise, one first concentrates on a bodily position, or to put it another way, consciously or unconsciously develops a program of action that would result in a particular placement of a segment of the body. Then that individual implements that program by the utilization of a minimum amount of energy to overcome the inertia and gravity of the arm. The fact that the arm is moving as one had planned is apprehended by the proprioceptors of the joints and muscles of arm and shoulder. In the terms of this chapter the arm has accommodated the intention of the program and the accommodation is noted through the agency of the proprioceptive senses.

The relationship between the amount of energy used and the accommodation reports is essential. If one intended to move an arm and had no manner of measuring the effects of force applied to that arm due to lack of proprioceptive feedback, one would tend to use disproportionate amounts of energy to the action intended or one would tend to give up entirely and not make an effort in an area where one's efforts were inconclusive and unmeasurable. Accommodation in this course is generally associated with emotional movement and the group's confirmation that an emotional expression has been effectively carried out, since an emotional movement is not completed within the framework of the single individual as it is in voluntary movement. Emotional movement places one in relationship with the outside world, even though the emotion is a direct response to an inner environmental stimulus, need, or drive. That *outer* world must provide the individual with the information that his efforts have had effect. This information is generally provided visually, sometimes aurally, and sometimes tactilely. Psychomotor training attempts to control those three methods of information feedback in a structured way called accommodation.

Just as in voluntary movement, when the essential feedback is lacking one tends to overreact or react not at all, so in emotional movement one tends to overreact or not react at all when the accommodation is lacking. Accommodation, in the final analysis, is a prerequisite for the satisfactory expression of emotional movements. Since psychomotor training is concerned with the expression of repressed and conflicted emotions, one can see the absolute necessity of the structured responses of the group and individual toward this end. This is one aspect of accommodation.

Another aspect involves the use of accommodation in provoking an emotional response. Each individual in psychomotor groups learns which spatial placements and gestures program or provoke an emotional response by practice in the exercises noted earlier. When an individual wishes to recall a specific emotion, he instructs his accommodator to assume those placements and gestures to stimulate the process of recall and emotional response. When that individual experiences the onrush of emotions relevant to the projection of feelings on those placements of the accommodator, that individual can make moves that are emotionally relevant to those feelings and relevant to the body of the accommodator. The accommodator can then respond appropriately to the actions of the individual as formulated above to enhance the sensation of efficacy in the expression of his emotions. Those emotions might be positive or negative, and the accommodator is appropriately considered either a positive or negative accommodator. Negative accommodators stimulate and respond to the negative emotions, generally fear or anger, and positive accommodators stimulate and respond to the positive emotions, generally love, nurturance, socialization, and joy.

Both types of accommodation must be practiced by the group in relation to specific instructions given by the individual who is called the "enactor." Accommodation should increase the responses of the enactor. However, poor accommodation, that is, actions not timed properly to the actions of the enactor, can decrease the responses of the enactor and lead to frustration. There is also the danger of creative attempts to supply the enactor with imagery actions that he has not called for which would produce other responses than those expected.

The group leader can describe the foregoing to the group and for practical purposes select a member of the group with whom to demonstrate accommodation. The major repressed emotion in our society is anger; therefore, the major emotional expression in the early phase of the course is anger. Thus the most important form of accommodation to be practiced is the response to anger. The accommodator must respond in such a manner as if the anger and hatred of the enactor is having its desired effect and that is pain, injury and death. Simply, the accommodator should give the appearance of being in pain, suffering injury and dying at the express moment the enactor wishes to see such graphic effects and results of his anger. At first suggestion this procedure can be shocking to an individual who does not feel that anger is a good thing and who is certain that he harbors no such wishes for the disposition of his enemies, or more mildly, the people he does not particularly like. Such people have to be led slowly to the examination of their anger and the concrete results of its expression, and this should be accomplished in the earlier practice of skills and exercises related to spontaneous emotional expression. If this is not the case for all members of the group, the group leader will have to move cautiously so as not to disturb the self-esteem or the sensitivities of those individuals.

For some it is one thing to move in an angry fashion or do movements like the temper tantrum and another to see someone fall to the ground as a result of a blow originating from oneself and to hear that person crying out in pain. In psychomotor therapy and training, one is not only facing the experience of his emotions but the logical consequence of the enactment of those emotions. Fortunately it is not in reality that this cause and effect relationship is played out, but in a structure.

The reader may be wondering, after all that practice with proximity and touch does one in psychomotor training literally connect in one's punches and hit the accommodator? The answer is not at all.

Touching is only permitted in a positive context and never in a negative context. Therefore there has to be a leap of the imagination or a suspension of an expectation of contact in such endeavors so that the real-life feedback of the felt target is not anticipated. For those individuals who discover that they need the actual contact of *something* in order to experience the efficacy they seek, the group leader can offer other surfaces such as mats, pillows, and so on, in proximity with the action and sounds of the accommodator. That should suffice to produce the experience of contact and solidity, following a thrown punch, that these people require.

To some readers the above satisfactions may seem to be unduly sadistic and not at all representative of man's true, better or entire nature. I have no argument that this is not representative of man's true, better or entire nature, but it is certainly, at least to me, representative of an aspect of every man's nature. All of us, man, woman and child, have innately within us the inclusion of the capacity to render asunder that which is of threat to us. There is obvious survival value in this ability, just as there is survival value in the ability to render asunder the original form of that which is eaten by us as food. Although this digestive sundering is unconscious and organic, it is still an expression of our being. Should that which is metabolic extended to the realm of overt and conscious action, be considered diabolic? I think not.

Whatever the case may be, man should have the opportunity for exploring *all* that he is and feels in a controlled setting and not merely experience only that which he thinks he should experience or is told that he should experience. This course seeks to offer group members the chance to explore all that emanates from within themselves. The diabolic, if that is what it is to be named, and the godlike, for he is that too. If man does have innate evil, which as some may feel he has to overcome and transcend, does he transcend this by ignoring it? Doesn't the ignoring of it truly mean the ignoring of the convoluted or devious expression of this evil, meanness or aggression which is bound to be manifested one way or another? Psychomotor training permits open expression of this aspect of man, admits it without the sting, without the death, without the pain that real life enactment would produce. Thus, it can be seen that this course offers an arena for man's behavior and impulses that is different from real life and also different than the arenas of sport and art. The last two arenas permit a more indirect and symbolic expression of man's emotions. For this reason they are not as powerful as an educative or therapeutic process but more valuable as a process of maintaining equilibrium and stability. Art and sports provide sublimation, or in simpler terms the redirection and symbolic rendering of what originated as a direct impulse for motor expression.

The regaining and re-experiencing of those raw primitive emotions is one of the aims of this course. These powerful drives have not been experienced whole by many of us since our early childhood when they were in the process of being molded and modified to the requirements of our respective cultures and social inheritances. The psychomotor training experience can be seen as an opportunity for the recapitulation of the state of this original learning experience with the inclusion of the new factor of adult awareness and adult knowledge and perspective. No longer will it suffice that our emotional drives become automatically shunted by a process of conditioning or unconscious habit patterns. The energies available from the direct experiencing of an emotion can be consciously put to use in the manner that is selected by the adult experiencing those emotions. This aspect of the activity can be seen as a true psychomotor reeducation; this description is perhaps a suitable or more meaningful title for the entire endeavor. It is felt that following this reeducation process on the emotional level, the energy relationships will be such as to allow greater proportionate energies for more intellectual and more "elevated" human ends than previously experienced. This is mere hypothesis, but since there are survival values in the hierarchical disposal of organic energies, wouldn't it be likely that the highest and most recent cerebral process would fare best in a system where the lower and more emotional processes were in a more balanced and relaxed order? Enough of hypothesis; let us return to that poor individual who was selected for demonstration purposes and then left suspended.

The group leader can have that individual practice throwing a punch or swinging an arm at him, which swing or punch the group leader will respond appropriately to, as the enactor directs. Depending on who is selected, and depending on the composition of the group, that individual will find it hard or easy to throw a punch at anyone, the group leader included. That individual is instructed to see to it that at the termination of the punch or swing, his fist is eight inches or more from the body of the group leader. The group leader reacts as if hit in the area that the fist would have come in contact with if it had extended eight inches further. This could be a shout of pain, a clutching at the section noted above and a recoiling of that part of the body as if from the force of the blow. It should be mentioned that the swing of the enactor should not be pulled, that is, it should be allowed to have its full extension resulting in a fully locked elbow. The sensation of the snapped elbow can sometimes substitute for the feeling of landing on the target, for the locked, snapped elbow also provides a type of feedback. The pulled punch is ultimately unsatisfying because it is experienced as a holding back of the blow and produces more frustration than release. Therefore the group leader should see to it that his instructions to maintain distance are not interpreted as a request to pull or restrain the energy of a swing.

Some people may get the greatest sensation of a full swing by holding back, via the biceps, the full force of the blow. That snapping against the contracted biceps can possibly be experienced by them as the same feeling experienced by others utilizing the locked elbow. In either event the group leader should point out this factor in the seeking of satisfaction in throwing the punch and have the enactor explore which method works best for him. The enactor, following the first tentative punch and its effects on the group leader, might grow more confident and throw the second punch with more energy and more feeling. This second punch has an even more effective result than the first punch. The group leader matches his response with the force of the thrown blow. This second response might elicit a smile from the enactor and he might think or even say, "Hey, I'm all right, look what I did to him!"

These responses, the smile and the comment, highlight several important processes that accommodation produces. The first is that accommodation enhances the experiencing of function pleasure. This fact is underlined by the smile. The smile, indeed, may have other sources, such as self-consciousness, embarrassment, and so on, but experience shows it is more than just that. The smile is such an expected and regular reaction to this type of behavior that if one were not forthcoming it would point out that the group leader had picked out an individual for the demonstration who was not ready to express his anger. An important process that the comment highlights is that the enactor responds to the accommodation believing that he is being effective in his expression. More than that he is being successful in its implementation. This reinforces the enactor's expectation and readiness to feel and express an emotion as he is presented with numerous examples of his effectiveness through accommodation. If one in the past had an orientation toward failure, this orientation would be overcome and replaced by an orientation toward success by the contribution of this single element. It also highlights the completion of the communication process noted earlier, the response of the accommodator is noted by the enactor, and the loop is completed.

Following the first two punches the group leader can indicate that the enactor should continue and explore further manners of imposing punishment or pain and note which reactions he prefers over others. The enactor can do so and in the process one can observe that he is becoming equal to the task for his blows are getting stronger, more of his body is being involved in the effort, his expressions are beginning to show signs of the feelings he is experiencing. In short the accommodation is resulting in a greater experience as well as expression of emotion.

Accommodation can be looked on as a seducer of the emotion, and the accommodator as a partner in this seduction. As the emotion is more and more noticeably and continually effective, the enactor dares to expose more and more of the depth of his feelings. One would wonder if there would be any end to this rising crescendo of feelings. One would wonder that one had opened Pandora's box and that one had tapped feelings that were bottomless, endless and impossible to control and contain once exposed. This is not the case. As in all things organic, the crescendo reaches a climax and there is a lessening of tension. The sexual implication is intentional. Rising sexual feelings do not result in impossible and uncontainable and endless feelings— they result in a climax and a gradual return to normalcy. No organic drives are endless; homeostasis is the normalizer in all advanced organisms. One way to extend the angry feelings over a period of time would be to deny satisfaction to that feeling, just as one can extend sexual feelings over a period of time by postponing a climax. However, accommodation does the reverse of postponement of satisfaction and as in sex where too early ejaculation can provide disappointment, too early demolishment of the accommodator can provide disappointment. The accommodator cannot fall to the floor and die before the enactor is through with his angry feelings in respect to him.

This brings up the topic of the poor or ineffective accommodation, like dying too early in response to one blow. The group leader can discuss with the group the effects of poor accommodation and give a demonstration of it using the same individual as before. This time when the individual swings the accommodator can postpone for too long a time his response, or react as if hit in an entirely different part of the body from that indicated by the direction of the swing. The postponed response provides the enactor with a sense of annoyance. This increases his feelings of frustration and anger and the misapplied response suspends the enactor's belief in the entire process.

How can one speak of suspension of belief when the entire activity is so patently faked? The responses by accommodation are so close to real and the feelings felt by the enactor are so close to real as to satisfy the emotional processes. Perhaps the emotional processes are stereotypic, or to put it anthropomorphically, naive enough to "believe" the faked responses if they are close enough to the real thing. Something of this sort must be happening for there is no doubt through long experience and many reports from many individuals that there is great satisfaction experienced through watching the accommodator respond.

The enactor, following the poor accommodation, loses the sense of relationship with the accommodator. He loses the sense of closure of the communication loop and begins to distrust the accommodator. He begins to turn off his emotions, since they will only be frustrated further by this accommodator. This is what happens in real life when one's feelings are responded to incongruously or tardily. One turns away from feeling those feelings not wishing to feel them any more or looks to others for possible re-attempts to feel those emotions. This example should make it clear that poor accommodation, indeed, sabotages the entire process and can actually be used by some group members for unconscious and indirect manners of expressing hostility. Group leaders should be alert to those individuals and stop them before they damage structures.

Following the example of poor accommodation the group leader can allow the enactor to resume his angry expression with the group leader offering good accommodation utilizing suggestions for appropriate responses which the enactor may offer him. The enactor may now follow completely through with his angry feelings until he has exhausted them at which time he looks upon the accommodator as a pretty nice fellow. This highlights two important features of good accommodation: one, the building of trust and two, the sense of gratitude one feels toward the accommodator and to a certain small extent toward the individual the accommodator represents. The trust-building is an important feature in the development of the proper atmosphere which will enable complete expression of all that is felt without fear of embarrassment or shame in front of the group. The gratitude toward the accommodator following successful expression and resolution of strong emotions is a brick in the building of the edifice of one's optimism and good feeling toward one's fellow man, even, ultimately, toward one's enemies. What an interesting way to learn to love one's enemy, hate him first, kill him, destroy him, do what you will to him and you have stripped him of all you hate until he appears like any other man. Or, if one must, one can see this reversal as an expression of laws of nervous stimulation, the reverse effect appearing following high stimulation of nervous tissue.

The demonstration serves the purpose of giving an example to the group members of how to and how not to accommodate properly. It also serves as a license for the group to include authority figures as potential targets for their anger. The group leader can instruct the group members to pair off and have one member be the enactor and the other member of the couple be the accommodator. They are instructed to reverse roles following the satisfactory exploration of this relationship. The entire room, following the selection and sequence decisions becomes a mass of shouting, moaning, swinging, punching, falling individuals. The tone is lighthearted and humorous. There is much for all the members of the group to get accustomed to, and ample time should be allowed for this.

Female group members may feel as if it is distinctly unfeminine to be punching anyone and they are likely to feel awkward, foolish, embarrassed or just plain ridiculous. Some may say that this makes no sense because they would never behave this way and that it just isn't natural for them to be swinging a punch at anyone. The group leader can point out to them that this is not the way anyone in the group would behave in real life anyway but is an exercise in giving full vent to anger. If the female individual continues that if she were feeling full of anger she might want to scratch or bite someone, the group leader can recommend that she do just that and have her accommodator react as she would like him or her to.

In general there will likely be much laughter, probably very loud laughter, shouting, and much freedom in the average group. There may be those who are intensely angry and whose response to this opportunity may be of two extremes: he may restrain himself more strongly than most and only make minute pokes at his accommodator or he may attempt to go all the way with his anger only to frighten himself and perhaps some members of the group by its intensity, volume, force or extensiveness. This type of individual needs many, many opportunities for the expression of anger before the appearance of any recession in his seemingly endless reservoir of hate. This cannot be done in one evening and he should be appraised of that fact by the group leader who should assist him in portioning out the amount of anger he will attempt to dispel in a given evening.

This portioning, a poor word, is not a simple process. One cannot take a pound of hate, a yard of hate or a quart of hate, but one can take a small situation which provokes hate in that individual and attempt to work that through. Then take another small hateful situation and another before attempting to seek the source or the central theme of his hatred, for no single structure or even a large set of structures will resolve that type of situation quickly. Experience shows that some seemingly endless anger is really sexual in origin, but this cannot be handled at this stage of the group.

There may be other members of the group as the female noted above who may find that the exercise is difficult for them due to the fact that punching or swinging does not seem to fit their style of expressing anger. The group leader can assist those individuals by going through an inventory of possible ways of expressing a feeling of hatred. He can suggest slapping, kicking, biting, spitting, dismembering, vomiting, defecating, stamping, choking, poking, crushing, or any other form of mayhem of a certain order that might come to his mind. The astute reader will have noticed that none of the forms listed excludes the active use of the body or its parts. This is for a purpose. The most primitive impulses toward the expression of anger are naturally those which use the body as a tool and those are the ones that should be explored, since only they afford the correct combination of neural, chemical, and muscular release and expression sought for in psychomotor techniques. Shooting, stabbing, hanging, burning, poisoning, electrocuting, and other such punishments use agencies other than muscular for their effective enactment. Not that it is not satisfying to tell one's accommodator that he is to die of burning and watch him die a painful death. But this kind of emotional release is actually more passive and more of a secondary nature than the directly physical kind. This type of secondary expression of hostility might seem more appealing at first to some members of the group but it is wiser not to offer it until the group members have grown able to first move directly in the primary manner described.

It would seem from this description that many group members will be moving in a way that they predetermine and not in a directly emotional way and that is so. For the purposes of this exercise it is not necessary that individuals move under terribly strong emotional impulses. The level of expression can afford to be fairly pantomimic until safe distances are established between enactor and accommodator and until one learns which forms of action seem to match what one senses is the stronger version of the action that is being tested.

The observation of the accommodation level will show that it is not too high at this time, as can be expected. Few will be able to be very convincing in their responses either vocally or physically. Some will at once be better than others and some will be and will continue to be for some time fairly poor at it. Some may find it difficult to disassociate themselves from the target as they accommodate for others and find themselves unwilling to be defeated. Some may even attempt to swing back at their enactor causing some confusing emotions in the enactor. The group leader must make it clear to those individuals that they themselves are not being asked to be losers and that they should not take the accommodation as real. He can also point out that the accommodator will have his turn to swing shortly and he can win then.

There are those who are such losers that they find it hard to believe in any success and sometimes ask the accommodators in early sessions to beat them back. The group leader should not permit this and he should assist that individual to explore areas where he feels he can be a winner and work up from there. In some hospitalized mental patient groups the feeling of guilt is so strong that some individuals regularly request that the group all gang up and beat him up because he felt so strongly that he is bad and should be punished. In the light of this, the group leader can note this trait showing in normal groups and be prepared to look for and work in the area of guilt and a history of self-punishment, perhaps engendered by a previous history of cruel treatment at the hands of parent figures.

Some group members might find the role of accommodator just suited to their need for punishment and they can sometimes be seen smiling while accommodating. The smile is not satisfying to the enactor however, for he does not want his punishment to be turned into pleasure for others. It is not necessary to stop that individual from enjoying himself so long as his pleasure does not limit his effectiveness in accommodation and so long as he is capable of allowing himself to effectively be angry, and successfully so, when he is the enactor. If a group member has a great deal of unconscious guilt, accommodation may be a way for him to assuage that guilt as long as he doesn't request the role of accommodator just for the sake of getting beat up again and again reinforcing only that side of his being.

It should be clear then, that there is much to look for in observing how group members accommodate. The group leader can make assessments that will be valuable in offering suggestions in the future organization of structures that would tend to balance out different parts of the group member's personality, not allowing negative aspects to gain preeminence. Valuable, too, is the opportunity for determining individuals who would be most effective for certain kinds of accommodation and others who would tend to frustrate their enactors in an unconscious passive way. Poor accommodation is a way to be a passive aggressive. The group leader can guard against this and lead that individual toward a more direct expression of his anger.

Mental patients are poor accommodators and for this reason hospitalized groups should contain equal numbers of professional accommodators as there are patients in the group. Hospitalized patients demonstrate every one of the faults of poor accommodation. They may identify with the target they are playing when they are negative accommodators and may be reduced to tears by the enactor's anger. It should not be concluded that it is a regular feature to have patients be negative accommodators but occasional use of them in that role can be attempted if a patient seems well enough. For if they are, this type of giving and separation from the target can be important in their personality growth. Hospital patients may respond poorly or not at all to actions directed at them, and in the role of positive accommodators may find it difficult to be in a giving position. In light of this it should be clear that those who accommodate extremely well, both positively and negatively, are those who are furthest from showing the type of behavior found in hospital patients.

One of the factors that the group leaders should point out at the outset of this exercise is that the enactor should not utilize the personality of the accommodator to stimulate his anger. Then he would truly be angry at his accommodator and that would make it difficult for his accommodator to separate himself from the target for the simple reason that he *is* the target in this instance. To expedite the disassociation of accommodators from target figures it should be a standard ruling in all sessions that present-day feelings toward members of the group will not be explored or expressed. One may ask where that type of difficulty is handled, that is the difficulties surrounding real life feelings between members of the group and the answer is, in real life or in other types of structured activities that are geared for that field of inquiry. The most profitable field of learning, given the structure of the sessions, appears to be in early life experiences. Apparently resolution of early life emotional conflicts in structures appears to have some bearing on the smoother handling of interpersonal relations in real life situations indicating that membership in a present-day exploratory group and in a psychomotor group at the same time might prove highly profitable as a combined learning experience.

The group leader should note whether any individuals refuse to play both enactor and accommodator, seeing that no emphasis has been established for any individual to be only a giver or a taker. Following the reversal of roles for each couple, the group leader can instruct the group to form new couples so that each person gets familiar with the idiosyncrasies of every other person in their requirements for accommodation. With such change of coupling, each group member can have the opportunity of working with members of the same and opposite sex to explore the differences that arise in one's emotional expression as a result of this. When the rotation is complete, the group members should have learned something about their own peculiar form of angry expression. They should have learned which type of action most suited this feeling. They should have noted the differences between their potentially expressible anger between the sexes. They should have learned to make actions of response in the accommodator role and they should have grown more accustomed to feeling their anger. Immediately following this exercise it is wise to ask the group if they would care to do a group hug. If they do, it tends to give them an opportunity for feeling group acceptance for all that happened.

The next step in the accommodation process and practice is called the controlled rejection. This exercise utilizes some of the elements of the controlled approach concerning the field of potential programs surrounding oneself. The two roles in this exercise are the rejector and the rejectee. The rejector is essentially an enactor and the rejectee is an accommodator. The group is instructed to pair off into couples and to determine who is to be in what capacity first. The group leader can then demonstrate the exercise using one of the members of the group who appeared to be accommodating well in the earlier exercise. It is important that this type of individual be selected, for he will be playing the role of the rejectee to the group leader's rejector. The purpose of the group leader's choosing of the rejector's role is to give the group members an opportunity to see an example of a more spontaneous emotional outburst than they might have as yet seen from members of the group and to provide an example and a license for such forceful expressions emanating from themselves.

The group leader can explain that the exercise is to be initiated by each member's imagining an individual who would provoke the most

forceful feelings of anger should that individual be in a certain location where his presence would program violent repulsion feelings. The
rejector should then project those feelings on his rejectee and act accordingly. The group leader can conjure up such an individual in his
own life who would provoke such an outburst were one to move
directly and without restraint to one's feelings of revulsion and then
allow himself to experience the literal throwing-out of feelings that
this image engenders. His rejectee should be prepared to move as if
being thrown and to leave the room through the door. Or go as far
from the group leader as possible if the room is so situated that opening
a door would place the group's noise and activity in some other ongoing program in the building.

The group leader may shout, "Get out of here and stay out, you
. . . !" and include any epithet that rises to mouth. If the accommodator is good the group leader can not only throw him away but
chase after him swinging and punching until he is down on the floor
or out of the room. The group leader should be able to effectively
purge himself of his angry feelings by this outburst so that his feelings
of function pleasure should be welling up in him following the action.
If they are not and he is finding more anger within himself he should
indicate to his rejectee to return and repeat the sequence of feeling and
action once again until he is satisfied. When he finally gets satisfied
he can hug his accommodator. The hugging is not forced or required
but appears to be the natural outcome of such expressions of anger.

The response of the group to all this may vary to the extreme.
Some will feel like cheering on the group leader, vicariously enjoying
the expulsion, some will be shocked by such overt expression and feel
tugs of conscience or anxiety, some will identify with the rejectee and
be frightened of the group leader's anger potentially expressed at themselves, some will want at once to attempt the exercise and will have
plenty of people pop into mind whom they would like to expel. There
may be some who have reservations about doing anything like that at
all and who might feel it totally immoral to express and cultivate such
feelings and actions, some who claim that they have no one in their
lives with whom they would like to behave that way and if they did
they would simply turn their backs on such individuals and have
nothing more to do with them rather than stoop to the level of ex-

ploding in such a manner. In truth the last type of individual is in the minority at this point in the group. For by now that individual would have come closer to accepting his or her hostile feelings or would have left the group. The group leader should assess the tone of the group and say what needs to be said to reassure those individuals who have fears and reservations regarding this type of action.

Following the demonstration with the group leader in the rejector's role, the group leader can instruct his rejectee to take the rejector's role with the group leader taking the rejectee's role. The rejector can imagine for himself some individual who provokes feelings of revulsion in him and project those feelings on to the group leader. He can then do in his own way all the actions of expulsion directed at the rejectee that he wishes and the group leader can accommodate accordingly. The usual response to the accommodation is one of distinct pleasure. The rejector may make some remark that he has been waiting twenty years to do that to the person he has been imagining. His feelings of satisfaction may be so patently real that they are highly effective to the rest of the group members. They may feel that it is possible for the group leader to get such satisfactions because he is accustomed to moving that way. But when they see one of their own number get a like reaction they may anticipate that such would be true in their own case too. The sight of seeing the group leader falling to the floor under the blows of his rejector might be satisfying to those who had become frightened of the group leader following the initial demonstration and they may feel that it served the group leader right to be treated in the manner he treated his rejectee. In other words it allows the group members to see the group leader in both roles and offers an example for them to see themselves in both roles and find it acceptable. The rejector may ask for several turns before finding himself satisfied and he too may wish to hug his rejectee.

The group leader can now instruct his paired-off couples to attempt the exercise and to advise them to continue in the role of rejector until they feel emptied of their anger. The rejectee is instructed not to return to the rejector until the rejector commands, so that it might not appear to the rejector that the individual he has sent away so forcefully is now returning without his wishing it. The group leader can also point out that when the exercise is over, one is to think of hugging one's rejectee and not the individual whom one was throwing out. The thrown-out individual can be imagined still out and the rejectee can be invited back for a hug. The group can separate around the room and the exercise begun.

There will be those who will, under the new circumstances of projection on the rejectee, find enormous amounts of feeling being engendered and expressed. These individuals will get quite worked up in this exercise and subsequently quite relieved of angry feelings. There will be those who will choose to project an individual who is overly meaningful or powerful in their lives and whose death or absence, although desired, would be experienced with shock. These individuals might tend to be in conflict as a result of this exercise and they can be seen welling up with strong feeling and then finding themselves unable to act on it. If such is the case the group leader can suggest that those individuals cast about in their minds for some lesser individual to throw out. There are those who may be able to do the exercise but only in a mild degree. There may be those who are not able to do it at all. The group leader should be prepared to assist those individuals in any way he can to get them past the point of their difficulty.

There may be those individuals who, in the act of being the rejectee, might exclaim verbally, "What have I done? I'm sorry," in response to being told to get the hell out of the room. Those phrases tend to limit the responses of the rejector, for at once he is confronted with that evil person behaving other than he is expected to. He is sorry and wishes you wouldn't be angry with him. How can you demolish him now! For this reason it is suggested that rejectees refrain from verbalizing. The verbalization tends to become incorporated into the rejector's imagery and produce confusions there. It has been found that it is best to paint the rejectee as bad as possible, polarizing the target to expedite the arousal of emotions and their subsequent expression.

In real life there is always so much ambiguity, so much complexity in one's relationships that it is difficult to ever get a clearcut response to them. For the purposes of permitting the most satisfactory expression of emotions in this course, it has been found that all target figures are best responded to in their polarized form. Emotions are simple, but reality is complex. Hence for the sake of emotional expression clarity, situations are so constructed that one only focuses on one aspect of one's target figure, polarizing him for the moment so that one can finally act. It is understood that this is not the way to behave in reality but this reality orientation is suspended in structures for the sake of unloading excess emotional charges so that, paradoxically, one can assess reality figures more neutrally. The course sessions can be looked at as the emotional arena in which one consciously chooses to behave, temporarily suspending, by an act of the intellect, the reality and complexity in real life so that one can face that real life with one's emotions in a more balanced and less overloaded condition.

This type of juggling is not simple and requires the development of a point of view that permits it. This point of view is difficult for the seriously mentally ill who are convinced of the reality of their emotions and are not prepared to find other targets than the "real" ones for their actions. For them there is only one arena and slow work is required on the part of the group leader to develop for them the playful aspect that permits active involvement in what one knows to be fantasy.

The comparison with play is an apt one and one can make a good case for the similarity of the basic approach between play therapy and psychomotor techniques. It should be pointed out that because of the difficulty found in hospitalized mental patients that sufficiently slow approaches be used in consideration of their deficiency in ability to play or fantasize knowingly. The word "knowingly" is the key factor, for indeed they are not living in reality but in some inner world of their fantasies and emotions as if they were real. In respect to this it is best to work intensively with some of these patients in the voluntary movement areas. After that aspect of their being (control, mastery, rationality and conscious knowing) is developed it can be used to oversee the emotional expression that is to be subsequently pulled out and expressed wilfully. This is an important and complex area and is noted here simply to point out basic differences in the handling of normal, neurotic and psychotic groups without the intention of going into the complete details regarding the differences in handling.

One other feature worth noting is the importance of play in the life of a child. Without some form of play or fantasy exploration, the child cannot learn to get his emotions out in the open and subsequently under some form of control and modification. Those that have had a deficiency in play in their childhood show subsequent rigidity in emotional expression and lack of flexibility in their personalities.

When the entire group has played both rejector and rejectee the group leader can suggest that each individual hug every other individual in the room. This can have occurred earlier following the tactile exploration of the other members of the group or it can be postponed till now when each individual has expressed some of the strongest angry feelings he has permitted himself to express to date. This hugging of each individual separately followed by a group hug provides concrete acceptance of all of the feelings that have been aired, and further is concrete proof that one will still receive warm, secure, nurturant expressions from others. One of the reasons so many people do not express their anger is the fear that such expression will result in their abandonment, denying them the warm experiences they need and desire from others. In fact the individual and group hugs following angry expressions can be seen as a reinforcement of the act of expressing angry feelings in this kind of setting.

It is possible that, during the controlled rejection exercise, one or more individuals might have attempted to express more feelings than they were capable of externalizing, and as a result they might be experiencing some distress. The group leader can focus all of his attention on this individual, since this warrants careful handling. The individual might be crying or in a state of anxiety and the most important element in the handling of this is a tactile one. That individual should be held by other group members in a parental manner, making it clear verbally as well as physically that the individual is still loved and will not be alienated because of his action.

It is possible that that individual is crying not because he has expressed some anger but because he has found that he still has a great deal of anger of which he cannot relieve himself. In that case the group leader can assist in the structuring of that expression so that that individual can get relief. Usually such an event provides the group with a clear example of the potency of the emotions that will be experienced in the activity and triggers similar feelings in themselves. The satisfactory structuring of the emotions provides the group with a potential way out for strong emotions and is a good "outline" for future structures of their own.

By structuring of the emotions we mean the seeking of the more precise circumstances and figures involved in the emotion. Then, the concretizing of those feelings and polarization of those feelings provides emotional relief followed by experiences of input other than what the original situation provided. For instance, that individual may have been attempting to throw out an older sibling who was tormenting him in his childhood and found that he had an enormous amount of anger welling up as a result of this imagery and, in the face of the original figure, a feeling of helplessness that could not be dispelled. In this situation the group leader could provide that individual with an ally who could arrive on the scene. The ally could champion that individual and beat off the offending older sibling. Seeing the older brother in a situation of defeat and vulnerability would present the enactor with hope that he actually could defeat him. He might then dare to fight which could lead to his subsequent victory over the brother. This in itself would not be sufficient, since it does not include the new positive input. An "ideal" brother who would not have acted in such a tormenting manner can be provided allowing the individual to experience how it might have been in more fortunate circumstances. This experience might permit him to anticipate more agreeable relationships in association with older-brother figures in real life.

What came to light is the topic of the next chapter which deals with the development of structures and the polarization and concretization of target figures. This plunge into the future can be taken when individuals unexpectedly leap into deeper emotions than can be resolved by the controlled rejection exercise. The tone and the tenor of the atmosphere during the time of the controlled rejection exercise is still largely humorous and playful although feelings more potent than before are being encountered.

It is on the note of playfulness that the next exercise is entered, the bowling game. I feel it incumbent upon me to make mention of a factor that may be entering the mind of the reader, the factor of slowness in the development of the group. Some readers may feel that a much greater speed could be developed at once in a group, and this is certainly true for some of the individuals of the group. There are always those who seem at once able to work at the most intense level. However, it is not wise to move at their speed for they do not represent the entire group. It is safer to err on the side of slowness then to err on the side of speed. Even those speedier individuals can use the controls and caution that the slower method provides. There is nothing to be gained in a precipitate plunge into one's emotions, for the total process of change is inevitably a time-consuming one. If one could truly change so rapidly, one could just as quickly change back or into something else again. Change of a long lasting, positive type is not to be sought in quick, startling and dramatic endeavors. The human personality is far too stable to expect of it reasonable changes in a short period, peak experiences notwithstanding.

The bowling game is a way of stepping back from direct expression of hostility to a more indirect expression of hostility, a way of stepping back from specific targets of one's negative emotions to more symbolic targets of one's emotions. This stepping back permits a desensitization and a de-escalation of anger and its expression. It also permits a time for consolidation of gains in the area of emotional expression without wearying the individual by going straight onward to greater depth of expression.

The bowling game places the entire group at the disposal of a single individual, the same condition that applied when structures are done. The group leader instructs the group to line up in the formation that is consistent with the normal game of bowling, with each group member representing a pin. Each individual member of the group in turn has the opportunity of being the bowler with an imaginary ball that he throws at the people pins. That individual who is the bowler can tell the pin people to fall in any manner he wishes. He can ask the pins to fall quickly and with lots of noise. He can ask them to fall slowly and silently. He can ask them to fall as if in agony. He can ask them to fall down laughing or any other way he chooses.

It can be seen that this exercise provides much opportunity for imagination and fun for all concerned. The bowler can explore the effects of his ball rolling and determine just what kind of reaction he most prefers. The group can gain the perverse pleasure that is involved in falling down as if struck down in a playful situation. There is about as much fun in being a pin as there is in being the bowler. The group leader should see to it that the fun of the pins does not intrude on the wishes of the bowler. It is possible that one of the pins begins dying or falling for his own pleasure ignoring the instructions on how to die or fall given by the bowler. This can be frustrating to the bowler as described in poor accommodation and should not be permitted to occur. The group leader can point out to the individual the necessity of complying with the wishes of the bowler and indicate that one can ask for whatever one wishes when it is one's own turn. This emphasizes the importance of accommodation practice and the importance of good accommodation.

Each group member in turn displays his own brand of cruelty in asking for different responses. Each individual bowls two or three times to explore preferences. The bowling game provides a safer expression of anger. This is a relief to the group for it affords, by comparison with the controlled rejection, a simple outlet while pointing out the underlying hostility in the innocent game of bowling. The responses to this game are generally humorous and of a low-keyed intensity with high hilarity.

This game was received with some feelings of embarrassment and self-ridicule by a group of male hospitalized mental patients. It was easier for them to express their hostility in this manner than in the controlled rejection exercise. They objected to this game on the basis of its childishness and foolishness, indicating inability to participate in the playful attitude noted earlier. The reality of accommodation (although obviously playfully structured to a normal) was emphasized by one patient's fear that practice in accommodation was done for the purpose of training him as a patsy so that he would lose in real life fights with people! Careful introduction of the concept of accommodation in patient groups is necessary. Outside professional personnel should play accommodator roles until such time as patients are prepared to make the important distinctions. That step in itself would indicate improvement of their mental state.

Another game that can be used following the bowling game or used in its place at subsequent sessions is the atom bomb game. The atom bomb game puts into the hands of the group member the weapon that has no defense, the ultimate weapon, the atom bomb. Actually for some the weapon might not be a bomb but be a bolt of lightning, a gun, a ray or whatever they wish to imagine. The important consideration is that the weapon is fantasized as invincible. It varies from the bowling game in that each individual is pursued and defeated individually rather than all at once. The individual spells out the kind of responses he wishes to result from his weapon. These may vary from quiet slow deaths to violent agonizing noisy deaths. He may ask the individual victims to run away from him in terror for awhile before they fall—zap—victim to his power. He may vary his tactics from individual to individual testing responses to each type of death. He may project onto each individual some real life individual whom he despises. He may project onto each individual some abstract entity, as "society," institutions of higher learning, mothers, fathers, business organizations or what you will.

It is surprising the satisfaction that can be derived from such playful destruction. It brings to mind the satisfaction that must have been and still is felt when a voodoo practitioner places pins in some effigy of a hated person. However, in this case the hated person is apprehended squirming and writhing in pain from one's efforts and not dully and docilely receiving each pin with no changed expression. In the atom bomb game, emotional action is of a high intensity and not the effortless action of pushing a pin. Those natives have a thing or two to learn about the satisfying practice of black magic. Seriously, there is no doubt about the similarity of the wish and the need to do something effective about one's emotions.

The difference is that in psychomotor, the individual knows full well that he is suspending belief in reality for the moment to provide himself emotional satisfaction, whereas the native is not. For the native, the doll *is* the hated individual, or the spirit of the hated individual. What happens to the doll is *imagined* to be happening to that individual. In psychomotor, the individual is provided with a living doll, the accommodator. (The term "living doll" is purposely chosen to point out the affection one feels because of an accommodator's efforts.)

The kinds of responses that one sees in the atom bomb game are varied. Some go after the victim with great relish and force using their bodies as the tool. Others may simply point a finger at the victim but still feel emotionally that they have caused the reaction. When all have been killed off, one finds oneself standing alone amidst the unmoving bodies on the floor. If one had ever had the wish that everyone in the whole rotten world was dead except for oneself, one can explore that reality in the atom bomb game. Suddenly one is alone. Slowly as the silence sinks in one realizes that one indeed liked the company of others, if they were the kind of people one would like to have in one's life.

In this exercise one can spell out the conditions for resurrection of each individual. This is essentially what occurs in a structure where one first gives vent to one's undone or unexpressed negative emotions and then demands the kinds of responses or input that he would like to see or feel. He can tell each individual that they must be good, no longer hurt anyone, be kindly, and so on. This prepares individuals for thinking about how they would like to be treated by the positive accommodators in their structures, and prepares them for being receptive to positive situations in real life. Following the resurrection, a group hug is often desired. The group hug satisfies the individual's need to be accepted again by the group and removes the cold feeling of isolation, the picture of the dead world created. The total process of this exercise takes time. The group leader should arrange the pacing of the evening so that all get a turn.

It may be that a situation occurs when an individual might not be able to have a turn due to a limited amount of time. It is wise to give that individual the opportunity to kill off the entire group at once. In a sense this punishes the group for the loss of a turn. It might seem silly or childish but once the emotions in the person of the group member become alerted and are led to expect gratification, the frustration of that expectation can lead to discomfort and really unpleasant feelings. It is not being suggested that all emotions must now and forever receive instant gratification following a period of psychomotor instruction, but emotions once aroused and brought to the threshold of satisfaction should not be shelved carelessly.

It is similar to the condition that coitus interruptus produces. Once the sexual stimulation has gone a certain distance, there is a point of no return. The sexual excitement cannot be precipitously dropped from the point of imminent climax without suffering physical as well as emotional discomfort. The same can be said of emotional stimulation and its concomitant expression.

Individuals in advanced groups, prepared to do a particularly relevant structure and who subsequently were unable to do a structure for reasons of time, reported a week of discomfort. This included nightmares, irritability, anxiety palpitations or other types of psychological or physical discomfort. Following the week of frustration those individuals might arrive at the next group meeting in a state of restraint and reduced emotional and perceptual levels. They might feel as if they had the lid on and that they are numb. It is as if they did not dare to feel again for it had led to frustration of expectations and its ensuing pain. Those feelings must now be nurtured back to expression. Following a satisfactory structure those individuals report a complete change in emotional and perceptual states.

The importance of this is such that it is worth repeating: Once an individual has raised his emotions to the threshold of expression, any frustration of that expression will cause difficulties for a period of time until that individual has damped down his entire emotional system or has subsequently expressed those emotions. If the emotions are *not* raised to the point of imminent expression, no such reaction follows. Participation in a psychomotor group does not reduce the threshold of emotional frustration to a point where discomfort is felt at every frustration. However, participation does raise one's awareness of emotional responses to situations. The individual can decide whether or not to act on those responses as he wishes. One can successfully express oneself in situations more efficaciously than before, as one is no longer rendered incoherent or inarticulate by unwanted and unrecognized angry feelings. Angry feelings are not as frightening after one learns to channel them into appropriate and successful expressions. Familiarity with the explosive nature of more primitive charges follows participation in psychomotor structures.

Regular confrontation with one's most spontaneous, uninhibited, global, childish, primitive and powerful feelings in the controlled setting of psychomotor training teaches one that there are indeed limits to those feelings. He finds that he does indeed have the capacity to refrain from literally causing mayhem to others while in the throes of those feelings. The act of restraining oneself from coming in contact with one's accommodator in a structure even though the power of the feeling is as if real, teaches that one has not lost control and done injury. One finds that one does not become a murderer when one gives vent to murderous feelings in a psychomotor group. It tends to lessen one's fear of those powerful emotions in real situations, knowing that control is well within one's capabilities in situations of far greater intensity.

Occasionally, an individual in the atom bomb exercise may feel guilt and call for the group hug. The person whose turn it was can be held in the center of the group hug. He can be placed in a nucleus position in the group hug, held by a male and female figure on either side of him with the balance of the group surrounding that nucleus group. The warmth and security of that center placement, if it is already tolerable, is of a high order. It says, in ways that no words can say, that one is safe, loved and cared for.

An observer to the atom bomb game (although no observers are permitted in psychomotor training sessions) might be shocked at the display of feelings, negative and positive, that are being expressed. The shock might be great enough to produce tears and a sense of uncontrollable emotions. This would be a testimony to the distance that has been traveled by the group. This type of shock occurred in early situations where psychomotor training was demonstrated to a psychology course. Those who participate in the expression of the emotions are on safer ground for they are in a position to *do* something about their emotions. The ones in difficulty are those who merely observe, with no opportunity for their own emotional release. Demonstrations must be structured most carefully to guard against the discomfort it may produce in some in the audience.

The group has taken a part in an odyssey, and has arrived in a distant land passed through long ago in another age in another level of consciousness, almost in another body, a body that was smaller and saw itself in relation to giants who had great power to do good and evil and who knew and watched whatever that little body did. Through the power of imagination and recall coupled with an adult mind and perspective, that trip can now be made again but in a way that real life could never offer, in a way that satisfies the internal environment to the greatest degree. The pressures of old undone emotions and actions can be reduced, and the shoreline of the over-powering demands of the beasts of the lower depths can be as at low tide. The group has learned the language of the body, before the word, the language of flesh that was before the word was uttered by flesh, the language of impulse, of the body in response to gravity, of the body in response to inner need and feeling, of the nervous system that saw itself moving and tried to duplicate that moving in its own ways, for ways that its eyes understood. They have learned the language of their response to the patterns made by the people around them, the language of their program to these patterns before they became flesh or action. They have remembered and reawakened the language of flesh talking to flesh, the language of touch, the sense that was before they came to their senses. They have learned the integration, the whole-ness that comes of doing what they feel or wish to do. Seeing the world react to that doing, their internal response tells them that it was good. They have brought their feelings to other people, acting and interacting with them, and have found that they were alike. Each could no longer reject the other, and they met themselves in one an-other and the loop and cycle of life and communication was made complete.

CHAPTER

8

The group is now ready to spend the bulk of its time doing structures. A structure is a motoric recapitulation of past or fantasied events. In psychomotor, the recapitulation polarizes the target figures, permitting expression of what was not expressed in actuality. A real recapitulation of a past event would include the actual remembrance of that event in all its aspects. A structured recapitulation of a past event provides the proper environment and arena for doing whatever direct emotional impulses might have arisen in the original event but were not acted upon because of the negative results they would have produced at the time or because of impotence at the time.

Another aspect of a structure differing from an actual recapitulation is that it provides the individual with an alternative, a highly positive and ideal one, that could have provided the maximum pleasure and security had it occurred instead of the original unpleasantness. In a manner different from his original one, the individual in one stroke gains catharsis, insight, and experience, providing a new model for responding to similar present-day situations.

The first structure, to be worked on as an exercise by the group, is the child-parent structure. This exercise permits the expression of childhood fears with the new addition of an ideal parent-accommodator who would be available to comfort, protect, and care for the frightened child. This exercise permits practice in positive accommodation for the group. The group is instructed to split into two even groups with each group lined up on opposite sides of the room facing one another. The members of one group are instructed to recall a time when they were very young and terribly frightened but had no one to go to for help. They are to concentrate on that feeling in the species stance until the force of the imagery is such as to produce the action concomitant with it; that is, running, hiding, and so on. If an individual cannot recall an actual event when he was terribly frightened, he is to invent or imagine such an event out of a movie, perhaps, or a nightmare. The members of the other group play ideal parents who will be available to the frightened individuals. The parent figures are instructed to hold the child figures tightly, caressingly and parentally when called upon.

The frightened individual is instructed to consider the positive accommodator as an almost godlike figure who can, indeed, protect him, regardless of the extent of the fear or the extent of the threat. The use of the godlike image is not to introduce the notion of religion into the activity but to draw on the feelings of confidence, belief, security, safety and "it's all right" that are potential to the human species which are tapped and evoked by religious ideas. The parent figure is instructed not to use words in his positive accommodation unless the frightened figure specifically requests them by saying, "Don't ever leave me," and so on, whereupon the positive accommodator is to say such things as "No, I'll never leave you," and so on. Whatever it is that the frightened individual must know of the parent figure in terms of his solidity, dependability, eternal vigilance, and so on, the parent figure should respond in kind that he is solid and dependable. The child figure is not expected to say, "Are you solid?" but his needs will imply solidity.

The reader may wonder at the believability of the positive accommodation. Positive accommodation is offered in the same spirit as negative accommodation. When the situation was so structured that one's anger always "won" and one's negative accommodator always lost, it was explained that this was necessary in order to fully express one's hostility without reservation, and with full feeling of satisfaction. The feedback had to indicate the success of one's efforts. That is, one had to see the effects of one's blows on the person of the negative accommodator. Simply, the environment in that respect is so structured that the appropriate response is always available to each type of emotional expression. This is the purpose of accommodation. The accommodation shows that each emotional expression includes an expected response which matches it like a jigsaw puzzle. This is the communication loop mentioned earlier, and it indicates the successful culmination of that emotional expression.

By extension, this argument implies that all the emotional needs that are possible to a human can be met by human environments, even though the words that are used to express those needs are not taken literally. This understanding of words is illustrated when the enactor tells his negative accommodator to "die," and the accommodator falls limp to the floor. The response that he needs is the limpness and the stillness that the word "die" connotes, not the real death of the accommodator. For the emotion can "wish" and "ask" the accommodator to "die" several different times in a period of minutes without being contradictory or emotionally false. This implies the suspension of the intellectual understanding of reality, noted earlier, for the sake of emotional reality. This same suspension of reality in the handling of words is evident in the negative accommodation just described.

When the term "godlike" is used in positive accommodation the action element is meant and not the intellectual meaning of the term. The action element implies the stability, the protectiveness, the warmth and security of the term "godlike." When the child figure implores the positive accommodator to stay with him "forever," and the accommodator says, "Yes, I will stay with you forever," this is an emotional truth even though it is an intellectual lie.

When such a child figure is permitted to feel the presence of that positive accommodator as a human parent figure (with the godlike attributes noted above), the child figure might wish to experience that security for eternity. When his wish is granted the eternity feeling is satisfied in approximately ten minutes to a half hour or less. It is the emotions that are being addressed by the accommodation, not the intellect. One's intellect is rightly offended by being offered "eternity" by another human, but one's emotions know exactly what is meant. Every normal, fairly satisfied individual has experienced that eternity in his mother's arms when that specific input was needed. When that emotion is satisfied the organism goes on to something else.

We are foolish to give total credence to the intellectual meaning inherent in emotionally packed words. The words are not real but the emotion is. The positive accommodator is lying in reality, yet providing an emotional truth and permitting the organism satisfactions it needs and knows how to use, allowing it to then go on to something else, whatever it may be. This is the crux of accommodation and structures. Without the use of accommodation and structures, an individual in emotional need of a parent figure can only be offered the reality words that "you are too old to be treated that way; you must forget it and go on to something else." Satisfying those needs in emotional action, knowingly suspending one's reality understanding of one's true age, permits the forgetting and the ability to go on to something else. When we suffocate the cries of the child within us in our efforts to go on with the real world, we deaden the senses to the outside world, and awaken the sensitivity to the inside world in a distorted form so that it appears to be the outside world.

How long does one need to cling to one's childhood, cling to one's godlike parent? There is a weaning process involved in all growth and maturation. The weaning comes partially from the inside and partially from the outside. The idea that one is simply forced to mature from the outside is offensive if one understands the maturing process as an unfolding from the inside. A tree is not forced to grow by admonitions and to produce fruit by threats. Through satisfaction of its organic need for water, sunshine, and chemicals it flourishes, matures, and dies with no intervention from any outside agency. In the case of a tree the forces of nature can be seen as positive accommodators. Is there not the perfect match as in a jigsaw puzzle between the needs of a tree and what is supplied it?

What is the place, you might ask, of the human cultivator in the garden? Does he hinder the growth of the tree? Yes, if he does not supply the tree with its own unspoken needs. The gardener can also take a tree that is suffering because of some environmental breakdown such as insufficiency of soil or water, and by application of those needs nurture back that "sick" tree to a return to its own health and normalcy. The positive accommodator in a structure is such a cultivator, such a gardener. He is supplying what the environment may have been unable to fulfill, in the terms requested and needed by the individual, for only he knows what he lacks.

Is it lying to say to that sick individual, "Take this warmth, take this nurturance and place it where it is lacking," so long as he knows that he is no longer a little tree, no longer a little person? I think not.

It is to the satisfaction of those organic, emotional ends that accommodation and structures are applied.

What about the weaning process? An organism as complex as man must pass through several stages of growth where those things meaningful to one stage must be left and things meaningful to the next stage must be picked up. The transitions between stages are crucial in the human and there must be sufficient satisfactions made in the preceding stage before the attention can be raised to the oncoming stage. There also appears in the human the need of outside intervention and particularly assistance in making the transitions. If one were left entirely to himself, he might possibly remain at the lowest level or stage of growth. This would ignore the possibility of an inner drive to bring the organism to the fulfillment of its potential. At best, there seems to be a subtle interaction between inner and outer forces which results in the transition being made successfully. Yet, with any complex organism there is always the possibility of return to a less-complex level of organization (assuming that development through stages implies increased complexity), brought on by difficulties either physical or psychological. The nurturance back to health must include satisfaction of those inner needs once again with assistance in the transition process.

There is a point where discomfort must be faced, where one leaves the parent, where one leaves the point of safety and embarks to points unknown. This point is most easily met when satisfactions are sufficient and where the satisfying agents are prepared to relinquish their relationship with the recipient. Perhaps the outside agency supplies a belief in the individual who is in the process of making that transition by saying in effect, "You can do it. I believe in your ability to take care of yourself, and so on." The transitions can also be seen as a time when the individual finds himself saying, "I would like to take the next step, but I am afraid I cannot make it." The wish is an inner push, and the outside help is in terms of support and belief in the individual's ability to make that transition.

There is an oscillation between receiving from others and needing others, and relying on one's own resources, that characterizes the life and growth of man. The positive accommodator must play two distinct roles: one, as the individual who supplies the internal needs for as long as they are desired or needed; and two, as one who supplies the support and belief in an individual's ability to gain his own ends. While the positive accommodator is in the second stance, he must be prepared to resume the first stance if it should be deemed necessary. Some people cannot make the transition in one complete step and must drop back for a time to stage one in the transition and retrench while supplying themselves with sufficient input to feel able to "go it alone" again. We build up our capacity to be individuals by satisfying relations with others. Once we are individuals we do not remain isolated from others but become suppliers for others and producers or satisfactions to others and ourselves. The roles of accommodators have not been developed by theories such as outlined above, but have developed organically out of an attempt to satisfy expressed needs.

Let us return to the still-frightened individual who by now must have developed a most devastating fear. Some individuals in the group will be able to move directly to their imagery and will run in terror to their parent figures. They may clutch, sobbing, to the positive accommodator, holding on for dear life in an anguish of fear and desire to be protected and hidden. What is the state of the positive accommodator at this point? He may be flooded with a desire to protect and hold that individual in a rush of feeling that is surprising to him. He may find himself being protecting and reassuring in a way he has never felt before. He may be shocked by the individual's need, and possibly may identify with that individual so that he becomes frightened too, and feels like crying also. This would be emotional testimony to the fact that he has much fear-expressing to be done himself, and is not fully prepared to be the protecting individual.

He may find himself indifferent to the feelings of the child figure and simply hold him as he has been instructed. If this is the case, the child figure will feel that fact in the quality of the pressure of the arms and will be unable to completely give in to his feeling of need. For the protecting agent is obviously unable to supply what is necessary. In that event the individual might turn off his crying and become his own parent by internalizing or imagining the parent figure as himself, or else abruptly transition himself to a point where he experiences no need.

Some child figures may fall to the ground in terror and huddle in a ball of fear, unable or unwilling to move toward help. In that event the positive accommodator should rush to the aid of that individual, providing him with as much body contact as possible, holding that individual in an embrace where the enactor's arms are also embracing and his chest is in contact with the positive accommodator's chest. This position seems to be most satisfying in a fear situation.

If there is no solid object to wrap one's arms around and no contact with the front of one's torso there seems to be a feeling of something lacking or missing and one is not as soothed as one would wish. The individual who falls to the ground is expressing a sense of hopelessness that there is any help for him and is capitulating to his fear. The arrival of the concerned parent in the body of the positive accommodator is felt with relief, although with some doubt and fear that it will not be sufficient. The final acceptance, evinced by the embrace and the torso contact, is indicative of willingness to receive comfort and to have a more optimistic viewpoint regarding the receiving of satisfaction.

Some individuals may be unable to find the capacity to express their fear in an overt manner and can be seen standing frozen and uncomfortable. They have not been able to move either way, toward their positive accommodator in an act of panic, or toward the floor in an act of capitulation. They are also unable to accept positive accommodation. If an individual in that state is approached by his positive accommodator with arms outstretched, the positive accommodator is apt to be waved off with the words, "I'm not ready for that yet. I'm not feeling the fear fully enough yet." Or they may acquiesce and go through the motions of holding and being held, but it is obviously pantomimed and tasteless to both participants as there is little or no feeling involved. One can hardly feel the surge of nurturance wishes and programs without the stimulus of a crying or frightened individual. One can hardly act nurturative when one is feeling imposed on to do an externally assigned series of movements that one is not particularly inclined to do.

There are those individuals who may feel nothing in response to the fear imagery and who cannot imagine a fearful situation. They may observe the more active members of the group in a mixed attitude of envy and disdain. They may wonder whether the more active individuals are really feeling what they seem to be feeling, or whether they are simply putting on an act. Others may look down on those whose feelings seem to be out of control, complimenting themselves on their greater sobriety and dignity. There may be some who are shocked by the outburst and who see that behavior as a potential example of their own loss of control.

Those who have burst into tears and are frantically clutching their positive accommodators can perhaps experience some of the same concern even while they are giving vent to their emotions. One part of their awareness is seeing the entire situation within its total perspective. Their decision to give in to their emotions does not place them emotionally out of control, as they realize they can stop themselves any time they wish. Their awareness provides them with the knowledge that this is a structure, with the memory that they have chosen the frightening image themselves, consciously concentrated on it themselves, and consciously selected to give in to the emotional action. The awareness in this case does not inhibit, does not modify; it simply oversees.

This type of overseeing has been one of the aims of the early practice exercises in psychomotor training. It has all been developed during the emotional movement training and here it is put to good use. This awareness is one of the important elements in psychomotor training, and without it one should not go into depth structures. This is the reason depth structures are not attempted with certain hospitalized mental patients. Those who cannot make the distinction between reality and a consciously selected structure should not do emotional structures, because for them there would be a belief in the reality of the structure, just as there is a belief in the reality of their delusions or hallucinations. There would not be a conscious selection to return to a childish emotion, but an unconscious compulsion to literally become a child, mentally and possibly physiologically.

With certain classes of psychotics the situation is entirely out of hand. It is almost as if the need for the undone sensations is so great that it causes a bending of the entire structure of the life toward the past, making the individual a child again. There are ways of relating to those individuals within the framework of their delusional systems; however, it requires great care and sensitivity to always lead that individual toward the realization of what was actually occurring without reinforcing the pathological view of reality.

Psychomotor training has been utilized with withdrawn, inactive patients whose overt expression has always been repressed and who are not in manic states. Other patient groups that have had successful application of psychomotor training have included autistic and regressed patients. In their cases there has been a lessening of emphasis on the emotional expression except in a highly structured and modified manner with a concomitant greater emphasis on voluntary movement and sensory input, particularly tactile. It is not my intention to go into the particulars of working with certain classes of mental patients at this time, since that will be the topic of another book. It should suffice to say that the basic tools outlined in this book are adaptable and applicable to most classes of mental patients, with care taken to utilize only those tools, at the proper time, that would lead toward greater satisfaction and ultimate control of the emotions, taking into consideration the difficulties regarding awareness and the reality orientation outlined above.

By the time of this particular exercise, most of the group should be capable of some sort of action in relation to their emotion. Those who have gone the furthest will perhaps cry for some time. As they are being reassured and held, the crying tends to subside, the rhythms of the breathing begin to change, the tension in the arms and body begins to lessen. Finally a state of relaxation and peace begins to develop. A sense of euphoria may be reported with a feeling of peace and comfort seeming to emanate from the parent figures.

This is a pleasant and unexpected development to those who have been crying, and they comment on how peaceful and content and secure they feel. Some may say that they feel like going right out and "playing in the sandbox," testifying to the desire to go on to something else once they are satisfied, and also testifying to the force of the imagery and its relationship to childish memories.

Those who have gone furthest in the exercise may comment that they had recalled a situation in their past where they were frightened of a dream or of some situation. When they had run to the parent, the parent had refused to comfort them, telling them to return to bed and not to bother them. They may say that they have experienced the same kind of fear many times since and that they often felt the sense of isolation of the original situation. Following the satisfying experience in this exercise they may comment that they just don't feel as frightened as before and they don't believe that that particular fear will have the same power. Numerous occasions with groups have indicated that longterm involvement in a psychomotor training group does reduce anxiety and fear.

The comforted expressions on the faces of those who have expressed their fear most directly and who have accepted the ministrations of the positive accommodators is noteworthy. This shows the inactive group members in a concrete way that something must have happened to those members. They may wonder if perhaps they were missing something and were not so well off for maintaining their dignity and sobriety, giving them a motivation to be freer at the next opportunity.

The positive accommodators who found a rush of emotion directed toward the crying individual may feel something quite gratifying. First, they may express surprise at the force and quality of the emotional desire to be helpful that arose in them. Then they may comment on how helpless they first felt in being able to comfort their child figures. They may comment on how seemingly successful were their largely tactile ministrations. Finally they may comment on how good it felt to be useful and successful in their efforts, reinforcing them in the use of touch as a comforting tool.

Some accommodators at the first time may tend to say to their crying child figures, "There, there, don't cry. Everything will be all right," and that is a mistake. When the child figure is venting the crying the last thing he wishes to hear is to be told, "Don't cry." The positive accommodators should simply permit and accept the crying and make themselves available as a protector and warm, loving embracing individual. Even without words there are those individuals whose manner of holding and caressing in this situation suggests that the child figure should stop crying. These efforts at positive accommodation should be clarified without bringing embarrassment to those individuals who are doing it.

During the time of positive accommodation the child figure might say, "You're not going to send me away, are you?" and the parent figure of course should respond, "No, I will never send you away." The types of requests that are made of the positive accommodator lead one to learn how to be a positive accommodator and to recognize the common denominator in each type of situation. The individual wants to be certain that help is always there, that he will not be abandoned, that he is loved, that the positive figure is not going to die, that he is not bad, that he is wanted, that he is loved unconditionally. Ultimately one tends to demonstrate in one's own real life the same attitudes as one learns as a positive accommodator, and one becomes a better teacher, parent, or therapist as a result.

After the entire first group has completed the child-parent structure, the group is instructed to change roles with the individuals with whom they were coupled. In that way, those who were playing child figure can now explore the parental role, and those who were playing parent figure can now explore the child role. The switching of roles reduces the possibility of emphasizing only one aspect of one's being and reduces the possibility of focusing on only one individual as the giver and on oneself as only the receiver. The group becomes the therapeutic agent, rather than the group leader. The group leader does not become the focus of all the strong emotional feelings, although he certainly is an important figure in the operation of the group.

The group has now had some experience from the first attempt, and it does not take as long for the second group of child figures to work up their emotions to a point of action. When they do begin to move in terms of their fear, the positive accommodators know more clearly what to do, as they know precisely how they wished to be comforted when they were the child figures. There is less fear of embarrassment and less self-consciousness on the second attempt, as the first attempt ostensibly did not bring about any negative results. The group is a little more willing to plunge into the business of feeling.

The positive accommodation is usually better on the second attempt than on the first. The overall attitude toward the development of structures begins to become apparent. The trust within the group is rising even higher, for once the emotion of fear has been expressed and once tears have been shed and once those feelings have been alleviated, the group is firmly on its way to the careful and regular scrutiny of all those life situations and transitions that were not successfully met and traversed.

As one looks back into one's past, the thread of one's life is punctuated by the knots and tangles surrounding important events and feelings. Some people go over those knots and tangles religiously fingering them like a rosary, secure in the knowledge that they are all in the right place and all the pains are the expected pains. In psychomotor training, however, the intent is to unravel those knots and tangles, and, surprisingly for some, this unravelling is anxiety-producing. These people recognize themselves *as* themselves by the familiar bumps and pains on their psyches and are reluctant to give them up. Psychomotor training produces change, and change produces anxiety. One has to decide that the anxiety of change is preferable to the stultifying experience of restraint, fear, and immaturity. After one chooses change, the changes become the expected thing and one operates on a higher level, prepared to be more effective and successful in what is attempted.

The experience within the child-parent exercise can lead to the development of the first structure. There is a difference between a structure and the child-parent exercise that is worth noting. The child-parent exercise allows the entire group to respond simultaneously, and removes the center of attention from any one individual. A structure is done with a single individual expressing emotions and feelings. The group leader should be in a position to know which individual is most likely to do the first structure successfully without too much inhibiting self-consciousness.

In actual practice, the individual who is most prepared to do a structure is clearly evident. He may become aware of the possibilities inherent in emotional movement, accommodation, and structures, and may have a situation in his life that he wishes to experience emotionally. He may have to be helped to polarize the targets of his emotion in his structure. The group leader should lend himself to this effort.

If one is to do a structure involving a parent figure, one should concentrate only on the negative features of that parent, knowing full well that there is more to the parent than that. One should recall the action or inaction of the parent that provided the pain and frustration, and one should permit oneself to experience the pain and anger this fosters and to allow this to become action.

One might ask, "You mean structures permit group members to kill their parents?" The answer is an obvious "Yes," for the killing is of the same kind done in the controlled rejection exercise. It is not the intellectual reality kill, but the emotional reality kill. "But what about guilt?" can be asked. The guilt is handled by first having the knowledge that this is not a reality kill but an emotional kill; and second, by having an ideal parent figure hold and accept one following the expression of anguish and rage fostered by the negative parent figure.

The positive parent figure is not the real parent, just as the negative parent figure is not the real parent. Both are polarizations of reality elements. The ideal parent figure may contain elements of the real parent figure but should be largely invented containing all that the emotions wish him to contain: that is, unconditional love and support, understanding, approval, and belief in oneself. It is reasonable to ask, "Why must all the angry feelings result in a death? Can't someone get angry without killing in psychomotor training?" The answer seems to be "No." Anger on the primitive, global, unmodified level that is practiced in psychomotor training seems to demand the emotional reality death. If such is the case, it is easy to understand why individuals in real life do not express many of their emotions. How could they express the emotional death wish for the frustrating parent? Dreams do permit this, which brings us to the notion that psychomotor training structures are similar in content to dream material, but done in a less symbolic and censored way than in a dream. Dream analysis shows that most individuals have death wishes for loved ones, so it should not be too surprising when direct emotional expression of rage seeks the death of the negative accommodator.

Let us return to the group member who was prepared for and desirous of doing a structure. He may vividly remember having been frightened by a parental figure who came home drunk and threatened to kill him and his mother. The real situation may have resulted in an evening of terror, running from the threatening parent until the parent finally subsided and fell asleep, drunk. It may be assumed that this was one of many such situations with that parent and that this one situation is reminiscent of all the others. How is this handled in a structure? The standard approach to a structure is to provide negative accommodators for the negative elements in a situation and positive accommodators for the enactment of what could have been in an ideal situation to match the internal needs and expectations of a growing child.

Through practice in spatial awareness, the enactor can tell the negative accommodators the kinds of placements, actions, and gestures that would provide the essential negative stimulus. The enactor might decide to stand on his knees if he was small at the time of the original event. In any event, he would attempt to supply himself with the most powerful stimulus to his emotions relevant to that situation and his feelings. If this group member is fully prepared to do such a structure (and the group leader should see to it that he is before allowing it) the setting should be distinctly provocative. At some point when the negative accommodator was threatening either him (the enactor) or his mother, the enactor will likely rise in a fit of fear and panic and go running perhaps to the negative mother figure. At which point he will still not be safe, for that was probably how it was in reality. The threatening negative father figure would probably still pursue the frightened individual and the mother both, and then finally the enactor might turn on the father in a rage and finding a rising tide of hatred, attack the negative father figure ferociously.

The attack might go on for minutes, with a negative accommodator rolling about the floor, responding to punches, kicks, repeated in a bewildering pattern, just this side of loss of control. When, finally, the anger at the father has been satiated and the father figure is perhaps beaten with the bottles of his own whiskey, the enactor may face his feelings toward the negative mother figure. If in real life she had been brutal and unprotective, he may turn upon her all the frustrations her lack of care engendered. Or he may simply be furious at her for marrying such a horrible father.

He may feel some hesitation in attacking the mother figure, depending on the amount of love and warmth she represented in reality, and considering that it was deficient she would receive her share of angry expression. The moment she would finally be "killed" might be a crucial moment in the feelings of the enactor. He might suddenly be overcome by the feelings of loss and isolation and also be giving vent to all the years of misery and pain and begin to sob helplessly.

This points out the need for the existence of the positive accommodators. For once an individual has finally vented his hatred, does it not destroy the potential givers of nurturance, the potential protectors, one's only parents? No wonder people hold their feelings in check. There is no one to replace the miserable parents they have, as bad as they were.

The positive accommodators come to the side of the crying enactor and embrace him and hold him gently and tenderly until he stops crying. They may be asked, "You wouldn't beat me up, would you?" and they may answer, "No, of course not." This type of dialogue may go on or the entire scene may take place in silence with the enactor experiencing how it might have been with ideal parents. He may wish to see his positive accommodators hug one another as if they really loved one another. He may wish to have them both extend their arms to him and be held tightly by them. Whatever he wishes to experience with them they accommodate accordingly. He may wish to be taken for a ride or to be sitting down at the table for dinner or he may simply wish to be held.

When he is through, the group leader can ask him if he wishes to do anything else. This is a crucial moment, and one that should be understood on a nonverbal level much more than on a verbal level. There is a certain quality to a satisfyingly-finished structure that a group leader becomes accustomed to. The clues to it are subtle but recognizable, and shortly the group members know if a structure is truly "over" or not.

Some of the clues are in the obvious appearance of relaxation. The expression is more relaxed and the arms hang easily to the sides. This quality of relaxation can also be apparent in the positive accommodation in the structure. Does the enactor accept the warmth of the positive accommodators peacefully and contentedly? Is he smiling? Sometimes the group leader can actually hear the rumblings in the stomach of the enactor which seems to physiologically indicate the change of emotional tone and correspond to the moment that an individual will report that he is feeling better. After the structure is seemingly finished, does the enactor have a strained look about the eyes? Is he making short and abrupt movements of the hands while saying that he is finished? Are one or both of his hands fisted, one perhaps digging into the other? Is he rubbing his eyes with his hands in a manner that suggests tears? Are his hands involuntarily going to his mouth and is he biting his lip? These are some of the clues a group leader becomes accustomed to seeing.

If there are sufficient clues to convince the group leader that indeed, the structure is not over, and that there is an obvious residue of undone emotions, the group leader can suggest to the enactor that perhaps he still has some feelings that he has not completely expressed yet. And would he like to repeat the situation over again? In the event that he does, the negative accommodators pick themselves off the floor, where they have been lying prone all the while until the structure is actually over, and resume the actions and placements the enactor instructed them to have originally.

From his experience in the throes of the emotion, the enactor might have recalled even more specific events and actions in that same or other incidents that he can now include as a stimulus. Once again the negative accommodators can provoke him and once again he can go through the expression of the feelings. This second time can either be stronger or weaker than the first time, depending on the strength of the residue of feelings after the first time. It is possible that it is stronger and if the bulk of the angry feelings are finally purged, the positive accommodators can be responded to with more peace and comfort than before.

The enactor might then say, "That does feel better. Thanks for letting me do it the second time. I was afraid there wasn't enough time left, and I really did not get everything out." It is also possible that he may still feel some residue of feeling at which time he can go through it a third time. The group leader should be in a position to ascertain whether the enactor has done as much as he is capable of doing without imposing on him or placing pressure on him.

In the event that a third time is not sufficient and it appears that there is much yet to be done regarding these particular circumstances, the group leader can suggest that the group hug that individual and have him be held for some time until he feels a lessening of his tension.

The group leader would not have permitted the very first complete structure to be attempted if it was not conducive to easy structuring, so it is unlikely that the enactor would be in the unhappy position where he was still uncomfortable after three tries. Those deep-rooted and hard-to-resolve situations generally do not arise so early in the process of doing structures. A certain amount of unconscious selectivity goes on that produces the kinds of structures in the right order for an individual to resolve when he is ready to resolve them. It is rare that an individual plunges into deeper water than he is capable of swimming in. If he should do so, the group leader should contain him from diving into such waters until he seems ready.

Typically, the first structure tends to be completed satisfactorily, with the enactor physically and emotionally drained. Frequently, the positive accommodators are instructed to sit with the enactor for some time after the ending of a structure during what is called "gape time." Following a successful structure, the enactor often appears in a state of suspended external awareness during which time feelings regarding the past situation are being experienced in a new way. It is reported that this time is not characterized by conscious thinking but by a relaxed awareness of new perspectives and a sense of the reorganization of thought and action patterns. During this gape time the enactor should be held between the positive accommodators so that he does not feel vulnerable and so that he should continue to feel their comforting presence.

The reason it is called "gape time" is that the enactor appears relaxed, with mouth and face slack, with eyes open but not paying attention to what is being seen; in short, he is agape. I do not mean to imply that he is incapable of normal interactions at this time, but experience shows there is something valuable going on in the internal reorganization which should not be disturbed. This gape period can last from one to ten minutes, during which time the group can go on to other structures.

The group's response to this first structure will undoubtedly be varied. There will be those who will have experienced "echoes" in themselves of similar types of treatment. These people will be feeling very strongly as a result of this and they will not feel the sense of resolution the enactor has because they have not done anything about their own feelings and vicarious responses can only go so far. There will be those who are shocked at the amount of feeling and action that took place and who might be shaken by it without having it refer to anything particular in their own lives. There will be those who will be unaffected by what they saw, and such individuals are among those who have the most difficulty in expressing their own feelings.

Seeing one of their number in such depth of feelings usually produces a closeness of the group. The enactor's willingness to demonstrate strong and personal emotions is extremely important to many group members. They feel that, here in the session, it is possible to be entirely oneself without covering up or hiding and without being hurt as a result of it. The first structure tends to add another brick in the edifice of trust within the group. The many feelings of hopelessness that people carry about due to the distress of feelings that are unexpressible begins to be changed to a feeling of hope that perhaps one can truly relate and share oneself with others.

The group leader can offer to those who have reacted with the most echoes the opportunity to do a structure next. One of those group members may have a specific event pop into his mind as a result of watching the first structure. He may remember a situation when he had done something wrong as a child and his father had come home and threatened him with his belt and subsequently being beaten with that belt. He may recall that he was angry with his mother for not having stood up for him, and that in his own eyes the offense for which he was being beaten was quite minor. The structuring of this can be essentially the same as for the first structure: two figures to be the negative accommodators and two to be the positive accommodators.

The group leader can play either of the roles, positive or negative, depending on the size of the group, the number of males present, and the ability of group members to effectively produce the required stimulus and input. In any given session, the group leader may be in several structures or none, and he should see to it that he does not over-emphasize one aspect or the other in his selection of accommodation roles.

Once again the enactor can instruct the negative accommodators in the appropriate placements, gestures, and actions relevant to himself. Words can be used, but it has been found that they tend to disrupt the polarization process and inject other aspects into the situation than were experienced by the enactor, thus tending to reduce the intensity of the focus on the emotions. If words are to be used, they should be only precisely those requested by the enactor, which in this case might be, "Come over here boy, I'm going to give you what you deserve," repeated as indicated by the enactor.

Bringing the stimulus to a point of reduplication of reality is an impossibility. What should be attempted is the construction of the crucial elements as *felt,* whether they were the actual conditions or not, because those are what will be reacted to. The examination of the stimulus conditions on a reality base is not the aim of structures, but a reasonable inquiry into other, more verbal forms of therapy and learning. The complete reassembling of the conditions as they actually were and not as they were felt would probably lead to inaction as did the reality conditions. One would be inclined to say, "I suppose my father was right in trying to discipline me, and I guess I did wrong, so I should not be angry at him." This is intellectual reality and must be lived with. The emotional reality is that one was bombarded with emotional impulses that have never been acted upon. That is the point of doing a structure about it.

The structure makes available an arena where all those impulses can come forth in full force, suspending for a consciously selected time the reality conditions. For the successful expression of direct emotions, polarization of target is necessary, and the negative accommodation supplies just that. Following the successful rendering of such a structure, the enactor might very well say that his father was probably right in trying to discipline him, but now the emotions surrounding that situation and the father have been reduced and one can make a more neutral and relevant appraisal of the entire circumstance.

When the negative accommodators have been instructed and the positive accommodators are standing on the other side of the room in readiness, the enactor can do the species stance and focus on the sensations his memories produce. Then he can open his eyes and direct the negative accommodators to behave as previously instructed. As they do so he may find emotions welling up in him; he may particularly find himself reacting to his father's belt. Many group members have noted how powerfully they have reacted to objects which played a part in emotionally charged circumstances. First, he may feel horror and fear in response to the father and the belt. Then he may feel fury as the belt begins to descend, not upon him, but on the floor beside him, close enough to remind him of the actual stinging sensation of the blows themselves.

The moment of the transition from fear to fury is an important one though it was not highlighted in the description of the first structure. Some individuals find that they cannot make that transition and remain frozen and helpless in fear. They may say that they cannot possibly fight off the father or whoever is their antagonist. To turn and attack him, even if they know they have a right to be angry, would be untrue to their real feelings. It is clear then that fear cannot turn into fury if one believes that one's efforts will inevitably be useless. Angry feelings are not directly available to weak individuals. Fear is more of their province.

In the event that the present enactor finds that he cannot turn on the father, the available alternative would be to call for an ally. The justification for this is that one could have, or wished to have someone external see the injustice of the beating and intervene in behalf of the enactor. This kind of intervention is done by the positive accommodator. At the height of that beating when the enactor is in pain and fear, the positive male accommodator may grab the belt from the negative accommodator, and proceed to beat the negative accommodator in the enactor's behalf. This may give the enactor a feeling of hope and security. He may run to the positive female accommodator and say, "You wouldn't let him beat me, would you?" and of course the positive accommodator would say, "Of course not." No words may be exchanged, if the enactor wishes, and he may simply watch in vicarious joy and relief as the once invincible father is beaten down in defeat.

It is possible that the enactor might feel guilt or anger at the positive accommodator for beating his father. In that case, the enactor should instruct the positive accommodator to simply stop the negative father figure and have him sent out of the room without hitting at him. All elements should be carefully watched by the group leader so that the structure does not produce actions and feelings in the enactor contrary to what is intended. One should not simply follow out the basic form of a structure and expect it to be relevant and correct for every individual. One must always use the feelings of the enactor, honestly and directly experienced, as the final guide to the direction the structure will take.

One might ask, following an ally's coming to an enactor's defense, "Does this not make the enactor a passive dependent person?" It would if that was all that occurred, but an interesting thing happens following this championing by the positive accommodator. Either at that time or in following structures the enactor may find that he too can turn on the father figure for now he has the license and the example. Let us say that following the first rendition of the structure the enactor goes to the positive accommodators. He there experiences ideal parents who would not utilize beatings as a disciplinary measure, and who would be unconditionally loving to the enactor. Following the question, "Are you finished, is there anything else you might want to do?" the enactor might indicate that he would like to try it over again.

The second run-through of the structure might reach the same crucial point where the negative accommodator is beating the enactor, but now the internal state of the enactor may be different. The enactor has had the benefit of an ally; he has experienced the security and the relationship of other parent figures who would not condone this type of treatment; he has experienced another frame of reference; he has experienced an alternate form of treatment. The full force of the reaction to the pain and the injustice may descend on him. He may turn on the negative accommodator, grabbing the belt from him and find that this gives him a surge of power that is surprising and exciting. He may attack the negative accommodator and may find himself spontaneously devising all kinds of tortures to impose on the father with his own belt. He may demolish the father figure and chastise the negative mother figure for not defending him. He may even beat her, depending on how he feels on a direct emotional level, and go to his positive accommodators feeling like a stronger, worthier, more powerful individual. He may realize during his gape time that he had accepted a diminished value of himself relevant to his many beatings and that now that value is being revised upwards in his mind and feelings.

Psychomotor training structures change the emotional charge that one has in respect to certain circumstances. They permit the physical action relevant to that charge. They change the kinds of behavior that one anticipates relevant to oneself. They change one's self-image depending on how successful one can let oneself become in a structure and depending on the kind of treatment one experiences from one's positive accommodators.

The examples given above of the first two structures should not be seen as hard and fast formulas. Each structure has its own pattern, its own organization. The group leader can assist in making a structure, but he should use as his guide the feelings of the enactor, as they are verbalized to him, and as they appear in the body of the enactor nonverbally. All structures should be flexible with the enactor's inner sense of his emotional changes highly attentive so that he always moves from that center and not as a "formula" structure form might dictate. He should always act in the direction of his feelings, even if they seem contradictory to what would be expected. He should not act in response to the way he thinks he should act, for that would not be true to his emotions, and emotional truth is what is being sought in psychomotor training. The integrating force of doing what is felt is what is sought for.

The intellectual understanding on the reality level follows, not precedes, the doing of a structure. After gape time and at some point following the termination of a structure, an individual will verbalize voluntarily regarding finding a completely new way of looking at an event in his life. Insight seems to follow action, rather than action following insight. Although there is a suspension of reality in the doing of an emotional structure, the resumption of reality following it is of a higher order and not of a lesser order, as one might fear after seeing so much primitive behavior.

Each member of the group should have a turn doing a structure each evening, because the act of watching others' structures can be so stimulating to the emotions, in terms of one's own past feelings and relationships, that it is unwise to permit those individuals to wait a week before expressing them. In the first session that explores structures, it is extremely likely that one or more individuals will have nothing specific that they wish to experience, examine, or express on the motoric level; however, they should still be *offered the use of the group in some form* to experiment with feelings.

Sometimes without any prior expectation or notice, a structure will develop from the simple practice of setting up negative and positive accommodators with the enactor doing the species stance between them. This leads to the examination of the restraint structure which can be developed out of a simple provocation. The enactor is instructed to focus his mind on feelings of being held from doing what he wanted to do, and then the negative accommodators walk over to him and forcibly hold his arms down and keep him from moving. This action can generate very strong reactions which can lead at once to specific instances where one was restrained either literally or symbolically.

If the restraint has been figurative, there is an attempt made to concretize the stimulus. For instance, if the restraint was that of a mother telling a child that he could not go out until homework was done or some such innocuous or simple blocking, the negative figure could literally and bodily stop the enactor from leaving a specifically designated area. If the enactor would attempt to leave it, the negative accommodator would force him to comply unless he asserted himself aggressively and physically. The reason that this is done is that the emotions are never abstract, but always concrete. Even though a seemingly abstract situation can produce emotional responses, it is the *behavior implicit in the abstraction* that ultimately controls the feelings. This may seem to be oversimplified, but experience indicates that this is the way emotions and emotional behavior operate.

Another general area that can produce structures is imposition. It is not the restraint of doing what one wishes that is focused on here, but the feelings during the act of being forced to do other than one desires. This imposition is figuratively and emotionally experienced like a breaking of the membrane of the self. The imposed behavior can be understood as an invasion following the breaking of the membrane. Comments following this kind of stimulus indicate feelings of capitulation and being in the power of another individual, whether it is liked or not. The feelings of rage and helplessness that this engenders are extremely potent, much as restraint touches living organisms at their center. One's early history can be replete with imposition. From being forced to eat and swallow food when one was an infant to having an enema intruded into one's rectum when a parent decided that the feces were in there long enough. These impositions produce primitive organic rage both in reality and in the structures which emotionally mirror that reality.

With the arrival of the time of structures the group has reached what in a nuclear setting would be called the critical stage. The elements are so arranged and of such a quantity that the reactor becomes critical and heat and radioactivity is generated. The group is at a comparable point. The early elements are now so arranged and the quantity of the experience and the relationships are such that a descent into the world of the unconscious can be made. The unconscious has much power, just as the nucleus of the radioactive atoms has much power. Much control has to be applied before that power could be put to benign use. A nuclear blast can be likened to a full-blown psychosis. A nuclear explosion is not the aim of a psychomotor training group, and none are anticipated. A nuclear reactor to operate successfully takes a trained group of technicians. A psychomotor training group to operate successfully needs a trained group leader.

The two structures described are but a small fraction of the kinds of structures that are experienced in psychomotor training. Ultimately what an individual group member accomplishes in this activity is an exploration of all the emotions in every stage of life that have left memory traces of pain and irresolution.

All group members ultimately, some at one point and others at another, deal with the quality of nurturance in their lives. They find themselves re-experiencing childlike and infantlike needs for nursing and contact of an ideal mother figure. Out of this contact develops the sense of security and worth of each individual. If an individual did not get as much nurturance as he desired, his almost automatic response to this would be that he did not warrant any more than that because he wasn't good enough.

Each act of the environment toward an individual is taken as a sign of one's worth. If the mother figure in real life or in a structure goes away, the organic or thoughtless reaction is represented by the words, "She doesn't like me and is going to leave me." If a parent figure dies, it is seen as an abandonment or a punishment for one's badness, or the death might seem the result of one's own behavior and one would experience the shock of guilt as well as the loss of the needed individual. Structures in the grief situation reflect the anger that one feels toward the fact of departure of the needed figure which can be verbalized as "I need you, how dare you leave me. I hate you for leaving me. I'll leave you instead." These are not verbalized in structures, but are acted upon.

Some individuals have wanted to be reborn again by the group or by ideal parent figures as they recall being told throughout their lives that they were conceived by accident and that they were not wanted. These individuals want a fresh start. A structure where they assume a fetal position and where they "hear" the parents discussing their sought-for entrance into the world is satisfying to these individuals. This type of structure concretizes fantasies which one has developed as antidotes to the pain of the real world. The individuals feel compelled to literally come squirming through the group and then be held and nursed by a loving mother.

The nursing is not practiced with the breast of a female positive accommodator being placed into the mouth of an enactor. It is accomplished by the enactor placing his cheek against the clothed breast of his female positive accommodator and then making sucking movements of the mouth. Some enactors have felt the need of some internal sensation in this sucking process, and the fingers or the fleshy parts of the hand of the positive accommodator can be supplied. When the nursing ensues, vestiges of real infantile actions make appearances. The action of the sucking becomes somewhat reflexive, the breathing of the individual changes, and the hands show some of the squeezing seen in suckling infants. Group members who have experienced this comment that very childlike feelings come over them and that the action of the hands and mouth have a much different quality than ordinary. Those movements feel internally originated. Very likely vestigial reflex actions can be recalled by providing the appropriate stimulus.

Since psychomotor training presents an arena where all emotions can be expressed motorically, all human emotions are seen in that process. One of the uses of psychomotor is to help the individual "unfuse" or clarify basic emotions, and to unfuse and clarify the targets of those emotions. Experience showed that many confused fear and anger, anger and sexuality, sexuality and nurturance, and nurturance and social affection.

The targets of those emotions were also seen to be suffering from confusion and lack of clarity and attempts were made to distinguish mothers from fathers, parents from peer and love mates, and siblings from parents. This brings us to the question of the sequence of structures and the development or maturation of the individuals involved. The overall goal is to solve the fusion and confusion. To do so, one must solve the earliest emotional needs and relationships.

No matter where one begins in this process, in the immediate present with reality problems and issues, or in historical structures, one must reexamine all basic feelings and relationships. This does not necessarily happen in a formal sequential way, going from birth structures on upward to sexual structures, but happens as the material becomes available or the feelings become available to the individual. The group leader can keep in mind the entire panorama of that person's history and present, helping to place each segment in the total picture as the emphasis shifts from session to session to many different ages and feeling states.

To put it in an oversimplified manner, in the process of growth an individual seems to grow from the infant, who has what appears to be amorphic emotional states, hinged about survival and satisfaction, which put him into relationship with an amorphous target—his mother, to an adult individual who has differentiated out of that amorphous emotion all his adult emotions, and out of that one basic target, all other targets. The process of "unfusing" in psychomotor might be similar to the process of differentiation in the maturation process with similar goals.

A person who is only partially matured, though physically adult, adds to this problem by ignoring what is patently an infantile nurturant problem, while attempting the solution on a sexual level— confusing nurturance with sexuality. This process of confusion is not a conscious or intentional one, but one that seems to rise spontaneously due to the structure of the human nervous system. Therefore one who has experienced a severe loss of nurturance as an infant or child might react to a sexual rejection as if his survival were threatened, arousing the anxiety of the infant or child he was at the original loss of his undifferentiated target, his mother.

It would seem that individuals carry about with them the vestiges of that undifferentiated emotion and invest it into undifferentiated targets in real life. Consider the reactions of some individuals following the loss of a job, a friend, or any reality loss that leaves them extremely shaken and anxious. It is possible to consider those reactions as pertinent to an earlier, truly earthshaking loss during early childhood or infancy. It is surprising how easy it is for individuals to project their feelings into any available target, within reality, or within a structure. This ease is perhaps demonstrated in the transference phenomenon in psychoanalysis. In structures the attempt is made to "populate" the transference using the accommodators and identifying them as positive parents, negative parents, and so on.

It is not within the scope of this book to go into elaborate detail regarding the sequences of structures and their developmental pertinence, but I will attempt to show some of the techniques used for separating the emotions and their targets, in hypothetical situations.

Let us say that in the preliminaries of a group meeting a female group member finds that her knees seem to be buckling and that she seems to want to fall. In psychomotor that is often understood as an unconscious or bodily request for support. The group leader can offer her positive parent figures who would be totally supporting. The female member might say no to this, on the basis that she would only like her positive father to hold her, as her own mother was weak and she did not trust her. If only a father were offered to her, it would be a reinforcement of the experience that mothers were weak and permit the female to have her father all to herself without a mother figure. It is suggested that she attempt to be caught by both parents as it would certainly be possible that one could have both an ideal father and an ideal mother.

In the subsequent buckling and being caught by both ideal parents she might find that she was tensing up and becoming angry at the mother figure. A negative mother figure could then be offered who is instructed to falter when she buckles and seeks to be held. When the negative mother falters and offers no support to her, she may either crumple to the ground in tears, whereupon the positive parent figures are instructed to go promptly to her and offer support, or she may flash out in anger at the negative mother and express violent fury. Whichever way the emotions go, the accommodators would be prepared to respond appropriately.

If tears and helplessness were the reaction to the faltering mother, she might accept the ministrations of the positive figures with relief and satisfaction for a period of time. She might comment quietly that she was never a safe or happy child, and never experienced the support of her mother. This recollection, in contrast with the present experience of support of the positive mother, might arouse indignant anger at the negative mother and she might get up and scream and strike at the negative, returning to the positive parents in a more relaxed manner. She might look at the positive mother and comment that she looked better to her now.

If rage were the initial reaction to the faltering mother, she might spend some time expressing it and then recall a specific event when her mother let her down, not necessarily in a concrete way, but in a meaningful, symbolic way. She is instructed to recall that event and then to tell the negative accommodator how to behave or what to say to provide herewith a stimulus to react to. Sometimes this stimulus is necessary, but at other times the mere recollection is sufficient to goad one into action. However, it is important that specific events be recalled in order to properly "uncharge" the memory by reacting effectively to it.

Following the angry reaction, she might be willing to attempt to trust the positive mother and try being caught by both mother and father together. This attempt might prove more satisfying than the first attempt but she might say, "I still like Daddy best," and smile coyly at him. This smile might be one that is recognized in psychomotor as an oedipal smile; that is, a smile that seems to show up in structures where one is consciously or unconsciously feeling sexually toward parent figures. This situation is an extremely intricate and complex one and I will attempt to show some sides of it.

If an oedipal situation seems to be occurring, the standard response for the parent figure is to say, "I am your parent and I will never have you sexually. It is all right for you to feel sexually toward me, but I love mother that way and I will only sleep with her. I will never sleep with you. I love you as a daughter and not as a wife." It is important for the parent figures to be standing with their arms about each other and not the least bit separated from each other.

(Any separation between parent figures acts as a magnet to the child figure to replace the absent parent. This seems to operate regardless of the sex of the distant or missing parent. In a divorce situation, where the daughter is left in the care of the mother, it is possible that the child fantasize that she is now the father and engage in conscious or unconscious sexual wishes for the mother. This is a kind of reverse oedipal situation and if not paid attention to can confuse and mystify as to what emotions are going where. However, it is possible for the child to fight off the sexual arousal by getting angry at the attractive and too available parent and "hating" him or her.)

Depending on her emotional growth, the child figure might react in various ways to the statement of the parent figure clarifying the love relationship. She might deny that she had any feelings toward her father and say that as a matter of fact I really hate him and find him disgusting, although he was always there when I needed him. If so, she might be directed to recall a time when she did find her father disgusting and hateful and to react to her negative father accordingly. This is a very interesting moment, for if her hate of her father is fused with sexual feelings, she will not be able to discharge the anger no matter how long she keeps on acting angry. She might eventually turn with weariness to the group leader and say, "I am still furious, but I cannot seem to get enough of getting angry and I'm exhausted." Long experience with this type of unending rage has led us to learn that it is sexual in essence. This rage is called "fuck anger" and the endless expression of it toward the negative father called "a negative wedding."

An attempt can be made to offer the female a contemporary figure toward which to direct the sexual feelings. She may find the contemporary figure attractive and embrace him, whereupon the positive parent figures state, "It is good to see you with your very own man. He is a good man." This might induce feelings of insecurity in the female figure, for it marks a real separation from childhood and from the parent figures. She might wish to return to the parent figures, but as a young child and for the moment return to nurturant needs. There is a direct relationship between unmet nurturance or dependency needs and one's ability to have a genuine love relationship with a contemporary. When the step toward marriage is made in a structure, the need or lack of need for filling nurturant and dependency deficits becomes apparent.

Another way of responding to the statement of the parent figures, defining who is the sexual love object and who the protective love object may be with humor. If this occurs, it generally indicates that the problem is well on its way to being solved. In the humorous or absurd response, the child figure may say, "Why don't you go to bed with me, what's wrong with me? I'm much more attractive than that old bag. You know you love me better than her," and so on. This is done in a spirit of absurdity and is often followed by a furious tug of war with the child literally attempting to pull the father away from the mother. I must add that this is not planned and done in a purposeful manner. What occurs is that a certain state of mind or mood seems to descend on some in this occasion, and it is a moment of real hilarity and absurd reactions. Persons in this structure comment afterwards that they found themselves saying and thinking these things and behaving that way while a part of themselves is looking on in open-mouthed amazement.

If at any time it appeared that the father might really successfully be pulled away from the mother, an aversive response might become apparent. It is only when the child is certain that she will not succeed that she can permit herself to consciously experience those wishes. Although, if the child in reality did seem to be able to win the father away from the mother, it can be certain that that individual will have a difficult time accepting a love relationship with anyone her own age, and may even find it difficult to have a satisfying sexual relationship whatsoever.

During the time that a child figure is attempting to pull apart the parent figures, she can vent anger at the positive figures for staying together. This is the only time in psychomotor that positive figures become the targets for angry feelings. The response here from the positive figures is to accommodate as if struck, but without falling or "dying," as is usual for anger, but to follow it with, "We still love you even though you are angry at us for this." Following the angry expression and the realization that she cannot split them and gain the father, the child figure might say, "Well I'm getting out of here, there's no sense in my hanging around this place." At this juncture she is offered a contemporary figure whom she embraces and once again the parent figures can approve.

It becomes clear that many parents withhold approval of the figures that a child might bring home as potential mates, making it evident to the child that no one is acceptable as her mate, leaving only the parents as the alternatives. Some families make it understood that only love within the family is to be contemplated.

Some individuals may wish to regress immediately after accepting the contemporary figure and either bring the boy home to be embraced by the parents or say goodby to the boy temporarily and wish to curl up on the parents' lap. If this occurs, the group leader should point out that if any sexual feelings arise while a person is ostensibly being a younger child, that the contemporary figure should be brought back and related to. Most often this regression is an expression of a real wish to experience the loving support that might have been lacking.

Sometimes the wish for the father can be so great that even after many encounters of trying to separate the two, the female figure might yet be unwilling to accept a contemporary figure. This has been seen to occur in situations where the mother has been seriously lacking in ability to nurture and the child at a very early age learns to look toward the father as a source of love. This missed love, although oral and nurturant when it had the mother as its target, becomes confused and includes sexuality when the father becomes the alternate. To give up the father as a love object is experienced in the same way as a loss of the breast to an infant. In this way the penis and the breast can become confused as organs of giving and the mouth and vagina can become confused as organs of receiving.

If the mother had been unloving and if there had been a real life rift between the mother and father, with the father making unconscious advances toward the daughter, the situation can become much intensified. In such cases the daughter becomes extremely attached to the father with a force that is awe-inspiring. If the father should die before the child is fully matured, wishes to rejoin the father in heaven, conscious suicidal feelings, and feelings of being unable to live without the father can be expected. Once again we are viewing an individual who reacts as an infant might when it is deprived too soon of its mother. The infant may view the breast with a religious or magical attitude, for such girls view the father with a religious or magical attitude, feeling that life cannot go on without him.

The attachment for father can only be solved with the child becoming able to trust and accept love from a positive mother figure at an infantile level. This can occur dramatically in a structure when the female figure, being figuratively weaned after many structures from the father as a sex object and unable to accept a contemporary sex figure, finally turns toward the mother and does a nursing structure.

When this does occur it can be expected that there will be a grief reaction, with the female mourning the loss of her father. This grief must be allowed to run its course. A similar grief occurs when a female figure, who has been fantasizing a meeting in heaven with the dead father figure, finally gives up the wish that she will actually have the father and turns toward the positive mother figure, or toward the contemporary love figure. Sometimes this grief will unexpectedly follow an embrace with a contemporary figure, in a structure which has not indicated any overly strong attachment to father. The comment may be made that, even though it felt so good to have a sexual love object, one felt an overriding sadness that seemed to come from nowhere. This can, perhaps, explain the tears that sometimes follow sexual intercourse, that has been more than usually intense. By making an emotional commitment to one's contemporary, one also loosens the fantasy attachment to one's parents.

Occasionally, a father may become unconsciously threatened by his sexual feelings toward his daughter and in an attempt to deal with them become angry with her, perhaps beating or spanking her. This physical violence seems to be experienced as sexual on some level by the female. It can be understood as the "fuck anger" mentioned earlier and it is comparable to rape in some respects. Fathers beating their sons may produce similar results, as experience has shown that such boys, when they grow up, tend to have masturbation fantasies involving strong males whom they overcome.

It becomes clear to members of a psychomotor training group how important it is for a child to be properly cared for when it is young. The child needs both parents for different reasons and both parents should see to it that they do not "seduce" the child. Some of the subtle forms of seduction include treating the child as a peer, telling the child about one's worries as if it were a parent, telling the child how difficult it is to get along with the mate, downgrading the mate in the eyes of the child and making the child feel more loved than the mate.

Even if the father has not become physically angry with his child, his brooding and potentially violent present can be sufficiently arousing to produce the aforementioned effects. One manner of dealing with this fusion between sex and anger is to permit, encourage or allow the female figure to physically wrestle with her contemporary figure, so that such violent body contact can safely and consciously arouse sexual feelings—this time with an appropriate figure. It is possible that such females, though aroused by forceful males, would find it impossible to give in to such males because they are so patently reminiscent of the hated, and secretly desired, father. Such wrestling encounters permit the welling up of sexual feelings and subsequent submission to the contemporary, for he is clearly not father. (Strong sexual feelings can be aroused in these structures and it is important that the group leader direct the group members to bring those feelings "home" to their real life situations and not attempt to act them out with group members outside the group session. The aim of these structures is not promiscuity and affairs but solid sexual relationships with meaningful and long-term partners.) In such an event, it is important to have the positive mother and father figures standing with their arms about each other nearby, so that the female can concretely see that her contemporary figure is not her father figure.

It might seem simplistic to state that merely seeing the difference between contemporary and father could be significant, but experience shows that this is so. Sometimes female figures who have melted together all men, that they are equally unavailable, as all men become her father, can be given a situation such as this: Two men stand one in front of the other, one is designated as the contemporary and one as the father. The females who have done such a structure comment that it produces an uncanny reaction when they see one male face peering over the shoulder of another male. When they are separated and one places his arm about a positive mother figure, indicating that he is father, and the other reaches toward her indicating acceptability, it can be the turning point in the process of this important clarification.

These are some of the highlights in the process of developing structures and clarifying the emotions and the targets of the emotions. Each aspect could well be the chapter of another book and that is the intention of the author. Such a book will deal in detail with the above topics, including the development of models, self-esteem, self-control and uses of voluntary movement as well as significant case studies.

Is this a process of therapy or a process of education? Obviously the answer is both, depending on the extent to which one's energy batteries have been depleted or short-circuited, one is either being cured or educated. What is more important is that there are tools available for finding that energy, for containing it, and for directing it in a new manner. What this has created is another arena, another place to be, between the external world and the world of the emotions. Art and sport are a step in that direction, but only enough of a step to be a safety valve. Following experience in psychomotor training, art and sport can be enjoyed more for their own sake and not for purposes of sublimation.

Each psychomotor training session in an advanced group is a recapitulation of the entire process previous to reaching the point of doing structures. All the preliminary stages are practiced, the species stance, the reflex modality, the voluntary modalities, and the emotional modalities. They are done so that one continues to gain skill in relaxation and giving in to one's reflexes; so that one continues to gain mastery over how one moves one's body and one's ability to act without affect or emotion in an abstract, functionless way; so that one continues to gain emotional spontaneity in order to respond directly and at once to emotional impulses, if one desires. The spatial awareness exercises are repeated so that one can forever examine anew what programs are being developed in response to what placements. All these are done not only to develop skill, but also to determine what state the individual is in at the time of the session.

The individual can ascertain for himself where the tension arises in the species stance: can he give in to the fall catch, or is he holding on today? can he indeed move without affect or is he finding it hard to concentrate? in the emotional exercises, which emotions come the easiest and which come not at all this session? All these questions lead toward assessing the state of the psyche and assist in the development of a structure, not from a rational examination of one's state of affairs, but from a look at the irrational nonverbal manner in which one moves one's body.

With this, I will close this segment of the investigation. It is hoped that this exposition will prove helpful to others in opening up awareness of nonverbal behavior in themselves and in those with whom they work.